RECLAIMING THE NATION:
MUSLIM WOMEN AND THE LAW IN INDIA

VRINDA NARAIN

Reclaiming the Nation

Muslim Women and the Law in India

UNIVERSITY OF TORONTO PRESS
Toronto   Buffalo   London

© University of Toronto Press Incorporated 2008
Toronto Buffalo London
Printed in Canada

ISBN 978-0-8020-9278-6

∞

Printed on acid-free paper

Library and Archives Canada Cataloguing in Publication

Narain, Vrinda, 1965–
Reclaiming the nation : Muslim women and the law in India / Vrinda Narain

Includes bibliographical references and index.
ISBN 978-0-8020-9278-6 (bound)

1. Muslim women – India – Social conditions.   2. Muslim women – Legal
status, laws, etc. – India.   I. Title.

HQ1236.5.I4N373 2007   305.48'6970954   C2007-905055-7

University of Toronto Press acknowledges the financial assistance to
its publishing program of the Canada Council for the Arts and the
Ontario Arts Council.

University of Toronto Press acknowledges the financial support for its
publishing activities of the Government of Canada through the
Book Publishing Industry Development Program (BPIDP).

Contents

Acknowledgments

I thank Kaleem for everything, but mostly for keeping it real, and Zai and Vir for reminding me of life's priorities. I am grateful to my family in Delhi, my parents and my sister for their love, and Shahla Haidar for her contribution to this project. I thank Colleen Sheppard for combining intellectual exchange with friendship. I am grateful to the Asian Institute, Munk Centre for International Studies, at the University of Toronto for a research fellowship to complete work on this book. I thank Virgil Duff of the University of Toronto Press for his support. I am grateful to Catherine Frost for her diligent copy-editing. Finally, I thank Homa Hoodfar for her encouragement through my academic and activist endeavours.

RECLAIMING THE NATION:
MUSLIM WOMEN AND THE LAW IN INDIA

1 Introduction:
Situating Indian Muslim Women

In India, the location of Muslim women at the intersection of gender, community, and nation exposes the inclusions and exclusions of postcolonial nationalist ideology, the mendacity of equal citizenship, and the inherent dangers of a forced identity based on primordial, essentialist definitions.

Despite formal constitutional guarantees of equality, Muslim women's lives within the family are regulated and structured by explicitly discriminatory laws.[1] The legal regulation of women is central to the negotiations between community and nation to establish the boundaries of the group and the scope of state authority to regulate religion. Family and religion, through personal law, are emphasized as the definers of collective identity and are sought to be protected against state intrusion and the imposition of the norms of the wider society.[2] The status of Muslim women is central to the self-definition of the Muslim collectivity. They are both the border guards of the group and the transmitters of cultural values. Their roles are sought to be regulated and controlled, as they are seen as both the instrument and the symbol of collective identity.[3]

---

1 Zoya Hasan, 'Minority Identity, State Policy and the Political Process,' in Hasan, *Forging Identities*, 59 at 61–3. Under Muslim personal law, women are disadvantaged, compared with men, in matters relating to marriage and divorce, custody and guardianship of children, and inheritance and succession.
2 Marie-Aimée Helie-Lucas, 'The Preferential Symbol for Islamic Identity: Women and Muslim Personal Laws,' in Moghadam, *Identity Politics and Women*, 391 at 393, 396.
3 Nira Yuval-Davis, 'Identity Politics and Women's Ethnicity,' in Moghadam, *supra* note 2, 408 at 413.

The Indian *Constitution* guarantees equality and freedom from discrimination based on gender or religion.[4] It also guarantees religious freedom.[5] In addition to these fundamental rights, the *Constitution* directs the state to enact a uniform civil code (UCC) for the citizens of India.[6] At the same time, India continues to have a system of personal law governing family relations, which applies to individuals based on their religious identity. The major religious groups in India – Hindus, Muslims, Christians, and Parsis – are governed in family matters by their respective personal law,[7] which is based on a combination of religious laws, customs, and practices, as modified by state legislation and judicial precedent. Personal law is the only

---

4 The *Constitution of India*, 1950 (hereinafter the *Constitution*). The fundamental rights are provided in Part III of the *Constitution* in Articles 12 through 35. 'Article 14: 'Equality before law. – The State shall not deny to any person equality before the law or the equal protection of the laws within the territory of India.' The relevant provisions of Article 15 are as follows: Article 15. Prohibition of discrimination on the grounds of religion, race, caste, sex, or place of birth. – (1) The State shall not discriminate against any citizens on grounds only of religion, race, caste, sex, place of birth or any of them. (3) Nothing in this article shall prevent the State from making any special provision for women and children. (4) Nothing in this article or in clause (2) of article 29 shall prevent the State from making any special provision for the advancement of any socially or educationally backward classes of citizens or for the Scheduled Castes and the Scheduled Tribes.'

5 Article 25, Freedom of religion, *Constitution*. Article 25. Freedom of conscience and free profession, practice and propagation of religion. – (1) Subject to public order, morality and health and to other provisions of this Part [the fundamental rights chapter] all persons are equally entitled to freedom of conscience and the right freely to profess, practice and propagate religion. – (2) Nothing in this article shall affect the operation of any existing law or prevent the State from making any law – (a) regulating or restricting any economic, financial, political or other secular activity which may be associated with religious practice; (b) providing for social welfare and reform or the throwing open of Hindu religious institutions of a public character to all classes and sections of Hindus.'

6 Article 44 is a Directive Principle of State Policy, not an enforceable fundamental right. According to the *Constitution*, Directive Principles of State Policy are not enforceable. They lay down the aims of state policy and are recommendatory rather than mandatory. 'Article 37. Application of the Principles contained in this Part [Directive Principles of State Policy]. – The Provisions contained in this Part shall not be enforceable by any court, but the principles therein laid down are nevertheless fundamental in the governance of the country and it shall be the duty of the State to apply these principles in making laws.' 'Article 44. Uniform civil code for the citizens. – The State shall endeavor to secure for the citizens a uniform civil code throughout the territory of India.'

7 Parashar, *Women and Family Law Reform*, 17.

law in India today that explicitly differentiates between individuals on the basis of religion and further differentiates on the basis of gender. Personal law is discriminatory to women and denies women equal rights within the family to varying degrees.[8] In a situation where religion is tied to organized national minorities, this discrimination dictates a system of 'differential citizenship' based on ascriptive belonging.[9] The personal law system creates both differential rights within the family for Muslim, Hindu, and Christian citizens and inequality for women. The right to religious freedom as an integral part of the protection of minority rights is cited as justification for the denial of gender equality in, and lack of reform of, religious personal law.[10] This separation between the formal rights guaranteed in the public sphere and the lived experience of women's disadvantage in the private sphere is maintained by the state and supported by community leaders as an expression of group autonomy, and it serves to deny equal rights to Muslim women.[11] The existence of the personal law system simultaneously reflects the Indian *Constitution*'s commitment to protecting group life, while it represents the state's unfinished agenda to reform religion and its obligation to introduce a uniform civil code.[12] It is this contradictory embrace of individual rights and group rights within the framework of the *Constitution* that renders extremely complex the critical re-examination of the disjuncture between the state's address to Muslim women as citizens and its legitimization of their unequal status under the personal law.

The state's address to Muslim women constructs them as unequal, gendered citizens with a prior religio-cultural identity. Such a con-

---

8 *Ibid.* at 18, 145, 201; Zoya Hasan, 'Introduction: Contextualising Gender and Identity in Contemporary India,' in Hasan, *supra* note 1, vii at xvii. Whereas Hindu law and more recently Christian law have been reformed to grant women greater rights, Muslim personal law has not been reformed to enlarge women's rights within the family. Under Muslim personal law, women have far fewer rights than men in corresponding situations. Women thus are disadvantaged compared with men in laws regarding marriage, divorce, inheritance, succession, custody and guardianship of children, among others.

9 Nancy L. Rosenblum, 'Introduction: Pluralism, Integralism, and Political Theories of Religious Accommodation,' in Rosenblum, *Obligations of Citizenship*, 3 at 6.

10 Parashar, *supra* note 7 at 188.

11 Hasan, *supra* note 1 at 60–1.

12 Sunder Rajan, *Scandal of the State*, 148.

struction places them in an anomalous position with regard to constitutional guarantees of equality and freedom from discrimination. In its
anxiety to retain the loyalty of minority communities to the ideology
of composite nationalism, the post-colonial Indian state has emphatically neglected its constitutional commitment to women, most notably,
to Muslim women.[13] Seeking to end invidious discrimination on the
basis of religion, caste, creed, and gender, the state has emphasized its
commitment to equality through the constitutional guarantee of fundamental rights. At the same time, in order to retain minority allegiance to the state, personal law, although explicitly discriminatory,
has been preserved as an aspect of group identity.[14] Inevitably, in this
situation the state contradicts itself.

Whereas nationalists sought to resolve the question of women's
rights by privileging the anti-colonial struggle over gender issues, in
the post-colonial state the pre-independence cooperation between
feminism and nationalism has not resulted in an aggressive pursuit of
women's rights by the state. The state has refused to reform Muslim
personal law on the grounds that the initiative for reform must come
from within the community.[15] Yet Muslim women's demands for
change have been marginalized.[16] So far, the state has taken no initiative to enact a UCC or to reform Muslim personal law to address the
vulnerability of women.[17] The Indian state's avowed policy of non-
interference in the private sphere of Muslim personal law on the
grounds that the call for change must come from within the community has meant, for those in the community who are already disadvantaged, specifically women, the abandoning of women's concerns

---

13 Parashar, *supra* note 7 at 196.
14 Rajeev Dhavan, 'The Road to Xanadu: India's Quest for Secularism,' in Larson, *Religion and Personal Law*, 301 at 309.
15 Parashar, *supra* note 7 at 19.
16 *Ibid.*; Hasan, *supra* note 8 at xiv, xvi. For example, despite the strong support for the
   Shah Bano decision by Muslim women's groups, including the Muslim Satyashodak
   Samaj and the Committee for Protection of Rights of Muslim Women, Muslim
   women's voices were not included in the debate on maintenance provisions.
   Another example is the refusal by the state and by community leaders to reform
   the divorce laws, despite demands from Muslim women's groups.
17 The early post-colonial state did take the initiative to enact the *Special Marriage Act*,
   which may be regarded as the kernel of a UCC, as a first step toward providing a
   uniform law without regard to religious affiliation. However, this preliminary
   optional solution is far from adequate, and the state has done little to address the
   systemic gender discrimination in all personal laws.

and the privileging of the voice of those already powerful within the community.[18]

The system of personal law perpetuates the subalternity of Muslim women who have been denied the power to speak or to define their needs, let alone the right to claim gender equality.[19] The manner in which presumed community interests are prioritized over women's concerns as a matter of political expedience has had profound consequences for the equality rights of Muslim women. The acceptance of male, conservative leaders of the Muslim community as the sole authentic voice of the group has led to a superficial, essentialized understanding of the accommodation of difference that serves to mask power relations and hierarchies within the group while buttressing dominant cultural norms that are oppressive to women.[20]

The status of women has served as a crucial signifier of the development of states. British colonialists used it to legitimize their civilizing mission and the imperial project. The nationalist government was conscious of the status of women as an index of modernization, crucial to its self-definition as a member of the community of developed, modern nations.[21] Accordingly, law reform was an important aspect of the modernizing nationalist project, and the Indian *Constitution* mandates the role of the state as a social reformer. Indeed, as Rajeswari Sunder Rajan argues, the early post-colonial Indian state deployed its social reformer role on behalf of women primarily to initiate social reform in continuation with the colonial state's claim to establishing civilizational modernity. The state now claimed 'to rescue, reclaim and rehabilitate women in the fervour of a nationalist identity politics.'[22] Today, the Indian state is called upon to meaningfully address the systemic gender disadvantage of Indian women of all communities, as women's groups have insisted on emphasizing the status of women as an integral part of the state's agenda.[23]

---

18 Galanter, *Competing Equalities*, 23. Drawing from Galanter's analysis that the British policy of non-interference, while leading to formal equality for lower castes, also led to increased advantages for the higher castes.

19 Subaltern is defined as a person of inferior rank, a marginalized subject relating tangentially or in opposition to the societal universal norm. Pathak and Sunder Rajan, 'Shahbano,' 565.

20 Razack, *Looking White People in the Eye*, 9.

21 Sunder Rajan, *supra* note 12 at 2, 3.

22 *Ibid.* at 3.

23 *Ibid.*

While women have been granted equality in terms of civil and political rights, equality continues to be denied in the realm of the private through the perpetuation of the personal law. The state's claim to grant equal citizenship to women is contradicted by women's disadvantage under the personal law system based explicitly on differences of gender and religion. India's political climate of rising Hindu right-wing chauvinism, Islamist fundamentalism, and politicized religious identity has impeded progress towards family law reform and the enactment of a UCC.[24] This suggests the need to separate the question of gender justice from religious politics. The challenge before us is to disrupt hegemonic ways of seeing group interests and gender justice that serve to reify these relations of power and reify women's subordination.[25] To forward women's rights, it is important to bring women's lives, experiences, and identities, hitherto excluded or hidden, back into the purview of state-citizen relations and to demand state accountability to women as equal citizens.

This book focuses on the relationship between gender and nation. Specifically, it seeks to interrogate the manner in which Muslim women are simultaneously granted and denied an equal citizenship in the post-colonial Indian nation. Inevitably, it is personal law reform – specifically, the gender issues involved – that forms the core of this debate. The state, by retaining the personal law system, has reneged on its constitutional promise to the women of India, particularly to Muslim women, who, owing to the lack of reform of Muslim personal law, are further disadvantaged.[26] Rather than describing the specific discriminatory provisions of Muslim personal law, my aim is to situate the claim for Muslim women's equality within the context of the Indian *Constitution*.[27]

Citizenship is a contested concept. It has been variously understood as a status ascribed by the state, as a set of rights, as an exercise of agency through political participation, and also as rights emanating from cul-

---

24 Dhavan, *supra* note 14 at 318, 319.

25 Razack, *supra* note 20 at 10.

26 Zoya Hasan, 'Gender Politics, Legal Reform, and the Muslim Community in India,' in Jeffery and Basu, *Resisting the Sacred and the Secular*, 71 at 72, 73.

27 *Ibid*. 71 at 71. For a discussion of the specific provisions of Muslim personal law, please see Fyzee, *Outlines of Muhammadan Law*; Pearl, *Textbook on Muslim Personal Law*; Coulson, *History of Islamic Law*; Derrett, *Religion, Law and the State*; Diwan, *Muslim Law*; Bhattacharjee, *Muslim Law*.

tural or group identification and membership. I discuss the idea of citizenship as a dialectical relationship between the classic understanding of it as both a status and a set of rights and the feminist and multicultural notion that it cannot be reduced to one single aspect of identity, in order to forward a gender-pluralist concept. I rely on an understanding of citizenship informed by the feminist challenge to a notion of citizenship that has hitherto excluded women from the enjoyment of equal rights. I base this understanding on the insights gleaned from feminist and multicultural citizenship literature. I have chosen the *Shah Bano* controversy as the lens through which we can explore how the relationship between gender and nation is constituted as it illustrates the manner in which the intersection of gender and religious identity excludes Muslim women from the privileges of equal citizenship.[28]

The *Shah Bano* case, decided by the Supreme Court in 1985, caused an unprecedented furor and pushed the nation to the brink of a constitutional crisis over the question of maintenance for divorced Muslim women.[29] The Supreme Court ruled in favour of Shah Bano, holding that the question of spousal support for Muslim women must be decided in accordance with financial need, and that personal law cannot override the secular law in matters of social welfare and public policy.[30] This decision, however, was not welcomed by Muslim fundamentalist leaders, who orchestrated a massive campaign against the decision, which ultimately resulted in the enactment of the only postcolonial Muslim personal law legislation, the *Muslim Women's (Protection of Rights on Divorce Act)*, 1986.[31] By enacting this law, the ruling Congress Party for the first time in modern Indian history, abrogated a

---

28 *Mohammed Ahmed Khan* v. *Shah Bano Begum*, AIR 1985 SC 945. Jayal, *Democracy and the State*, 7. There is a vast literature on the several understandings of citizenship. I rely on the insights and ideas articulated by Lister, *Citizenship*; Lister, 'Feminist Theory,' 5; Yuval-Davis, *Gender and Nation*; Phillips, *Democracy and Difference*; Young, *Inclusion and Democracy*; Young, *Justice and the Politics of Difference*; Mouffe, 'Democratic Citizenship'; Shachar, *Multicultural Jurisdictions*; Kymlicka, *Multicultural Citizenship*; Nedelsky, 'Citizenship and Relational Feminism'; Jan Jindy Pettman, 'Globalisation and the Gendered Politics of Citizenship' in Yuval-Davis and Werbner, *Women, Citizenship and Difference*, 207; Pnina Werbner, 'The Politics of Multiculturalism' in Saunders and Haljan, *Whither Multiculturalism*, 47; Bhabha, *Nation and Narration*; Bhabha, *The Location of Culture*.
29 Pathak and Sunder Rajan, *supra* note 19 at 558.
30 *Shah Bano*, *supra* note 28 at 948.
31 Hasan, *supra* note 1 at 64. *The Muslim Women's (Protection of Rights on Divorce) Act* (hereinafter *Muslim Women's Act*); see 'Statutes' in Bibliography.

Supreme Court decision. Politicized religion was able to prevail over constitutional principles in the electoral calculations of party politics, and Muslim women's interests were subsumed under the presumed interests of the Muslim collectivity.[32]

The *Shah Bano* case raises issues that go to the heart of the complex question of the legal status of Muslim women: gender justice, minority rights, and the duty of the state to introduce a uniform civil code. This case presented, and in its aftermath continues to present, a dilemma to Indian feminists. The various political convergences and contradictions among those who support a UCC for women and those who seek to use the notion of a uniform family law to undermine minority rights raise the spectre of majority Hindu chauvinism. They have led many in the women's movement to reject a UCC for fear that advocacy would, in the current political context, serve only to alienate the minorities and escalate their anxiety regarding their rights as citizens and the assimilationist impulse of the majority community.[33]

The Shah Bano Narrative

Mohammed Ahmed Khan v. Shah Bano Begum

The question of spousal support for Muslim women has been a matter of contention between the state and community leaders. Whereas the state and the judiciary have attempted to widen the scope of the law to include Muslim women, fundamentalist leaders, by contrast, have consistently sought to circumscribe Muslim women's rights by curtailing the application of general laws to Muslim women. The conflict centres around the provision for maintenance under section 125 of the *Indian Criminal Procedure Code* (hereinafter CrPC).[34] Enacted in colonial

---

32 Hasan, *supra* note 31 at 67.
33 Amrita Chhachhi, 'Identity Politics, Secularism, and Women: A South Asian Perspective,' in Hasan, *supra* note 1, 74 at 89; Sunder Rajan, *supra* note 12 at ix.
34 *The Indian Criminal Procedure Code*, 1973 as amended by *The Criminal Procedure Code Amendment Act*, 2002 (hereinafter, CrPC); see 'Statutes' in Bibliography. The relevant provisions of section 125 of the CrPC are as follows: 125. '(1) If any person having sufficient means neglects or refuses to maintain – (a) his wife, unable to maintain herself ... a Magistrate of the first class, may, upon proof of such neglect or refusal, order such person to make a monthly allowance for the maintenance of his wife as the Magistrate thinks fit. Explanation – For the purposes of this Chapter, – (b) "'Wife' includes a woman who has been divorced, or who has obtained a divorce from her husband and has not remarried."'

times, it was intended as a welfare measure to provide, in summary proceedings, maintenance for destitute wives to prevent vagrancy.[35] Muslim men, however, were able to evade responsibility for payments by divorcing their wives under their personal law. To address this vulnerability of Muslim women, in 1973 the state sought to amend the maintenance provisions of the CrPC, to include divorced wives.[36] The law was amended to include divorced wives, but Muslim leaders won an escape clause, providing that if Muslim husbands fulfilled their obligations as required under personal law, they were not liable to pay maintenance.[37]

However, the Supreme Court interpreted the provisions for maintenance for women to include Muslim women within their scope. *Bai Tahira, Zohara Khatoon*, and *Fuzlunbi* were decided in response to the state's compromise with Muslim fundamentalist leaders, who sought to resist state efforts to guarantee maintenance rights for divorced Muslim women.[38] *Shah Bano* was the logical culmination of this judicial interpretive process that sought to expand the rights of Muslim women, following this trilogy of cases decided by the Supreme Court on similar questions of maintenance for Muslim women. Yet it was *Shah Bano* that provoked an outcry and generated tremendous controversy, while earlier and, indeed, subsequent decisions, essentially similar in law, provoked little reaction. Arguably, it was the timing of *Shah Bano* decision and the context of political uncertainty, spiralling Hindu right-wing chauvinism, and increased Islamist fundamentalism that led to this virulent reaction.

Shah Bano was in her seventies when her husband, Mohammed Ahmed Khan, forced her out of their home after forty-three years of

---

35 Section 488 of the Code of Criminal Procedure, 1872.
36 This provision is not meant to be a substitute for civil proceedings for spousal support upon marital breakdown, but is a provision for support for women under the criminal law procedures, which are quicker. This provision for maintenance applied to women irrespective of personal law.
37 Section 127(3)(b), CrPC: 'Where any order has been made under s.125 in favour of a woman who has been divorced by or has obtained a divorce from her husband, the magistrate shall if he is satisfied that: the woman has been divorced by her husband and that she has received, whether before or after the date of the said order, the whole sum which under any customary or personal law applicable to the parties, was payable on such divorce, cancel such order.'
38 *Bai Tahira* v. *Ali Hussain Fidalli*, AIR 1979 SC 362; *Zohara Khatoon* v. *Mohammed Ibrahim*, AIR 1981 SC 1243; *Fuzlunbi* v. *Khader Vali*, AIR 1980 SC 1730.

marriage. She filed for maintenance under section 125 of the CrPC.[39] A few months later, her husband divorced her under Muslim law through the method of triple *talaq*, which allows husbands unilateral, unregulated divorce. The magistrate ruled in favour of Shah Bano. Astonishingly, however, Shah Bano was awarded a mere Rs. 25 per month, amounting to less than $1. It is interesting to note that her husband's declared income was Rs. 5,000 per month. The High Court of the state of Madhya Pradesh enhanced the maintenance amount to Rs. 179.20 per month.[40] Her husband then filed an appeal in the Supreme Court of India.[41]

The questions that the Supreme Court had to consider were whether Shah Bano, as a divorced Muslim woman, was eligible for maintenance under section 125 and, correspondingly, whether Muslim men were exempt from the provisions of this law on the basis of personal law. Mohammed Ahmed Khan claimed that he had discharged his obligations to his now ex-wife under Muslim law, and that as he was a Muslim, the secular law of maintenance was not applicable to him. He argued that his personal law overrode the secular law in this matter.

The Supreme Court decided in favour of Shah Bano, relying on a purposive interpretation of the provisions of section 125, CrPC, and based on established case law. The court ruled that, in keeping with the social welfare object of section 125, the religion of parties was not relevant.[42] Further, the court held that, in case of a conflict between secular law and personal law, the secular law must prevail.[43] The court also held that Muslim law did not preclude maintenance for divorcees.[44] Finally, the court called upon the state to enact a UCC to address gender discrimination under the personal law system.[45]

---

39 Less than $20 per month. In Shah Bano's time, there was a fixed maximum amount of rupees. 500.
40 About $10. *Shah Bano, supra* note 28 at 946–7.
41 The Supreme Court of India is the highest court in the country; below it are the various state High Courts, and below the High Courts, the District Courts. Shah Bano filed her claim for maintenance under s.125 of the CrPC in the District Court and appealed against the amount awarded in the High Court; her ex-husband then filed an appeal in the Supreme Court of India.
42 *Shah Bano, supra* note 28 at 948
43 *Ibid.*
44 *Ibid.* at 951, 952.
45 *Ibid.* at 954.

The Muslim Women's (Protection of Rights on Divorce) Act, 1986

Shah Bano made clear the complexities in attaining gender equality within the family.[46] The judgment was harshly criticized by fundamentalist and conservative Muslim leaders for its reference to the UCC, which was understood as a sweeping criticism of Muslim personal law.[47] They were concerned that the Supreme Court had taken it upon itself to interpret the Koran, and they rejected the judgment as an illegitimate interference with Muslim personal law. They saw it as an assault on Muslim personal law and, as important, as an assault on the their understanding of India's democratic secular consensus based on the privacy and autonomy of the sphere of personal law.[48] The government initially supported the Supreme Court decision, hailing it as an important victory for women. However, when a ruling party candidate lost a by-election to Syed Shahbuddin, one of the fundamentalist leaders of the anti-*Shah Bano* campaign, the government quickly changed its stance.[49]

Ignoring the voices of progressive Muslims, Muslim reformists, feminists, and Muslim women's groups, all of whom supported the *Shah Bano* decision and opposed the proposed legislation, the government

---

46 Hasan, 'Minority Identity,' *supra* note 1 at 65.

47 *Ibid.*

48 Dhagamwar, *Uniform Civil Code*, 24.

49 Hasan, *supra* note 1 at 66. Pathak and Sunder Rajan, *supra* note 19 at 559. Radha Kumar, 'Identity Politics and the Contemporary Indian Feminist Movement,' in Moghadam, *supra* note 2, 274 at 277. Hasan, *supra* note 26 at 89. Parashar, *supra* note 7 at 173–6. A bill to enact legislation specifically to exclude women from the secular law of maintenance, the Muslim Women's Bill, had been introduced by a Muslim League member of Parliament, Mr Banatwala. The government persuaded him to withdraw his bill and introduced its own bill, the Muslim Women's Protection of Rights on Divorce Bill which was passed into legislation in 1986, specifically to undo the *Shah Bano* decision. It was based on the contentions of the Ulema (Muslim religious leaders) and the All India Muslim Personal Law Board's interventions in *Shah Bano* that rejected a Muslim husband's liability to support his ex-wife beyond the prescribed *iddat* period. (Under Muslim law, a man is required to pay spousal support to his divorced wife for a period of three menstrual cycles, or three months. This is known as *iddat*. If the divorced wife is pregnant, then the *iddat* period runs till the birth of the child. Fyzee, *supra* note 27 at 108.) The All India Muslim Personal Law Board was the self-appointed arbiter of Muslim personal law, founded in 1973 specifically to safeguard Muslim law against any reform, to protect what the members deemed the true *shariat*. It was an intervenor in the *Shah Bano* case on behalf of her husband, Mohammed Ahmed Khan.

rushed through the enactment of the new law.[50] It was called, ironically, the *Muslim Women's (Protection of Rights on Divorce) Act, 1986*.[51] In
fact, it curtailed Muslim women's rights and was far from being a
demonstration of the state's commitment to gender equality. It
excluded Muslim women from the application of the general law of
spousal support, which had been applicable to them hitherto and continues to be applicable to all other Indian women. By contrast, men's
rights within the family were reinforced, unequal gender relations
were buttressed, and patriarchal structures of authority were strengthened. Men's right to unregulated, extrajudicial divorce was reaffirmed,
and their right to polygamy remained unchallenged. Muslim husbands were absolved of the duty to support their ex-wives beyond
their obligation to repay the dower amount and to pay maintenance
for the three-month *iddat* period. After this time, divorced Muslim
women were to be supported by their children, their parents, their
future heirs, or, in the last resort, by the Wakf Boards (Muslim charitable institutions).[52]

---

50 Parashar, *supra* note 7 at 177–9; Hasan, *supra* note 1 at 68.
51 *Muslim Women's Act, supra* note 31.
52 Section 4 of the *Muslim Women's Act* 'Order for payment of maintenance. – (1)
Notwithstanding anything contained in the foregoing provisions of this Act, or in
any other law for the time being in force, where a Magistrate is satisfied that a
divorced woman has not remarried and is not able to maintain herself after the
iddat period, he may make an order directing such of her relatives as would be
entitled to inherit her property upon her death according to Muslim law to pay
such reasonable and fair maintenance to her as he may determine fit and proper,
having regard to the needs of the divorced woman, the standard of life enjoyed by
her during her marriage and the means of such relatives and such maintenance
shall be payable by such relatives in the proportions in which they would inherit
her property and at such periods as he may specify in his order. Provided that
where such divorced woman has children, the Magistrate shall order only such
children to pay maintenance to her, and in the event of any such children being
unable to pay such maintenance, the Magistrate shall order the parents of such
divorced woman to pay maintenance to her: Provided further that if any of the
parents is unable to pay his or her share of the maintenance ordered by the Magistrate on the grounds of not having the means to pay the same, the Magistrate may,
on proof of such inability being furnished to him, order that the share of such relatives in the maintenance ordered by him be paid by such of the other relatives as
may appear to the Magistrate to have the means of paying the same in such proportions as the Magistrate may think fit to order. (2) Where a divorced woman is
unable to maintain herself and she has no relatives as mentioned in sub-section (1)
or such relatives or any one of them have not enough means to pay the mainte-

The circumstances of the enactment of the *Muslim Women's Act* demonstrates the use of the rhetoric of protection by state and community in conflicts over Muslim women's rights.[53] The discourse of protection was used to mediate the tension between Muslim women's rights and group rights and was deployed in the use of personal law to regulate gender roles and community identity.[54] The notion of protection further demonstrates the use of the public/private split to reinforce women's subordination. The state presented the *Muslim Women's Act* as offering greater protection to Muslim women, rescuing them from dependence on uncaring husbands and instead allowing them to depend on their children, parents, or heirs, or on the charity of religious institutions. By iterating that, indeed, Muslim personal law better safeguarded Muslim women's rights than the general, secular law of maintenance, the state was able to claim to be simultaneously protecting the interests of Muslim women and the Muslim community.[55] Muslim fundamentalist leaders' opposition to the *Shah Bano* decision and their support for the new Act was articulated around the notion of protecting Muslim women, Islam, and group identity from state interference. The Hindu right, not surprisingly, supported the *Shah Bano* decision and opposed the *Muslim Women's Act* as being state appeasement of minorities. For them, this controversy was an opportunity to challenge minority rights, as they, too, used the notion of protecting Muslim women from the backward and outdated Muslim personal law and, following from that, protecting Muslim women from Muslim men.[56]

The *Muslim Women's Act* illustrates the symbiotic relationship between community leaders and the state, reflecting the inherent ten-

---

nance ordered by the Magistrate to be paid, the Magistrate may by order, direct the State Wakf Board established under section 9 of the Wakf Act, 1954, or under any to her law for the time being in force in a State, functioning in the area in which the woman resides, to pay such maintenance as determined by him under sub-section (1) or, as the case may be, to pay the shares of such relatives who are unable to pay, at such periods as he may specify in his order.'

Wakf Boards are Muslim charitable institutions that administer funds and land donated by religious Muslims for the upkeep of Muslim religious institutions. The administration of Wakf Boards is overseen and regulated by the state and the members of the Wakf Boards are nominated by the state.

53 Pathak and Sunder Rajan, *supra* note 19 at 569.
54 Narain, *Gender and Community*, 34.
55 Pathak and Sunder Rajan, *supra* note 19 at 568.
56 Hasan, *supra* note 1 at 64–6.

sions within contradictory state policies of the protection of women's rights, the commitment to secular laws, the perpetuation of the personal law system, the pressures of Hindu right-wing politics, and minority anxieties. Discussions of Muslim women's rights, rather than retaining a focus on gender equality, are invariably displaced by discussions of minority rights.[57] The rights of Muslim women were debated in terms of religion but not in terms of constitutional law or their rights as equal citizens of the nation entitled to equal protection under the law.[58] The debate around Muslim personal law reform converted what was an issue of women's rights to one of minority rights, erasing the lived experience of Muslim women and ignoring their claims to equality and personal law reform. As Zoya Hasan argues, 'These displacements and subversions treated Muslim women as emblematic of personal law or minority identity, and the high stakes of real Muslim women in equality were overlooked.'[59]

By enacting the *Muslim Women's Act*, the state showed itself willing to give into demands to preserve discriminatory personal laws in return for minority political support. The Act reinforced state legitimization of community control over Muslim women. The state thus buttressed patriarchal structures of authority within the Muslim community by allowing leaders to circumscribe Muslim women's rights, thereby increasing their dependence upon the community. The unwillingness to enforce the principle of gender equality emphasizes state collusion with the politically more powerful interests within the Muslim community, invariably those of the male clergy. The state was complicit in curtailing the rights of Muslim women as citizens by allowing religious law to override even minimal constitutional entitlements for Muslim women, as the rights of cultural community were privileged over the rights of citizenship for women.[60] In passing the *Muslim Women's Act* restricting Muslim women's rights to spousal support, the state did not address the economic vulnerability of divorced Muslim women by either regulating men's right to unilateral extra-judicial divorce or reforming spousal support provisions in Muslim law.

---

57 Mukhopadhyay, *Legally Dispossessed*, 23.
58 Vasudha Dhagamwar, 'Women, Children, and the Constitution: Hostages to Religion, Outcaste by Law,' in Baird, *Religion and Law*, 215 at 255.
59 Hasan, *supra* note 26 at 85–6.
60 Jayal, *supra* note 28, at 148 on.

The fundamentalist All India Muslim Personal Law Board (AIMPLB) led the campaign against the *Shah Bano* judgment.[61] Although the discourse of Muslim fundamentalists was cloaked in the language of opposition to state intervention in the internal affairs of the community, the *Muslim Women's Act*, which they welcomed as a victory, in fact implied greater state intervention in the management of Muslim community affairs, in relation to both the functioning of the Wakf Boards and the restrictions on Muslim women.[62] They claimed to be protecting the rights of Muslim women through their rejection of the Supreme Court *Shah Bano* judgment and by their insistence on the *Muslim Women's Act*. Yet, in so doing, fundamentalists were reasserting their control over the women of the community. Significantly, this reassertion of community control was occurring as a response to the reality that Muslim women increasingly were resorting to the secular law to widen their rights within the family, as reflected in a rise in cases filed by Muslim women seeking property rights, spousal support, and even divorce.[63] Arguably, women's challenges to traditional structures of authority are met with renewed efforts to reassert these controls, as women are the symbols of the group, and personal law is regarded as the primary signifier of group identity.[64]

Shah Bano's subalternity was determined by her multiple identities: she was lower class, she was a woman, and she belonged to a minority community. Yet she disrupted traditional stereotypes by seeking legal intervention in a family dispute and brought the apparatus of the state into the private sphere of the family, which community leaders have tried to maintain separate from the intrusions of the public sphere of state regulation.[65] It is significant, however, that Shah Bano was forced to retreat from her challenge by publicly rejecting the Supreme Court decision in her favour. Conscious of the Hindu right-wing support for her and its opposition to the *Muslim Women's Act*, Shah Bano rejected the offer of 'protection' from Hindu fundamentalists and chose to forward the presumed interests of the group over her

---

61 Parashar, *supra* note 7 at 174. There were nevertheless also several Muslim women who supported the AIMPLB's position and rallied around the cry of Islam in danger. Hasan, *supra* note 26 at 84.

62 Chhachhi, *supra* note 33 at 89.

63 Hasan, *supra* note 26 at 88.

64 *Ibid.*

65 Kapur and Cossman, *Subversive Sites,* 64.

interests as a woman.[66] In an open letter she declared that the Supreme Court judgment was contrary to Islamic law and was an open interference in Muslim personal law. 'I, Shah Bano, being a Muslim, reject it and dissociate myself from every judgment that is contrary to the Islamic Shariat. I am aware of the agony and distress to which this judgment has subjected the Muslims of India today.'[67]

Shah Bano thus complicates simplistic understandings of a subaltern consciousness. While at one level she was able to challenge her subject position, at another she was restricted by her location. Yet Shah Bano's story points to the possibilities of the transformative power of subaltern resistance. It is this complicated location that challenges us to problematize assumptions about analytic categories of 'woman,' 'Muslim woman,' 'minorities,' and 'others.'

Situating Muslim Women

The Muslim woman as the post-colonial gendered subject is rendered disadvantaged – as a woman, as Muslim, and as a Muslim woman. The location of Muslim women at the intersection of multiple axes of discrimination has meant that, even sixty years after independence, they continue to be among the most disadvantaged, impoverished, and politically marginalized groups within Indian society. Their economic and social vulnerability combined with the denial of equal protection of the law as citizens, makes the re-examination of their situation critical.[68] Muslim women occupy a unique location, forcing us to disrupt the complacency of Manichean dichotomies through which we understand the validity of the protection of both women's rights and the protection of group difference. To forward Muslim women's rights, we need to move the focus away from false binaries such as modernity versus tradition, personal law versus uniform civil code, and community versus nation.[69] The challenge before us is to bring the margin to

---

66 Pathak and Sunder Rajan, *supra* note 19 at 572.
67 Engineer, *Shah Bano*, 211, 212.
68 Kazi, *Muslim Women*, 2.
69 Before going any further, I should acknowledge borrowing from Martha Minow an explanation of my use of the word *we*. 'My use of "we" … represents an invitation to the reader to assent, to disagree, but above all to engage with this focus. I use "we," moreover, to emphasize the human authorship of the problems and solutions at hand and to avoid locutions that eliminate human pronouns.' 'Foreword,' 10 at 15.

the centre, and to demarginalize the intersection of gender and religion to give Muslim women voice, to articulate their needs, to compel the state to respond to their signals for change, and to realize the constitutional promise of equality and freedom from discrimination.[70]

The difficulties inherent in pursuing women's rights in the context of colonialism and nationalism greatly impacted the agenda of the women's movement and shaped the struggle for women's rights. In the years preceding India's independence from Britain in 1947 an important aspect of organized women's struggle was the challenge to existing laws and the demand for law reform to give women more equitable rights within the family.[71] The law was a site of intense discursive struggle as women fought to claim rights and to challenge male privilege. Upon independence, it appeared as if Indian women, too, had been liberated. Indeed, the women's movement's primary objectives of universal adult suffrage and law reform had been conceded. However, this was not the whole picture.

Women's issues were subsumed under what were considered more pressing, politically fraught issues such as minority rights and establishing a secular state. Indeed, it is here that the public/private divide appears to have been reinstated by leaders, and women were placed once again squarely within the patriarchal family. For Indian women, and especially for Muslim women, the discourse of nationalism and citizenship seemed to stop short at the family. As Partha Chatterjee notes, 'Equal citizenship is qualified by the existence of the different personal laws.'[72] Whereas women faced little resistance to their demand for equal civil and political rights – winning the right to vote – their demand for family law reform was met with fierce opposition, and law reform was still not established.

The state has displayed a certain ambivalence towards enforcing the principle of gender equality, most particularly for women of minority groups. The state's claim of reforming personal law to make it more gender equitable is itself open to scrutiny. While Hindu law was reformed to some extent, the post-colonial state did not similarly reform minority personal laws. Muslim personal law remained unchanged till the passing of the retrograde *Muslim Women's (Protec-*

---

70 Crenshaw, 'Demarginalizing the Intersection of Race and Sex.'
71 Forbes, *New Cambridge History of India*, 113.
72 Partha Chatterjee, 'Secularism and Tolerance,' in Bhargava, *Secularism and Its Critics*, 345 at 375.

tion of Rights on Divorce) Act in 1986 in response to the *Shah Bano* decision.[73] This is not to say, however, that the state has a good record of
enforcing women's rights in the majority Hindu community.

Women's groups' and social reformers' campaigns to reform Hindu
personal law did meet with partial success as some measure of gender
equity was recognized in reformed Hindu law. The nationalist government did reform Hindu law despite opposition from conservative
Hindus, including the president of India himself. Between 1954 and
1956 a series of separate Acts were passed to reform Hindu family
law.[74] However, this was in a more modified form than originally
envisaged.[75] Not only was the reform partial, but, by leaving property
and power relations within the Hindu joint family unchallenged it did
not go to the root of women's disadvantage under Hindu law. This
partial reform of Hindu law, while being far in advance of the treatment of minority laws by the new post-colonial government, did
nothing to challenge the structures of oppression; so, as a feminist
project, it remains incomplete. Perhaps the greater significance of this

---

73 *Muslim Women's Act, supra* note 31.
74 Basu and Ray, *Women's Struggle,* 67. 'These Acts were: The *Hindu Marriage Act,*
    which abolished polygamy, fixed the marriage age of both boys and girls and
    granted the right of divorce to Hindu women; the *Hindu Succession Act,* which
    granted women the right to inherit and hold certain kinds of property. In the past
    women had possessed only a limited right over inherited property, that is, they
    could not sell it or bequeath it by will. Also, the daughter had no claim in her
    father's property, but now property was to be divided equally between the sons
    and the daughters. An unmarried daughter, a widow or a woman deserted by or
    separated from her husband, was granted right of residence in her father's home.
    The *Hindu Minority and Guardianship Act* made the guardianship of a woman over
    her children become at par with her husband's and she could appoint a guardian
    for her children by will. The *Hindu Adoption and Maintenance Act* allowed for the
    adoption of a son or a daughter. The consent of the wife now became necessary for
    adoption.'
75 Gerald James Larson, 'Introduction,' in Larson, *supra* note 14, 1 at 5: 'A first attempt
    at the development of a uniform civil code came shortly after independence in 1948
    with the introduction of the Hindu Code Bill, a bill designed to codify the myriad
    of regional Hindu customs and laws as a first step towards a uniform civil code for
    all. There was much Hindu opposition and the bill was set aside without passage
    in 1951, this led to the resignation of the distinguished law minister, Ambedkar.
    The Hindu code was later introduced piecemeal in the mid-50s when Nehru had a
    more pliant Parliament, and was passed as the *Hindu Marriage Act* (1955), the *Hindu
    Succession Act* (1956), the *Hindu Minority and Guardianship Act* (1956), and the *Hindu
    Adoptions and Maintenance Act* (1956).'

reform lay in its symbolic value as a first step towards the reform of religious personal law and the separation of religion from law to move towards a UCC as part of the post-colonial state's wider commitment to family law reform to address systemic gender discrimination. Arguably, the reform of Hindu law must be seen not only as a measure to address the status of women, but equally as an exercise in modern nation building and as a demonstration of India's post-colonial claim to modernization and secularism.[76]

An explanation for the lack of reform in Muslim personal law may be sought in the circumstances of India's partition along religious lines at Independence. In this context and the subsequent creation of the state of Pakistan as a homeland for Muslims, the new nationalist leaders strove to define India in terms of its secularism and commitment to diversity. The immediate challenge facing the newly independent state was understood as being the creation of a secular, pluralistic democracy that recognized and accommodated religious difference through the protection of minority rights. For the nationalist government, in its anxiety to retain the loyalty of minority communities to, and especially Muslim confidence in, the new state, guaranteeing minority rights took precedence over the protection of women's rights. In return for Muslim adherence to the ideology of nationalism, leaders were complicit in postponing a re-examination of the rights of Muslim women within the family. In the negotiations between community and nation, religious identity was accorded a prior claim and the interests of Muslim women were marginalized.[77]

The colonial state had created the myth of the autonomous personal sphere that was untouched by colonial hegemony to appease the nationalist imagination. Excluded from legitimate areas of political participation in the public sphere, the private sphere became the only space in which 'the natives' could exercise authority. Inevitably, the focus of attention was on the family and personal law, which remained the only spaces where religious leaders could exercise control. In the immediate aftermath of independence and continuing in the present, the superimposition of the emancipation/national liberation discourse on the discourse of 'the home and the world' persists. The imperatives of gover-

---

76 Rajeev Dhavan and Fali S. Nariman, 'The Supreme Court and Group Life: Religious Freedom, Minority Groups, and Disadvantaged Communities,' in Kirpal et al., *Supreme but Not Infallible*, 256 at 257.
77 Parashar, *supra* note 7 at 195–7.

nance, reflecting the anxieties of the post-colonial state, most especially the concern to build a pluralist, secular republic, have resulted in the studied neglect of Muslim women's equality rights, owing to the state's reluctance to interfere with minority personal laws.[78] The colonial government's expression of the group principle through the preservation of personal law was readily appropriated by the post-colonial state, and thus religion was irrevocably appropriated to political life in independent India.[79] At the same time, the idea of home and the world, wherein the Muslim community fiercely guards the personal law against state hegemony, continues, the difference being only that this is not the colonial but the post-colonial national state.

As a consequence, for Muslim women in India, citizenship is invariably mediated through their religious identity. In post-colonial India, the personal law system continues, legitimized and sanctioned by the state as a measure of its commitment to minority rights, secularism, and pluralism. The Indian state continues the colonial policy of a public/private split, upholding a dual legal structure that recognizes the system of discriminatory personal laws, while at the same time the laws applying to the public sphere are free from the burden of invidious distinctions of caste, creed, religion, and gender. Muslim women are particularly vulnerable in this dual legal structure that, on the one hand, affirms the equality of women in public life, while, on the other hand, perpetuates the personal law system, which is explicitly based on gender and religious differences.

The post-colonial state, like the colonial state, has formulated its policies with the notion of an undifferentiated, homogeneous category of 'Muslim,' without regard to differences of gender, class, custom, and region, among others. As a result, Muslim women have suffered from a lack of comprehensive analysis of their gendered subjectivity, which instead has been understood as mediated by religion alone, and the systemic nature of gender discrimination in India has been disregarded. In considerations of public policy, Muslim women invariably have been viewed as a category apart, with religion seen as the main oppositional force in their lives. We need to have an analytical framework that does not separate Muslim women from other Indian women solely on the basis of religion.[80]

---

78 *Ibid.* at 145.
79 Dhavan and Nariman, *supra* note 76 at 275.
80 Lateef, *Muslim Women*, 104–5.

It is critical to understand that the category 'Muslim women' is defined not simply by religion, but also by other situated and locational experiences that affect all Indian women equally. The analytical category of Muslim women highlights the need to pay attention to other experiences that are brought to bear simply by their existence in the lives of such women. Their ability to participate in (the making of) their culture is affected by their experience of religious fundamentalism, patriarchy, nationalism, as well as communalism. All these experiences together have shaped the struggle for greater rights. Nevertheless, it must be acknowledged that the legal aspect of change is perhaps the single factor that differentiates Muslim women from women of other communities in India.[81]

Questions of the status of women and women's rights within the family are 'central to post-colonial national culture and politics,' making gender a critical category of analysis.[82] The *Shah Bano* case sparked off a constitutional crisis and reignited the debate on a UCC, reiterating the centrality of women's issues to the national debate. Yet, while women's issues are central to the definition of community and state, at the same time, women are addressed as the subjects rather than the objects of debate and women's interests are erased.[83] Muslim women's claims to gender equality are framed by the state and by community leaders within a discourse of protection that results at once in stripping women of their agency and seeing them primarily in terms of their victim status. This serves to circumscribe Muslim women's rights and to frame them narrowly within discussions of personal law reform and equal citizenship. Indian feminists have questioned the role of the state as the guarantor of women's rights in light of the state's failure to address systemic gender discrimination.[84] The state upholds the dual legal structure that disadvantages Muslim women, while at the same time professing to be the emancipatory ally of all Indian women. As *Shah Bano* highlights, the state, in fact, has been an accomplice in the subordination of women within religious

---

81 *Ibid.* at 107; Kazi, *supra* note 68 at 4: 'Muslims, therefore, are not a single homogeneous community in India. According to the Anthropological Survey of India, over 350 regional or ethno-linguistic Muslim groups exist in India.'
82 Rajeswari Sunder Rajan, 'Introduction' in Sunder Rajan, *Signposts*, 1 at 3.
83 Sunder Rajan, *supra* note 12 at 166.
84 Paul B. Courtright and Namita Goswami, 'Who Was Roop Kanwar?' in Larson, *supra* note 14, 200 at 210.

communities, relying on arguments of cultural specificity and internal autonomy of groups to deny Muslim women's claims to equitable family laws.

When considering the situation of Muslim women under personal law, we must be careful not to trivialize their struggles for change, while recognizing their efforts at challenging male privilege through everyday acts of resistance.[85] We must be careful to retain the cultural, political, and socio-economic context of Muslim women's lives, where challenging certain aspects such as polygamy may lead to unwanted consequences such as abandonment, which may well be a worse fate, given the reality of non-existent spousal support provisions. The point of this example is to emphasize that while criticism of cultural practices sanctioned by religion (such as polygamy) may seem self-evident, any lack of challenge by Muslim women themselves must be understood in its correct context if we are to retain an understanding of why they challenge some aspects of their lives but are unable to challenge others. This knowledge should lead us to more clearly comprehend what the state, feminist reformers, and social reform advocates need to focus on in the struggle to forward Muslim women's rights.

In this particular example of polygamy, for instance, we can learn that while the issue of unregulated polygamy is indeed a problem for Muslim women, the greater underlying issue is their economic vulnerability. It is this wider systemic disadvantage that the state must address by reforming the law to include provisions for spousal support in the event of desertion, separation, or divorce. Another important lesson we can draw is that it is possible to be loyal to the interests of one's community while at the same time being conscious of the problems of gender discrimination and patriarchal privilege within the community. Indeed, the anxiety of anti-Muslim hostility complicates Muslim women's struggle for gender rights. The fact that the Hindu right casts itself in the role of the rescuer of Muslim women from the men of the community, as it did in *Shah Bano*, only heightens the fraught nature of Muslim women's resistance to gender patriarchy. Inevitably, given the political context of Hindu hostility, Muslim women are forced to turn inward to demonstrate group integrity. However, this should not signify to others, especially to the state, that they are unaware of the problems of systemic gender disadvantage.

---

85 Yuval-Davis, *Gender and Nation*, 118.

Indeed, the state must recognize that Muslim women's attempts at resistance signal a call for change.

An exploration of the contradiction of discriminatory personal law in a secular democracy avowedly committed to principles of equality and non-discrimination results in a recognition of multiple axes of discrimination that Muslim women have to contend with. It is therefore critical that we remain always attentive to the social and economic context in which they make their choices. A nuanced understanding, not only of the comparative rights of religious communities, but of the very premise of the protection of religious freedom and the role of the state in accommodating difference, together with the rights of women across the public and private spheres, leads to the reconceptualization of women as agents rather than a unidimensional framing of them as objects in the democratic dialogue. As Rajeswari Sunder Rajan argues, 'By pushing the terms of the debate on personal law beyond the dispute between the state and the rights of religious communities, Indian feminism has already identified women as not merely the subjects but the rightful agents of change.'[86]

To understand Shah Bano purely in terms of her oppression is to erase her acts of agency, at the same time we must be careful not to valorize her oppression. It is as important to resist framing women such as Shah Bano, who challenge traditional norms, as all-powerful heroines. In seeking to recover the authentic voice of Shah Bano, we must avoid the pitfalls of prescripted identities. Rather, her claim for rights must be understood within the particular social and political context in which it was made – the spiralling religious fundamentalism, together with the rise of the Hindu right wing. However we understand Shah Bano and the choices she made, we must continue to pay attention to the context of these choices. We have to understand her as a historically contingent character in order to avoid reification of the category 'Muslim women.' As Gayatri Spivak argues, the subaltern has not spoken, not because she cannot speak, but because she does not have a position to speak from. She becomes either an object of rescue or a self-determining transparent subject.[87]

Indeed, we have to complicate our understanding of the multiple identities of Shah Bano and her sisters, 'as a subaltern, as a victim of

---

86 Sunder Rajan, *supra* note 12 at 173.
87 Spivak, 'Can the Subaltern Speak?' 299–306.

religious patriarchy, as a pawn of the Hindu right, as a victim of the Muslim conservatives, as the discursive object of narratives of community and of nationalist identity, as a heroine of feminist struggle. It would seem that she was all things at once, and at the same time none of these things attributed to her personhood.'[88] It is this 'ambivalence and complicated personality which gives Shah Bano her credibility, her moral authority as a voice that signals the demand for change, a voice that must be heeded by those responsible for shaping public policy and for formulating strategies to combat inequality.'[89] To forward women's rights, it is critical to challenge the representation of women as either abject victims or unworldly heroines. Such stereotyping ultimately serves to reinforce the traditional characterization of Indian women as backward, unable to exercise agency, and trapped within communal, patriarchal structures. Indeed, such an understanding of Muslim women has the effect of removing them from history, freezing them in an essentialized time and space, and 'eternally constructing them as politically immature.'[90]

The *Shah Bano* controversy is significant for its demonstration of the discursive displacement of the question of Muslim women's rights onto several other discourses while managing to avoid questions of both state and community responsibility to address systemic gender disadvantage. These discourses of state and community use the ideology of protection to frame Muslim women narrowly and to circumscribe their rights. At the same time, arguably, within these discourses there lies also the possibility of resistance. We need to complicate our understanding of notions of representation, of agency, and of the location of Muslim women. We need to recognize that women, even while living within and participating in an oppressive patriarchal society, do, at some level, exercise control and agency in their lives. An example is Shah Bano, who turned to the law to mediate what was essentially a family dispute. It may be said that this exercise of agency by a subaltern figure is in itself a challenge to the discourse of protection. Just as important, it emphasizes the possibilities of the margin as a site of resistance.[91] At the same time, Shah Bano's story cautions us not to conflate the resistance of individual women with the exercise of

---

88 Courtright and Goswami, *supra* note 84 at 221.
89 *Ibid*.
90 Yuval-Davis, *supra* note 85 at 118.
91 Pathak and Sunder Rajan, *supra* note 19, 562.

agency. Her story highlights the importance of using agency in collaboration with others and constructing coalitions with other marginalized groups. In the absence of such coalitions of resistance, stories like Shah Bano's might simply reflect individual attempts to redress a specific grievance, leaving untouched the larger structures of systemic gender discrimination.[92]

Overview of the Book

In this book I seek to apply a feminist understanding of law to analyse and critique the issues raised by the state's address to Muslim women as citizens with a prior religious identity. The feminist critique emphasizes that women's perspectives, hitherto marginalized, must be included in the formulation of public policy. Further, it emphasizes that the accommodation of difference must not be premised on the continued subordination of those already marginalized within minority communities, particularly women.[93] A feminist methodological approach is useful in understanding and revealing how the law has maintained gender hierarchies and why it is unwilling to restructure the power balance within the family in any substantial way. It is critical to address the systemic discrimination against women, and it is imperative that the law take into account the reality of women's vulnerability as a manifestation of the general devaluation of women in Indian society while simultaneously seeking to rectify it. The insights of this methodology are crucial to an understanding of the extent to which gender roles and family relations are shaped by the law and legal institutions. A contextualized, experiential methodological approach helps us to understand how the 'position of women reflects the organization of society rather than the inherent characteristics of women.'[94] It expands the scope of our analysis by revealing that women's equality is not simply a matter of private arrangements between individuals, but rather an issue that implicates a broad range of responses, emphasizing that oppressive social structures that serve to perpetuate women's subordination need to be problematized.

---

92 Patricia Jeffery, 'Agency, Activism, and Agendas,' in Jeffery and Basu, *supra* note 26, 221 at 222.
93 See Cook, *Human Rights of Women*; Shachar, 'Religion, State'; Shachar, *Multicultural Jurisdictions*.
94 Bartlett, 'Feminist Legal Methods,' 552.

In addition, this book draws from the insights of post-colonial theory, primarily in its interrogation of misleading oppositions of east/west, modernity/tradition, feminist/true Muslim woman. Post-colonial feminism challenges the framing of Third World women within a rhetoric of victimization and seeks to reframe discussions of their alterity. By challenging both the notion of an essential authentic cultural identity as well as a universalizing discourse of global sisterhood, post-colonial feminism disrupts simplistic divides of us/them. It recognizes the continuing impact of the colonial past on the postcolonial present.[95] The recognition of the hybridity of cultures and the acknowledgment of the interdependence of the margin and the centre are crucial to articulating an emancipatory feminist politics. These insights serve to undermine challenges to a feminist agenda that question its legitimacy in the Third World, using arguments of cultural relativism to reinforce the public/private split and to shield the family from public scrutiny. Post-colonial feminist legal theory cannot be characterized as a grand, monolithic, theoretical framework, in view of the great diversity of post-colonial societies as well as the heterogeneity of feminist theories and practices in postcolonial nations, yet its theoretical insights and the understanding of the subaltern as a peripheral subject are critical to a better understanding of the situation of Muslim women in India.[96]

This book is not focused on offering a grand normative theory or on formulating legal strategies for emancipating the subaltern Other; rather, it is a call to challenge received notions of subaltern subjects, to better understand the choices to be made in forwarding the struggle for Muslim women's rights. To that end I focus on how, in the context of Muslim women in India, concerns about nation, community, and gender impact and challenge the post-colonial state's claim to an uninterrupted narrative of modernity and progress. The chapters of this book are presented as some aspects of this larger, overarching question.

In chapter 2, 'Feminism, Nationalism and Colonialism,' I present the relationship between feminist struggle, nationalism, and colonialism in the years immediately preceding India's independence from Britain in 1947.[97] Looking at the campaign for women's suffrage and the

---

95 Kapur, *Erotic Justice*, 5.
96 *Ibid*. at 3.
97 India gained independence from Britain in 1947. It was divided into two independent states, India and Pakistan.

struggle for personal law reform, I consider the manner in which the movement for women's rights was both implicated in and impacted by the imperial agenda as well as the nationalist project. The status of women was used by both the colonialists and the nationalists, although in different contexts, to justify their respective political agendas. Ironically, in this contestation of power and hegemony, women were the discursive terrain upon which ideas of imperialism and nationalism were sought to be legitimized and justified, and yet women themselves were not equal participants in either discourse. Nevertheless, both discursive paradigms were critical to the shaping of the women's movement and the struggle for women's rights.

Inevitably, the 'woman question' was intricately tied in with the national question.[98] Equally important, the colonial response to the 'woman question' framed the way in which the Indian women's movement developed.[99] For Muslim women, the situation was especially challenging. Their participation in the mainstream national women's movement was fraught with the tension of Muslim separatist politics, which inevitably prioritized the goal of Muslim political power and cast the objective of gender rights of Muslim women in a dichotomous relation to the goal of Muslim autonomy in an independent India.[100]

I go on to explore the framing of women as victim subjects, denied agency and a complex subjectivity, even as they were central both to justification for imperialist intervention and to the nationalist response to it. I argue that the framing of women as either victims who need protection or as unworldly heroines who do not need it serves to obfuscate the extent to which the larger structures of state and community are responsible for systemic gender disadvantage. The way Muslim women are viewed by the state's addresses to them as citizens, by judicial discourse, and by community controls shapes, in turn, their response and how they must present themselves to claim their rights. We must be wary at once of strategies that are premised upon the saving of 'Other' women and those that profess to save the 'Community' through saving 'Our' women. It is important to understand the manner in which the saviours and the saved are implicated in historical relations of power and subordination if we are to disrupt these structures.[101] Equally

---

98 Liddle and Joshi, *Daughters of Independence*, 20.
99 *Ibid.* at 24.
100 Forbes, *supra* note 71 at 199; Lateef, *supra* note 79 at 94.
101 Razack, *supra* note 20.

important, we must acknowledge Muslim women's own strategies of resistance to oppressive practices.[102]

In chapter 3, 'The Post-Colonial Predicament: Muslim Women and the Law,' I examine the status of Muslim women within the constitutional context. The Indian *Constitution* includes both negative and positive rights to ensure state power to pursue substantive equality with regard to certain historic formations in Indian society, such as caste and gender hierarchies. The realization that mere provision of formal equality would not suffice to bring about the desired equality of status and of opportunity led to the adoption of these affirmative action provisions. The *Constitution* confers fundamental rights on individual citizens in their personal capacity, not as members of communal groups. Therefore, the scope of affirmative action involves tension between individuals and groups as objects of state policy. The constitutional embrace of the seemingly antagonistic principles of equal treatment and affirmative action, individual rights and group rights, confronts both government and courts with the problem of reconciling them in specific settings.

The courts have played a major role in shaping policy in this area by defining the constitutional boundaries of preferential treatment. Recent developments in Indian constitutional law point to the possibility of the success of a constitutional strategy to forward women's rights. In this chapter, I examine the assumptions built into law and legal discourse and enquire into the contradictory promise of law. Looking at leading judicial decisions, I explore whether legal challenges to discrimination under the personal law have served to undermine or to uphold women's rights, I consider the extent to which law both upholds gender stereotypes and challenges them. These judicial decisions arguably underscore the fact that the law is both a site where women's rights can be forwarded and a site for the reification of existing hierarchies of patriarchy, class, religion, and gender, not least through the use of the rhetoric of protection.

In constitutional challenges to the personal law, women are invariably treated as dependants of men or of the state because of the nature of the personal laws, while in contrast, men are constructed as the subjects of the state. The law is as complex as it is contradictory. As Carol Smart writes, this understanding of the uneven development of the

---

102 *Ibid.* at 7.

law 'allows for an analysis of the law that recognizes the distinctions between law-as-legislation and the effects of law, or law in practice. It rejects completely any concept of law as a unity which simply progresses, regresses, or reappears as a cycle of history to repeat itself. It perceives law as operating on a number of dimensions at the same time. Law is not identified as a simple tool of patriarchy or capitalism. To analyze the law in this way creates the possibility of seeing law both as a means of liberation and, at the same time, as a means of the reproduction of an oppressive social order. Law both facilitates social change and is an obstacle to change.'[103] In chapter 4, 'Reclaiming the Nation,' I examine the problematic nature of citizenship for Muslim women in light of the contradiction between equal citizenship in the public sphere and explicit discrimination within the family. I suggest the reconceptualization of a uniform civil code of family laws as a process and as a dialogue about the rights of Muslim women as citizens within the context of constitutionally guaranteed rights. I advocate the notion of transversal politics as a way to negotiate the boundaries between gender and community. I suggest that this notion of universality in diversity has the potential of constructing progressive coalitions across difference and points to the possibility of opening up citizenship as a secular space for Muslim women from which they can recover a selfhood free from essentialist, primordial definitions of gender and identity.

In post-colonial India, questions of group identity, gender justice, and secular law versus a uniform civil code inevitably converge around conflicts over the status of women under the personal law. By accepting the contention of Muslim conservative leaders that the preservation of (discriminatory) personal law was essential to the guarantee of minority rights, the state overlooked the gender aspect of such accommodation of difference. The implications of this policy were important for Indian women, in particular, for Muslim women, as the state guarantee of equal citizenship was not extended to the 'private' sphere of personal law. As Maitrayee Mukhopadhyay points out, 'The discourse of the UCC implicates the nature of personal law, gender justice and citizenship.'[104] Demonstrating this conflict and convergence of issues, the *Shah Bano* case raises questions of the gendered aspects of the state's

---

103 Smart, 'Feminism and Law,' 117.
104 Mukhopadhyay, *supra* note 57 at 204.

address to Muslim women as citizens. These are critical issues for feminist politics and praxis. The aim here is to provide insights into the complexity of these issues without pretending to provide any easy answers.[105] In order that we may better understand the larger implications of these issues and the way these debates have framed women's subjectivity far too narrowly, the issue of gender justice must be situated squarely within the context of women's rights as equal citizens of the nation. Such contextualization opens up the space for an emancipatory dialogue and the possibility of a progressive politics. As Rajeswari Sunder Rajan argues, 'The challenge before us is to "recognize Indian women as 'national subjects' outside these options that are constructed so narrowly, yet so comprehensively."'[106]

A uniform civil code signifies different things to different people. For the British, a UCC was a means to rationalize and standardize the law to facilitate colonial administration. For the nationalists, it is an expression of India's secularism and is seen as a way to promote national integration. For social reformers, it is a means to enfranchise the disadvantaged and marginalized, freeing them from oppressive religious and patriarchal control. For women particularly, it is a means of disengaging the definition of women's rights from conservative male interpretations of religious laws that sanction women's disadvantage. For religious minorities, it signifies an attempt to erase particularity and difference, thus threatening their identity and culture. For Hindu nationalists, it is a means of assimilating minorities and undermining the recognition of difference.[107]

The UCC debates encompass the wide range of positions adopted by the state, by political parties, and by the women's movement itself regarding gender rights. This tug of war between either a UCC or the personal law system has been differently mobilized over time, depending on the historical, political context. It is important to pay close attention to the political and social contexts when evaluating the tension between the two, to better understand the tension that continues in today's climate of aggressive Hindu nationalism as it confronts the state

---

105 Vanaja Dhruvarajan and Jill Vickers, 'Introduction,' in Dhruvarajan and Vickers, *Gender, Race and Nation*, 3 at 13.
106 Sunder Rajan, *supra* note 12 at 37.
107 Susanne Hoeber Rudolph and Lloyd I. Rudolph, 'Living with Difference in India: Legal Pluralism and Legal Universalism in Historical Context,' in Larson, *supra* note 14, 36 at 54–5.

imperative of governing a multicultural nation. Whereas for the colonial power the recognition of groups as the constituent basis of society was compatible with its imperial mission and religious division served this ideology, for the post-colonial state the recognition of group rights was important to foster allegiance to the ideology of the nation-state.

In this final chapter, I explore the question of women's rights while recognizing that a UCC and a personal law system are not either/or positions. I suggest that we need to view a UCC not as a fixed, ahistorical concept, but rather as a continuing, evolving, politically contingent historical process. *Shah Bano* highlights the fact that the UCC arena is likely to represent a process rather than an enactment, a continual negotiation rather than a unilinear progression. This struggle between a UCC and personal law remains at the centre of public debate in India, and at the centre of this debate lies the question of gender equality. I seek to understand more clearly why, for reasons of gender equality, a UCC is imperative, while retaining the knowledge that the politics surrounding the UCC calls for the problematizing of political alignments.[108] Strategies for forwarding Muslim women's rights in India include challenging and transforming binary understanding and categories of us/them, colonial/post-colonial, and tradition/modernity. It includes taking the perspective of traditionally excluded groups and including the perspective of the marginalized.[109]

It is with an awareness of the sensitivity and complexity of the issue that this book has been written. What is offered is not an explicit agenda for law reform; on the contrary, it poses questions for the directions that the struggle for gender equality might take, and it is an attempt to identify the critical issues involved in debates around women's rights in the family and in personal law.[110] It is a call to understand the question of a UCC and personal law reform within the context of gender equity and a caution to negotiate the challenge while being attentive to the particular social and political context in which Muslim women find themselves. It is also a call to make the living experience of Muslim women, as affected by personal law, the locus for understanding current debates on the need for gender-just family legislation.

---

108 I refer here to the unfortunate predicament of the women's movement: in recommending a UCC, it might be seen as aligned with the Hindu right and its call for a UCC, although of course on completely different premises.

109 Minow, *Making All the Difference*, 16.

110 Sunder Rajan, *supra* note 12 at 3,4.

2 Feminism, Nationalism, and Colonialism

During the years preceding India's independence from British rule in 1947, the women's question and the question of national freedom, were inextricably intertwined, in a manner that led to promises being made regarding the reform of the status of women and a guarantee of fundamental rights to equality and freedom from discrimination in the *Constitution of India*. However, despite participation in the nationalist movement, which women leaders hoped would result in an acceptance of the principle of gender equality upon independence, women did not gain equal rights within the family in the post-colonial state. Sixty years after independence, women continue to be denied the constitutional promise of gender equality, most notably in the form of discriminatory personal law. The contested nature of women's contribution to the nationalist movement was such that women's agency was both enabled as well as silenced. At the same time, women were simultaneously victim and subject, imbricated in the discourses of colonialism and nationalism.[1]

While the question of women's suffrage received nationalist support, and the independent Indian state granted women civil and political rights, the question of personal law reform was met with bitter opposition. Arguably, while suffrage did not threaten the basis of male patriarchy, the extension of equal rights within the family was seen as a direct threat to male privilege and a challenge to the gender status quo. The idea of a uniform civil code based on the principle of equality, which would give women greater rights to property and

---

1 See Homi Bhabha, 'DissemiNation: Time, Narrative and the Margins of the Modern Nation,' in Bhabha, *Nation and Narration*, 291 at 297.

inheritance and equal marriage and divorce rights, was unacceptable even to those leaders who were willing to concede political empowerment for Indian women.[2]

In this chapter, I trace the trajectory of the women's movement's demand for legal rights. I discuss the development of a feminist consciousness among Indian women and examine the beginnings of women's struggle for greater rights during the pre-Independence years. I look at the manner in which the discourse of women's rights impacted and was implicated in the contemporary discourses of colonialism and nationalism. The aim is to trace the continuities with and to draw lessons from the difficulties inherent in pursuing women's rights in the context of nationalism and colonialism, for women's claims to equal rights today. I shall set the context for current struggles for women's rights, examining the way in which two issues that feminists considered key to the status of women in a free democracy, universal adult suffrage and equal rights within the family through personal law reform, were dealt with by the British and by nationalist leaders. I examine the way in which women's status was central to both colonial and nationalist politics with consequent implications for the shaping of women's rights struggles. Finally, I consider how both discourses framed women as victims, denying them a complex subjectivity, which ultimately resulted in their exclusion from the discussions surrounding their rights.

Pursuing Women's Rights in the Context of Nationalism and Colonialism

The struggle for women's rights was shaped equally by colonialism and its approach to women's issues and by the context of the nationalist movement. As a colonized people, Indians faced two key challenges. One was to achieve national liberation and the other was to replace colonial domination with democracy and a vision of social justice that countered the structures of social oppression of a traditional society and the invidious distinctions of caste and gender. In turn, these challenges raised questions regarding priority and timing. Should the question of national liberation take precedence over other issues; could the two challenges be tackled simultaneously; should

---

2 Sunder Rajan, *Scandal of the State*, 25.

there be an order of priority in achieving these goals; or should the task of national liberation be understood as the overarching and primary challenge?[3] These questions were of critical importance, especially to women leaders, who had only recently taken the lead in articulating women's demands. They were crucial to a feminist analysis of the 'woman question,' and inevitably the resolution of these questions, in turn, shaped the nature of women's struggle in the years leading up to independence.

For the colonial state, the status of women was used to demonstrate the civilizational backwardness of India and thereby to legitimize colonial rule. At the same time, British efforts to improve the status of women were selective and carefully designed to preserve those aspects of patriarchy that contributed to the preservation of British interests.[4] The status of women was central also to the nationalist project, which saw the reform of the status of women as an index of 'modernization' and development.[5] Thus, the status of women was used by both the colonialists and the nationalists, although in different contexts, to justify their respective political agendas. Ironically, in this contestation of power and hegemony, women were the discursive terrain upon which ideas of imperialism and nationalism were sought to be legitimized and justified; yet women themselves were not equal participants in either discourse. Nevertheless, inevitably, both discursive paradigms were critical to the shaping of the women's movement and the struggle for women's rights.

Women leaders recognized that an either/or choice between feminism and nationalism would have only adverse effects on the pursuit of women's rights. Opting for an alliance with the nationalists allowed them to develop and flourish in partnership with the male-dominated nationalist movement. The construct of 'feminist nationalism' allowed Indian women to pursue both feminism and nationalism in a way that did not force them to choose between the two.[6] Arguably, this construct had its drawbacks, primarily that it prevented the development of a radical ideology that would challenge the root of patriarchal oppression. On the other hand, it might also be seen as a pragmatic

---

3 Jayawardena, *White Woman's Other Burden*, 10.
4 Sunder Rajan, *supra* note 2 at 2, 3.
5 *Ibid*.
6 Margot Badran coined the term 'feminist nationalism' with respect to Egyptian women. 'Dual Liberation,' 20.

choice in the context of the chaotic and emotional political climate of nationalist fervour of the 1930s and 1940s. At any rate, women leaders understood that as long as women's demands coincided with nationalist demands, nationalist leaders welcomed them. However, if they questioned the gender status quo and challenged inequitable family law, these demands were met with suspicion. Suspicion not only by nationalists, but also by the British, who were no more sympathetic to women's rights than, in fact, the nationalists. Such were 'the difficulties inherent in pursuing women's rights within a colonial framework.'[7]

Inevitably, the woman question was intricately tied to the national question.[8] Just as important, the colonial response to the woman question framed the way in which the Indian women's movement developed.[9] The British approach to women's issues shaped the way in which the women's movement understood its role and defined its goals. Although this approach was ambiguous, it was of great importance because 'it affected whom the women defined as the main enemy, which in turn affected the analysis of how liberation could be achieved and at what point the major goal had been reached.'[10]

As Joanna Liddle points out, the status of women was used to justify and perpetuate colonial rule. The British used the abysmal status of Indian women to justify and perpetuate colonial rule, arguing that Britain's 'civilizing mission' justified the imperial plan.[11] Kumkum Sangari and Sudesh Vaid argue that the degeneration of Hindu civilization and the abject position of Hindu women, requiring the 'protection' and 'intervention' of the colonial state, were two aspects of colonial politics. The third aspect was the 'effeminacy' of Hindu men, who were unfit to rule their own country. On all three counts British rule in India could be justified on grounds of moral superiority.[12]

Britain claimed to be a liberating force, most especially for the women of India. The British used the articulation of women's (as well as the lower castes') discontents to argue that India was not ready for

---

7 Forbes, *New Cambridge History of India*, 93.
8 Liddle and Joshi, *Daughters of Independence*, 20.
9 *Ibid.* at 24.
10 *Ibid.*
11 *Ibid.*
12 Uma Chakravarti, 'Whatever Happened to the Vedic *Dasi*?' Orientalism, Nationalism and a Script for the Past,' in Sangari and Vaid, *Recasting Women*, 27 at 35.

political change. They were careful to have an official policy of non-interference in personal law, yet, in fact they showed little hesitation in reforming those aspects that suited colonial interests. Arguably, the British were not unambiguously in favour of women's rights.[13] They liberalized the law for some groups of women, by outlawing sati, for example. Yet they imposed constraints on other groups of women by removing their sexual and economic rights, for example, by abolishing the legal and social structures of matriliny among certain Hindu communities in South India.

The need to preserve empire, above all, is crucial to understanding Britain's ambivalent approach to women's rights in India. The colonial policy of selectively interfering and simultaneously preserving the status quo was suited to the preservation of British interests. As David Washbrook suggests, Britain's reluctance to interfere with family law was linked to the evolution of British control over India and efforts to secure political and economic ascendancy.[14] Legal structures were altered to enable the indigenous elite to maintain control over agrarian producers. In turn, these changes permitted the British to retain control over this indigenous elite, who were the intermediaries of colonial power. The parallel enunciation of private and public governed by separate rules was premised on contradictory objectives. Whereas the public law was reformed to facilitate the freedom of the individual in a market economy, the private sphere was now subject to only those changes that would reinforce patriarchal controls over women and strict social control over individuals within the community so as not to upset those groups upon whom the British relied for the collection of revenue.

For Britain, the women's cause served to legitimize colonial rule as well as to demonstrate British superiority. Thus, while they were invested to this extent in reforming the status of women, at the same time they necessarily had to emphasize the subordinate status of Indian women in order to underscore British superiority, and, as a corollary, to reject nationalist demands for self-rule.[15] At the same time, it is important to note that, whereas for the British women's

---

13 Liddle and Joshi, *supra* note 8 at 30.
14 Washbrook, 'Law, State and Agrarian Society,' 660.
15 Liddle and Joshi, *supra* note 8 at 239–40.

emancipation was an important issue in the colonies, in the metropolis the British establishment opposed feminism.[16]

The British influence on the nationalist movement was contradictory.[17] On the one hand, colonial criticism of the status of Indian women put nationalist leaders on the defensive, compelling them to defend 'tradition' and culture. On the other hand, it also forced a self-conscious re-examination of existing caste and gender relations. An unintended effect of British criticism of Indian male patriarchy was that it fostered an alliance between the women's movement and the nationalist movement against a common enemy. In the words of Dr B.R. Ambedkar, 'I am afraid that the British choose to advertise our unfortunate conditions, not with the object of removing them, but only because such a course serves well as an excuse for retarding the political progress of India.'[18]

These words of Ambedkar might be applied equally appositely to the *Shah Bano* issue of today. Parallels can be drawn here with the current situation where Muslim women, faced with the hostility of the Hindu majority community and its criticism of Muslim male patriarchy, have felt compelled to turn inwards to an alliance with Muslim men in an effort to demonstrate a united front against Hindu right-wing polemics and the harsh reality of communalism. The Hindu right has appropriated the defence of Muslim women, as an indicator of the backwardness of the Muslim community and as a critique of minority rights in India's pluralist democracy. At the same time, today we have male leaders of the Muslim community defending 'Islam in danger' and justifying inequality in personal law using the defence of cultural relativism. We have once again the false demarcation of public and private, avowed official non-interference in the 'private' domain of Muslim family law, and the fiction of a private sphere of autonomy untouched by state hegemony.

The woman question was central both to the colonial power and to the nationalist project. However, the notion of this centrality differed in significant aspects. Whereas the British claimed to be an emancipa-

---

16 Jayawardena, *supra* note 3 at 6.

17 Liddle and Joshi, *supra* note 8 at 235–6.

18 *Ibid.* at 24. Dr Ambedkar, a freedom fighter and champion of the oppressed lower castes, the 'untouchables,' known now as dalits, was one of the principal drafters of the Constitution. Presidential Address to the All-India Depressed Classes Congress, August 1930. Quoted in Dutt, *India Today*, 262.

tory force for Indian women, saving them from the ills of Indian male patriarchy and oppressive cultural traditions, for nationalists it was the idea of saving women from the unwarranted interference of a foreign power that resonated with the 'masses.' As Partha Chatterjee notes, 'The refusal of nationalism to make the women's question an issue of political negotiation with the colonial state' was due to the fact that it seemed to 'deny the ability of the nation to act for itself even in a domain where it was sovereign.'[19]

Precisely because British rulers justified their domination over India using the degraded status of women as a crucial signifier of India's backwardness and inability to govern itself and because they used social reform of women's status as evidence of their efforts to 'save' Indian women, the fact of women's participation in the nationalist movement challenged the notion of Britain's moral purpose and legitimacy in ruling India. Simultaneously, by supporting the freedom cause, women granted a certain legitimacy to Congress as the rightful leaders of the country.[20] At the same time, women's participation in the nationalist movement was critical in shaping the nature of the women's movement itself. Not only did this participation give them the opportunity to articulate their own demands, it forced the nationalist movement to take their demands seriously, and, most important, it legitimized their claim to a role in independent India.[21]

By linking the cause of women's liberation with that of national liberation, the women's movement was able to win support for its cause, and thus was formed 'the freedom alliance.' Women's participation in the nationalist movement helped to defuse male opposition to the principle of gender equality. This principle was accepted by Congress leaders and was eventually written into the *Constitution* as a fundamental right. However, the acceptance of the principle of gender equality was not unqualified and not all leaders within the nationalist movement agreed on it. In practice, nationalist leaders supported women's demands when they were seen as forwarding the cause of liberation, but where these demands were seen as a challenge to male interests, nationalist support was not forthcoming.[22] Nevertheless, these leaders understood the value of women's participation in the

---

19 Chatterjee, *Nation and Its Fragments*, 132.
20 Forbes, *supra* note 7 at 150.
21 *Ibid.* at 154.
22 Liddle and Joshi, *supra* note 8 at 33.

nationalist movement in challenging the legitimacy of colonial rule while simultaneously legitimizing the nationalist movement itself. For women leaders, this alliance gained for them, at least temporarily, the approval of Indian men.[23] However, as Geraldine Forbes eloquently states, 'Feminist demands for equality with men were never fully integrated into the nationalist program even though nationalism was feminized.'[24]

Mahatma Gandhi was instrumental in bringing women into the mainstream of the nationalist movement. Early on, he understood the importance of women's participation in the movement and encouraged them to join. At the same time, he did not envisage their participation as a radical departure from conservative, traditional ideology. Rather, he emphasized male guardianship over women, even within the movement, assuring husbands and fathers that women's political activism was not directed against prevailing gender ideology or the sanctity of the family.[25] For Gandhi, women's political activism was to be limited to the cause of national liberation. It was never intended as a social revolution or as a challenge to traditional gender roles.[26] Thus, nationalism subsumed the women's movement, co-opting the woman question.[27] The discontents and aspirations, not only of women but also of other dispossessed groups, such as the lower castes, were sought to be directed towards a common enemy, the British, and the cause of national liberation was deemed to be the larger one.

Women's stake in nationalism is complex. Whereas, on the one hand, nationalist movements draw women to participate more fully in collective national life, on the other hand, they set the boundaries of culturally acceptable limits of feminism. Gender interests are to be articulated within the terms of reference set by nationalist discourse, thus underscoring the fact that feminism, rather than being autonomous, is actually significantly bound by the national context.[28] Arguably, the nationalist movement was ambivalent on the issue of women's rights. Certainly, opinion among the nationalists was not unanimous. Whereas leaders such as Nehru were committed to the

---

23 Forbes, *supra* note 7 at 121.
24 *Ibid.* at 7.
25 *Ibid.* at 125, 134, 7.
26 *Ibid.* at 25.
27 Liddle and Joshi, *supra* note 8 at 34–5.
28 Kandiyoti, 'Identity and Its Discontents, 48, 49.

principle of gender equality and law reform, others, like Rajendra Prasad, who later went on to become the first president of free India, were strongly opposed to the reform of Hindu law. Gandhi, although a strong proponent of 'women's uplift,' was ambivalent in his attitude – encouraging women's participation in the nationalist movement, but at the same time reiterating his belief in complementary gender roles rather than advocating radical social change, and displaying an ambivalence towards women's participation in public life.[29]

While the alliance between feminists and nationalists contributed to the growth of the women's movement, this alliance also held drawbacks for the women's movement. Most important, by subsuming the woman question under the nationalist question, it denied, or at the very least delayed, a critical examination of systemic gender discrimination in India. Whereas the nationalist alliance undoubtedly contributed to the growth of the women's movement, at the same time, this alliance served to limit the scope of the movement, not least because of nationalists' ambivalence to women's demands that did not directly further their own cause of freedom from colonial rule.[30] The British were no less ambiguous in their support of women's emancipation. Their approach to the woman question and the nationalists' attitude to women's rights converged to the extent that both supported those women's rights that coincided with their respective political agendas.

Consequently, the women's movement's own agenda was severely circumscribed, ironically, by both the British and the nationalists. Women activists had to wage their struggle perforce on the dual platform of anti-imperialism and national liberation. As Liddle argues, this peculiar context meant that women's interests had to be articulated so that they fit in with the goals of national liberation. This prevented the development of a critique of indigenous patriarchy and traditional structures of oppression, which was understood to be, in effect, a betrayal of the greater causes of national unity and anti-imperialism.[31] Similarly, in the contemporary Indian context, Muslim women are forced to subsume gender interests under the presumed greater cause of group integrity, fearing that criticism of male privilege will result in exposing the group to criticism from the larger society; that such criti-

---

29 Everett, *Women and Social Change,* 75, 76.
30 Liddle and Joshi, *supra* note 8 at 38.
31 *Ibid.* at 39,   .

cism will be subverted by the the forces of communalism and will thus undermine rather than uphold the integrity of the Muslim community as a whole in the face of majority community hostility; and that to do so will expose the community to charges of backwardness, inviting state interference in the imagined private sphere of Muslim family law.

The context of colonial rule forced Indian women activists to address their claims to the British.[32] Yet the nationalists were not necessarily more sympathetic to the women's cause and displayed an inconsistency with regard to their claims. Nevertheless, women activists chose to support the nationalist project, perhaps at the expense of pursuing women's rights. Arguably, this was a calculated choice women leaders made, fully aware of the complexities of their location. They understood that in the contemporary political context, women's goals were not salient, and, moreover, that women's issues had to be fought for on more fronts than the political one. From this choice and from their understanding of the need to contest the issues on more than one front, we can learn valuable lessons applicable to the struggle for greater equality for Muslim women today.

Most important, we are taught that the sites of contestation for power must be not only the state, but also everyday resistance, community, and family. For subaltern voices to be heard, we need to acknowledge the importance of alternative sites of resistance.[33] We learn the importance of building strategic coalitions. We learn the importance of understanding that the struggle for women's rights must be linked with the larger cause of greater rights for all dispossessed groups within society. We learn that any alliance of disparate groups around common issues must necessarily confront not conflate, those issues that are not common, as indeed the national question sought to conflate the woman question without a serious examination of the deeper causes of women's subordination.

Women Organizing

A look at the campaigns of the women's movement around the issues of suffrage and personal law reform illustrates the difficulties in pursuing women's rights in the context of colonialism and nationalism. Women leaders understood that British support for reform was con-

---

32 Forbes, *supra* note 7 at 119.
33 See *supra* chap. 1, note 19.

tingent on imperial politics, and it was also clear that the nationalist movement did not unequivocally support women's issues. National liberation did not necessarily mean women's liberation. It was this understanding that prompted women leaders to seek change through the reform of personal law.[34] The nationalists were united around the issue of women's suffrage but were divided over personal law reform, thus illustrating the contradictory attitude towards women's rights.[35]

In the early twentieth century women formed a number of national women's associations, many of which, interestingly, were initiated by British women.[36] Foremost among these new women's organizations were the Bharat Stri Mahamandal founded in 1910; the Women's Indian Association (WIA), founded in 1917; the National Council of Women in India, founded in 1925; and the All India Women's Conference (AIWC), founded in 1927.[37] The emergence of the new women's organizations led by women, and their participation in the nationalist movement served simultaneously to challenge the essentialist notion of the 'helpless' Indian woman, to undermine British claims of the legitimacy of imperialism through the discursive paradigm of the rescuing of native women, as well as to challenge nationalist leaders to take women's demands seriously. From this point on, women were active in a number of social and political movements, including the elections of 1937, the nationalist campaign of Quit India in 1942, and the campaign for the creation of a separate homeland for Muslims.[38]

By the 1930s the AIWC had gained prominence to become the most important national women's organization.[39] The AIWC decided to remain an apolitical organization, and its main objectives were to lobby and influence government policy regarding women, especially in the areas of personal law, suffrage, education, employment, and health.[40] However, AIWC leaders realized that their work was developing on two fronts – they were concerned both with issues that directly benefited women as well as with issues that affected the entire nation. While their work regarding specifically women's issues

---

34 Liddle and Joshi, *supra* note 8 at 40.
35 *Ibid.* at 34–5.
36   See Jayawardena, *supra* note 3.
37 Everett, *supra* note 29 at 68–9.
38 Forbes, *supra* note 7 at 191.
39 Everett, *supra* note 29 at 75.
40 *Ibid.* at 75.

focused primarily on the removal of legal disabilities of women, their concern for the freedom of the nation led them to support and participate in Gandhi's movement for reconstruction and social action.[41]

The situation of the AIWC illustrates the way in which the pursuit of women's rights in colonial India was often tricky and subject to the contradictory pulls of feminism and nationalism. Their concern with the removal of legal disabilities for women compelled women leaders to seek legal reform by petitioning the British and collaborating to this extent with the indigenous political elite. At the same time, their sympathies with the nationalist movement and, in particular, the draw of Gandhian politics for the reconstruction of Indian society with the promise of the enfranchisement of the rural poor and the lower castes drew them into the nationalist movement. Nevertheless, the AIWC was more an elite representational group than a grassroots movement with the ability to mobilize the masses. The AIWC was criticized for not representing all Indian women, despite its claims of sisterhood and solidarity.[42]

There were divisions even among the leaders of the movement regarding program and strategy. Whereas the AIWC was committed to legal reform, this was not as popular with Muslim women, who did not want to interfere with the Muslim personal law. Finally, although some effort was made to widen the membership base to include poorer rural and urban women in the organization, there was no real attempt to develop programs that would specifically address their needs.

In the Indian context, nonetheless, the emerging women's organizations were indeed remarkable for their time and place in history. Their primarily middle-class and upper-middle-class membership meant that their agendas reflected their class concerns, and they were further limited by the lack of any real grassroots connections that might reflect and focus their attentions on issues that affected the majority of India's rural women. Notwithstanding, these national women's organizations were significant for the development of the women's movement in India.

Despite their limitations, these organizations attempted to further women's causes in a harsh environment that did not reward women for non-conformity.[43] They were significant for many reasons. First, they were the first to be led by women, and for the first time, there

---

41 Forbes, *supra* note 7 at 81.
42 *Ibid.* at 81.
43 *Ibid.* at 91.

was the identification of women's issues by women rather than by the hitherto male-dominated leadership of women's causes, which had focused primarily on 'women's uplift.' Second, they were essentially secular organizations that welcomed an all-India membership, open to women of all religions and castes.[44] Third, they were careful to build links with other similar organizations. Most important, these women's organizations linked the woman question with the national question, thus bringing women's issues into the mainstream of national politics. Significantly, several of these women activists participated in both the nationalist movement as well as the women's movement, giving women the self-confidence to agitate for women's rights under their own leadership rather than under male tutelage.[45]

The AIWC was an all-India organization and claimed to represent women of all religions, castes, and classes. A number of Muslim women did indeed join. However, upper-class Muslim women also founded local associations.[46] Most met with opposition from the Muslim community, such as the school for girls started in 1906 by Sheikh and Begum Abdullah in Aligarh. Similarly, attempts by Muslim women to join the All India Muslim Educational Conference in 1926 were opposed. The most important organization with the aim of representing specifically Muslim women's interests was the All India Muslim Women's Conference (the Anjuman-i-Khawatin-Islam).[47] Claiming to speak for all Muslim women in India, they were committed to promoting Muslim women's education, which led the organization to oppose *purdah* (seclusion and veiling) restrictions and early marriage. Yet the members of the organization were upper-class women who themselves were reluctant to abandon the practice of seclusion and veiling.[48] Nevertheless, in 1917 the Muslim Women's Conference proposed a resolution against polygamy.[49]

---

44 Ray, *Early Feminists*, 81: 'The significant feature of the inaugural session was that the AIWA was joined by Hindu, Muslim and Christian women. It was presided over by a Muslim woman, Her Highness the Begum Saheba of Janjira, it was attended by another leading Muslim woman, the only ruling princess of India, Her Highness, the Nawab Begum Saheba of Bhopal.'
45 *Ibid*. at 83–7.
46 Everett, *supra* note 29 at 63.
47 *Ibid.*; Ray, *supra* note 44 at 89.
48 Ray, *supra* note 44 at 90.
49 Everett, *supra* note 29 at 63.

Although the resolution was not passed in the face of opposition from the more conservative members and the Muslim community at large, it marked an important step in Muslim women's identifying the source of their disadvantage: personal law. At the same time, Muslim women were able to advantageously deploy religious themes together with anti-British sentiment to enable their participation in nationalist politics. While their participation in mainstream nationalist politics was certainly not as wide as that of women in other communities, they used religious themes to their advantage, particularly to participate in those aspects of nationalist politics of specific interest to the Muslim community. Primarily, it was the Khilafat movement, which supported the Turkish Caliphate, that resonated deeply with Indian Muslims, who saw the deposing of the Caliphate as evidence of British hostility to Muslim interests. The Khilafat movement, strongly supported by Gandhi, represented Hindu-Muslim unity against British imperialism. Muslim women also were active in the non-cooperation movement of Gandhi.[50] However, the All India Muslim Women's Conference had a brief existence. It was primarily an upper-middle-class organization, reflecting in its aims the preoccupations of its membership, and it did not live up to its claim of representing all Muslim women. Despite supporting the nationalist and Khilafat movements, it was unsuccessful in organizing a national platform, and by 1932 it had become virtually defunct.[51]

Suffrage

The struggles around women's representation highlight the ambivalence of both the British and the nationalists towards women's rights. Although the ultimate political authority was the colonial power, the colonial context was such that the women's movement could also appeal to the indigenous elite in the British-controlled legislatures as well as to leaders of the nationalist movement. As such, the success of the women's movement was contingent upon a convergence of interests of as well as the interaction between the colonial authorities, the indigenous elite, and the nationalists with the interests of the women's movement.[52] Whereas, initially, the interests of the women's move-

---

50 *Ibid.*
51 Ray, *supra* note 44 at 89, 92, 93.
52 Everett, *supra* note 29 at 101.

ment and the British coincided, by the second phase of the campaign the situation was more complicated, owing to a shift in nationalist politics that resulted in a sharp disagreement between the Indian National Congress and the British.

The women's movement focused on political representation as a means of initiating social reform and called for increased representation on the same basis as men.[53] The campaign for suffrage and political representation in the legislature had two phases, coinciding with the British efforts for constitutional reform in India, and each ended with the passage of a new law.[54] The first was the *Government of India Act* of 1919 and the second the *Government of India Act* of 1935, both of which granted limited representation to women.[55]

THE FIRST PHASE

Women's right to vote was first raised in 1917, by the Women's Indian Association.[56] At first, the British, the Indian political elite, and the nationalists rejected this demand.[57] Initially, Gandhi did not support a campaign for suffrage, on the grounds that it would detract from the more important cause that demanded a united front: the campaign for national liberation.[58] Women leaders lobbied the Indian political elite and eventually gained the support of the India Home Rule League, the Muslim League, and Congress. All three groups passed resolutions in favour of women's suffrage in 1918. Jana Everett suggests that these political associations agreed to support women's suffrage, perceiving it to be an opportunity to demonstrate to the British how far advanced they were and therefore that they were capable of self-rule.[59] The British, after their initial opposition, conceded women's right to vote on a limited basis in light of the support it had from the indigenous political associations and the nationalist groups.[60] As a result, the Act of 1919 allowed for limited women's franchise.

The British agreed to allow women to vote for the Provincial Assemblies if the latter wished them to do so. By leaving this decision to the

---

53 *Ibid.* at 103.
54 *Ibid.* at 101.
55 See 'Statutes' in Bibliography.
56 Liddle and Joshi, *supra* note 8 at 35.
57 Everett, *supra* note 29 at 103; Forbes, *supra* note 7 at 93.
58 Forbes, *supra* note 7 at 100.
59 Everett, *supra* note 29 at 105.
60 Liddle and Joshi, *supra* note 8 at 35; Forbes, *supra* note 7 at 99–100.

Indian legislatures, the British were able to show themselves as progressive while simultaneously avoiding the risk of upsetting conservative opinion.[61] The British initially opposed women's suffrage primarily out of a desire not to upset orthodox opinion and a fear of consequent political instability. This fear is reflected in the British claim that it was premature to grant women the vote when the majority of male voters themselves 'require education in the use of a responsive vote.'[62] In addition, they were wary of upsetting *purdah* restrictions and its practical implications, which would make it virtually impossible to allow women to vote. Ironically, the British used the veiling of women as a reason for refusing them the vote, in spite of the fact that the women's movement leaders declared that not all Indian women were veiled and secluded, and that in any case *purdah* would not stop them from exercising their rights.

The *Government of India Act* of 1919 granted franchise to a mere 3 per cent of the adult Indian population for the Provincial Assembly and a negligible 0.06 per cent for the Central Assembly. Most Provincial Assemblies did choose to give women the vote. However, this move was more symbolic than a real gain for women: the property eligibility criterion disqualified the overwhelming majority of Indian women from the right to vote, as the right to own property was mediated by women's inequality in inheritance and succession laws. It was symbolic, however, because it permitted nationalists to claim that they were more amenable to women's rights than the British, who waited till 1928 before granting women in Great Britain the right to vote. This demonstration of their greater progressiveness meant that they were fit and able to govern themselves. Moreover, this concession to women served the nationalist cause by increasing Indian political representation in numerical terms, however minuscule.[63]

Yet women leaders were unhappy that the decision to enfranchise women was left to the Provincial Assemblies. They felt betrayed by the British government, which had hitherto portrayed itself as the champion of Indian women. This decision to restrict female franchise was seen by the women leaders as a demonstration of British support for only male minorities, and it underscored the strengthening of male authority over women. In addition, the use of the custom of *purdah* to

---

61 Everett, *supra* note 29 at 107.
62 *Ibid*. at 106.
63 Liddle and Joshi, *supra* note 8 at 35–6.

deny women civil and political rights seemed to reinforce this notion of women's subordination. Nevertheless, as a result of their campaign, women's suffrage and political representation in the legislatures were accepted in principle, by both the British and the Indian political elite.[64]

THE SECOND PHASE

The second round of negotiations by the women's movement for suffrage was prompted by the appointment of the Simon Commission in 1927 to evaluate the possibility of political reform for India. This process of constitutional reform culminated in the *Government of India Act* of 1935, which was, in effect, a colonial constitution for India. This second phase of the campaign for women's suffrage exposed the limits of both collaborating with the British and joining with the nationalists.[65] The women's movement demanded an extension of the franchise and representation in the legislatures. The movement was divided, however, as to the terms on which the franchise was to be extended and how women were to be represented.[66] Whereas one faction, supported by the Congress party, demanded universal adult franchise and rejected the notion of reserved seats, the other faction of the movement argued for franchise qualifications and reserved seats for women as well as for religious communities.[67] The British policy of creating communally reserved seats, which began in 1909, converged with the demands of the latter faction and was incorporated into the new *Constitution*.[68]

The Simon Commission arrived in India in 1929 and was boycotted by the Congress and other nationalist parties because of its all-British composition. The nationalist parties, led by the Congress party, drafted their own Constitution, with the objective of complete independence for India, known as the Nehru Report. This report, presented as the nationalists' answer to the Simon Commission, called for dominion status and responsible government for India, and, significantly for the

---

64 Everett, *supra* note 29 at 112.

65 Forbes, *supra* note 7 at 106.

66 Everett, *supra* note 29 at 113.

67 *Ibid.* at 102.

68 *Ibid.* at 115. Communal electorates were first established by the Morley-Minto reforms of 1909; Hindus and Muslims formed separate constituencies and voted for members of their own religious communities.

women's movement, 'it marked a change in nationalist strategy toward the political representation of women.'[69]

Also in 1929, the British government announced the First Round Table Conference to discuss political reform in India. The Congress party decided to boycott this conference, as the British refused to commit to implementing dominion status for India, agreeing only to discuss the issue. The party rejected British moves towards limited political reform and called instead for complete independence or *Swaraj* and launched the Civil Disobedience movement in January 1930. In response, the British outlawed the Congress party and imprisoned most of its leaders. As a result, the recommendations of the Nehru Report could not be implemented. The imprisonment of Congress leaders meant that women now were pushed to the fore and took over leadership and participated in unprecedented numbers in the political campaigns of the time.[70] Women's participation in the Civil Disobedience movement resulted directly in the inclusion of sex equality as a fundamental right in the Congress party's Declaration of Fundamental Rights of 1930, along with the principle of universal adult suffrage.[71]

The major women's groups supported the Civil Disobedience movement. However, the decision to support the nationalists' boycott was difficult for women's groups. The WIA had campaigned vigorously for extension of the vote for women, but because of their support for the nationalist movement, they now felt compelled to leave the negotiating table; reluctantly, they lost the opportunity to make their voice heard in the process of constitutional reform. At the same time, other women's groups had continued to petition the British, although by now there was a split in the women's movement, with those who supported the Congress party also boycotting negotiations with the British. This rift complicated the response of the women's movement leaders, who were divided over whether they should ally with the party and make no further representations to the British, or whether they should be pragmatic and continue to press the colonial authorities for change. This decision was further complicated by the fact that several prominent leaders of the women's movement were also active participants in the nationalist movement.

---

69 *Ibid.* at 113.
70 *Ibid.* at 114.
71 *Ibid.* at 115.

During this period, women's movement leaders were organizing to coordinate suffrage demands. The participation of prominent women leaders in the Civil Disobedience movement disposed them favourably towards Congress principles of equal representation and suffrage. Accordingly, they met to make a joint proposal for the principle of gender equality to be incorporated in political rights, employment, and adult franchise, and they rejected the idea of reservation for women. Everett has termed this group among the women's movement the 'equal rights faction,' as they were committed to a women's campaign based on the idea of equal rights.[72] Further, they were committed to placing the nationalist cause above the cause of wider female enfranchisement.

The position of another group within the movement, termed the 'uplift faction,' was more in keeping with the British stance. This faction asked for women's representation based on the idea of women's uplift and social reform. They supported women's reservation as being more realistic than open electorates, as they did not believe that Indian men were ready to accept women's equality, and they felt that women would be denied representation unless they competed for representation in reserved electorates. However, they too rejected communal representation. There was thus an apparent split in the women's movement, with one group solidly behind the nationalists and the other willing to compromise and cooperate with the British and willing to accept limited suffrage and special reservations as an interim measure.

The Congress party continued to oppose reserved, communal electorates. However, the British refused to accept the idea of joint electorates, insisting on communal electorates and reservation of seats for minority communities. Everett suggests that this position was partly due to a desire not to antagonize Muslims while at the same time wanting to minimize the Congress influence.[73] By 1931 the Congress party and the British reached a truce, and so began the second Round Table Conference to discuss constitutional reform for India. Women's organizations, following the Congress lead, also participated in the conference and sent a representative. The British nominated Begum Shah Nawaz and Radha Subbaroyan as their representatives. Begum Shah Nawaz, a prominent Muslim woman leader and member of the

---

72 *Ibid.* at 119.
73 *Ibid.* at 118.

AIWC, who opposed the AIWC policy of non-communal electorates, was committed to universal adult franchise, in agreement with the majority of the women's movement, although she was at odds with the mainstream women's movement regarding reservation of seats for Muslims. The other British nominee, Radha Subbaroyan, although a WIA member, did not agree with the WIA's policy opposing women's quotas and continued to support the idea of reserved seats for women.

A Franchise Committee was constituted to work out the details of extending the vote. This committee accepted a memorandum from Indian women's groups, although it did not meet with them in person. The women's movement pressed for adult franchise and rejected the idea of further qualifications on women's franchise; it also rejected the principle of reserved constituencies both for women and for religious communities. Although the Franchise Committee recognized the importance of enfranchising women in the interests of social progress, the idea of universal adult franchise was rejected outright, in view of the vast population and size of India as well as because of the high illiteracy rate of the population. [74]

However, in 1932 the British went ahead, despite Indian objections, and introduced the Communal Award, reserving constituencies on the basis of religious identity as well as gender. Women's organizations objected strenuously to the Communal Award, nationalists were bitterly opposed to it in principle, and Gandhi went on a hunger strike in protest. Eventually, the British reached an agreement with the Congress party, agreeing to Gandhi's demand to include the lower (untouchable) castes' reserved constituencies within the category 'Hindu' while retaining reserved seats for Muslims and women. This decision was not acceptable to the majority of women's groups, who now saw that the Congress party had abandoned the principle of universal adult franchise. Further, it had reached this compromise with the British without consulting the major women's groups, who were bitterly opposed to communal reservation, though here, too, the movement was divided. Some Muslim women, most notably, Begum Shah Nawaz, were in favour of reservation for Muslims. She convincingly presented the Muslim League's insistence on separate representation for Muslims, arguing for the necessity of the guarantee of reserved electorates. Muslim women leaders believed that because the Muslim

---

74 Forbes, *supra* note 7 at 109.

League and other community leaders supported Muslim reserved electorates, they too were bound to support reservation as an act of community integrity and also to promote religious harmony.[75]

The second phase of the women's movement's campaign for the vote had mixed success. The British government's acceptance of the extension of women's franchise was closer to the position of the women's uplift faction of the movement. However, the movement's position on communal representation did not find a place. The equal rights faction's demand for adult suffrage was rejected, perhaps owing to the British government's reluctance to extend the franchise in light of the unstable political climate and increased nationalist militancy. On the other hand, acceptance of the wifehood qualifications proposed by the uplift faction was more in keeping with British policy of property qualifications and extended the franchise to the wives of those already enfranchised by the property qualifications.

The *Government of India Act* of 1935 was designed to preserve colonial authority in India by appeasing the moderates without upsetting the conservatives. This was important in the political context of the time, as the British had to preserve empire by defusing the influence of the militant nationalists and retaining the loyalty of the indigenous elite. The Act extended franchise to women over the age of twenty-one who met the property or education qualifications. As a result, now 6 million Indian women could vote and stand for election to general or reserved seats.[76] However, though a greater number of women were enfranchised, it was still not considered adequate by the women's movement, which did not view this concession as a victory.[77] Women's organizations such as the AIWC objected to the rejection of the principle of universal adult franchise as well as to the limited enfranchisement of women that did not recognize the rights-bearing capacity of women as individuals or as citizens in their own right, or acknowledge them as being an integral part of the nation.

Women activists saw this limited extension of the franchise as a betrayal by both the British as well as the nationalists. For the British, this Act was a compromise measure designed to manage 'the woman question without challenging the status quo.'[78] The British had

---

75 *Ibid.*
76 *Ibid.* at 191.
77 Chaudhuri, *Indian Women's Movement*, 153.
78 Forbes, *supra* note 7 at 112.

appeared sympathetic to the women's cause and saw the women's movement as progressive; the Simon Commission noted in its report, 'The women's movement in India holds the key to progress.'[79] The British authorities saw the women's movement, in the contemporary context of increased religious antagonism and nationalist militancy, as a force of stability and social progress, with its emphasis on communal unity and its objectives of social reform and education. Yet they granted only a limited franchise to women.

Leaders of the women's movement, who had hoped that their participation in and support of the nationalist campaigns for liberation would result in greater nationalist support for women's rights, were disappointed. They were told by nationalist leaders that, whereas women had a duty to support the freedom struggle, the struggle for women's rights had to be waged by women themselves.[80] Indian male nationalist leaders agreed to the terms of the compromise with the British regarding limitations to the extension of franchise without first consulting women's organizations.[81] In protest, women's organizations issued a memorandum re-emphasizing their demand for adult franchise and their rejection of reservation and separate electorates. Nevertheless, they accepted this limited extension of the vote to women as a temporary measure and women did stand for election from the reserved constituencies. Thus, women increased their participation in the mainstream of the nationalist movement while simultaneously highlighting women's issues.[82] Yet, although women had now a marginally greater presence in election politics, they remained male dominated.

Law Reform

The issue of law reform was contentious, highlighting the split between women and nationalist leaders over the issue of women's rights.[83] Arguably, the nationalists would have liked to confine the principle of gender equality to civil and political rights, and they were reluctant to extend it to women's status within the family. Women,

---

79 Everett, *supra* note 29 at 118; Great Britain, Indian Statutory Commission, 53.
80 Forbes, *supra* note 7 at 193.
81 *Ibid.* at 112.
82 *Ibid.* at 193, 195.
83 This discussion is based on *ibid.* at 112–20, unless otherwise noted.

who had gained experience in political campaigns during the struggle for suffrage, now increasingly understood their dependent status and were increasingly aware of the force of male patriarchy. Although women had gained the right to vote, the percentage of women who could, in fact, vote was negligible and always contingent on their status as dependants of men. As such, the overwhelming majority of Indian women were excluded from the structures of representation.[84]

The women's movement campaigned for the reform of personal law during the period from 1934 to 1951.[85] All women's organizations were opposed to child marriage, as were Indian reformers and the British. A law against child marriage was passed, but rarely enforced. The age of consent was raised from twelve to fourteen for females and from fourteen to eighteen for males. However, although the law prohibited the solemnization of child marriages, they were not declared either illegal or invalid. Despite this being a consensus issue, the *Child Marriage Restraint Act* of 1929 remained a dead letter, which forced women leaders to recognize that collaboration and a common goal with Indian male reformers as well as the colonial power masked competing agendas and differing priorities.[86] Disappointed with this new law, the AIWC petitioned the government in 1934 to review the legal disabilities of women.

The AIWC was committed to legal reform and their goal was new laws for women of all communities based on the principle of equality. In 1934 the AIWC first called for a complete review of women's legal disabilities under all personal laws. The legal secretary of the AIWC, Renuka Ray, wrote a pamphlet entitled 'Legal Disabilities of Indian Women: A Plea For a Commission of Enquiry.'[87]

The legal status of Indian women was recognized by the AIWC as being 'one of the most inequitable in the world.'[88] It was recognized that legal change through reform of personal law was essential for the full participation of women in public life. Disregarding nationalist censure, women's organizations chose to continue to petition the British for legal change. Women leaders lobbied government, met with liberal Indian men in the legislature, as well as promoted the idea of law reform among Congress leaders. By the 1930s the discourse of

---

84 *Ibid.* at 113.
85 Everett, *supra* note 29 at 141.
86 See 'Statutes' in the Bibliography. See also Forbes, *supra* note 7 at 113.
87 *Annual Report*, AIWC 1935, Tenth Session.
88 Forbes, *supra* note 7 at 113.

equality was increasingly a major focus of the women's movement. The principle of equal rights was seen as critical to the forwarding of women's claims. It was the premise of the challenge of the women's movement to existing oppressive laws and social structures that subordinated women. There was a shift from the focus on women's uplift to a focus on the principle of equality as being crucial to engendering women's rights. Everett suggests that this ideological shift can be understood in terms of the impact of nationalism on the women's movement. The focus on law reform as being critical to women's advancement meant, in turn, that the principle of equality was the crucial premise on which to base claims for reforming personal laws.[89]

Though expressing its agenda for law reform in general terms, the AIWC focused primarily on the reform of Hindu law. Specifically, the focus was on reform of laws relating to marriage, guardianship of children, inheritance, prohibition of polygamy, and divorce rights for women.[90] Women leaders recognized that such change would not be endorsed by the majority of the people of India, quite apart from the male elite and the nationalists, and therefore they appealed to the liberal element of the indigenous political elite to initiate social change. By 1940 the AIWC was calling for a common civil code for all communities, based on the principle of equal rights.[91]

The changes demanded by the AIWC met with strong opposition from nationalist men. Although nationalist leaders had supported women's suffrage and the extension of rights to women in the public sphere, the primary motivation of this support arguably was that it forwarded nationalist goals of undermining British political legitimacy and also served to increase political representation of Indians. Nonetheless, the extension of the principle of equality together with greater rights for women within the family threatened male privilege and challenged the gender status quo; as such it was bitterly resisted.[92]

However, there was a small group of liberal Indian men who were reformers and were conscious of the need to address the status of women. This group was active in the British-controlled legislature and introduced a number of bills in the 1930s in regard to Hindu widows' inheritance rights and Hindu women's divorce rights; its members

---

89 Everett, *supra* note 29 at 82, 83, 92–100.
90 Chaudhuri, *supra* note 77 at 183.
91 Everett, *supra* note 29 at 149.
92 Liddle and Joshi, *supra* note 8 at 36, 37.

also presented the Muslim Personal Law Bill, the Muslim Women's Right to Divorce Bill, and the Prevention of Polygamy Bill.[93] Yet these proposed reforms were very limited in their scope and highlighted the differing agendas of this liberal male group and women's organizations. Despite the restricted nature of the reforms proposed, women leaders decided to support them, on the understanding that they would support every law that appeared to bring change, however minimal.

Male opposition to even such moderate reform remained strong. This resistance was based on religious beliefs and the fear of the chaos such legislation might bring to the home and to gender relations. The British government, whose support was critical to the success of these bills, seemed to support conservative male opinion. The nationalists were ambivalent in their support of women's legal rights in the personal sphere. Women leaders expected nationalist support for their legal reform campaign in return for their support of the nationalist project in the past, but nationalists leaders held that agrarian reform rather than personal law reform was a priority. Furthermore, nationalist leaders were opposed to the women leaders' petitioning British authorities for change and objected to their collaborating with the British for legal reform. Gandhi, despite being in favour of reforming the status of women, discouraged women from pressing for legal reform, arguing that the changes they demanded had little relevance for the majority of Indian women, who lived in rural India.[94]

The resistance to changes proposed accentuated the ambivalence of nationalist leaders to the woman question, highlighting the fact that neither nationalists nor colonial authorities were unequivocal supporters of women's equality. As far as the nationalists were concerned, this resistance to reform of women's legal disabilities highlights their understanding of gender roles in terms of the private-public split. While the rights of women in the public sphere were conceded, the private sphere was still zealously guarded, apparently not only against onslaughts by a foreign colonial power, but equally against internal challenges from women themselves.

It was against this background that an Indian member of the Central Assembly moved a resolution to set up a committee to investigate the legal disabilities of women. The Muslim League stated that it had no

---

93 Forbes, *supra* note 7 at 113.
94 *Ibid*. at 115

objection as long as the committee confined its inquiry to Hindu law. Congress leaders agreed to the setting up of a committee but were not in favour of any changes that might upset the traditional social framework of Hindu society.[95] Given the lukewarm response, if not the outright hostility, to this proposal, eventually the scope of inquiry was limited to residence and maintenance of Hindu women. Pragmatically, women's organizations decided to support even this truncated agenda in the hope of making at least some gains.

In the meantime, the bills proposed earlier suffered systematic defeat. This opposition was deplored by women leaders, who now framed their demands in terms of women's human rights.[96] Eventually the colonial government agreed to appoint a committee to look into women's legal disabilities under Hindu law, and the Rau Committee was appointed in 1941.[97] Women's organizations made tremendous efforts to gather information for the committee. They were rewarded with the inclusion of two critical recommendations in the committee's final report: codification of the law and comprehensive modification of the law. However, the political context of the time was not favourable towards implementing any change. India was in the midst of political turmoil. The nationalists' call for Civil Disobedience against British rule, the Congress boycott of the legislatures, and the Second World War ensured that the recommendations of the committee lay dormant.[98] Women were caught in a dilemma, and the causes of nationalism and feminism seemed once again to have competing agendas.

Any continued cooperation by women with the Rau Committee would be seen as anti-nationalist in the context of the Civil Disobedience campaign. Yet to abandon cooperation at this stage would jeopardize any hope for women's legal rights. Women had to choose between continuing the struggle for women's rights and joining the Congress party in the struggle for freedom. Many of the prominent women's leaders were also active in nationalist politics and women were divided on what action to take. Whereas some advocated that the nationalist cause should be prioritized to the exclusion of the pursuit of legal reform in collaboration with the British, others, such as Amrit

---

95 *Ibid*.
96 *Annual Report*, AIWC 1940, Fourteenth Session, 80.
97 Forbes, *supra* note 7 at 116.
98 *Ibid*. at 116–7.

Kaur and Sarojini Naidu, continued to support legal reform. Congress women in the legislature, despite being asked by Congress leaders not to support the work of the committee, also supported this work and called for the pursuit of legal reform.

In 1944 the Rau Committee was reconvened to formulate a Hindu law code. The Hindu Code was an issue that divided the Indian political elite.[99] Despite opposition, the Rau Committee pressed on and produced its draft of a Hindu Code Bill in 1947. While the committee was engaged in its deliberations, the women's movement continued to press for reform of Hindu law, both among the Congress leadership and in terms of increasing public awareness of the need for reform. The *Constitution* for free India was at this time being debated by the Constituent Assembly.[100] Two AIWC members, Hansa Mehta and Amrit Kaur, were also members of the Constituent Assembly Subcommittee on Fundamental Rights. Amrit Kaur was also a member of the Minorities Committee. The debates of the committees were an important arena in which the AIWC pressed for constitutional guarantees for women and to have guarantees of personal law reform incorporated in the Constitution.[101]

Indian women leaders took the lead in calling for personal law reform, and in 1946 the AIWC formulated an Indian Women's Charter of Rights, calling for gender equality to be the basis of citizenship rights in India. Demanding improvements in the status of women, the charter gave the highest priority to personal law reform.[102] The charter called for equal inheritance rights for men and women, equal rights of guardianship of children, banning polygamy, allowing divorce, and necessitating the consent of both parties for marriage, and legalizing inter-caste and interfaith marriage.[103] The AIWC supported the idea of a UCC and saw the efforts to enact the Hindu Code Bill as a first step towards a UCC. The AIWC sent the charter to the central and provincial governments in 1946 and attached a memorandum listing the demands concerning personal law reform that the AIWC believed could be most easily enacted.[104]

---

99   Everett, *supra* note 29 at 158.
100 The British government had set up the Constituent Assembly, composed of Indians, in 1946 to draft a constitution for India.
101 Everett, *supra* note 29 at 159.
102 Narain, *Gender and Community*, 56.
103 Chaudhuri, *supra* note 77 at 185.
104 Everett, *supra* note 29 at 158.

The final recommendations of the Rau Committee sought to reform Hindu law without upsetting the basis of Hindu society. Women's viewpoints had been widely accepted by the committee, but the changes envisaged were not as far-reaching as women would have liked. The draft Hindu Code Bill suggested only limited moderate reforms: widows were to get the same share as a son in the husband's property, daughters were to get a half share, polygamy was banned, inter-caste marriage was legalized, and divorce on limited grounds was made possible. The women's movement supported the Code although it fell far short of what they had wanted. At the same time, the Code provoked violent resistance from its opponents. Indian political elite opinion was divided. Although agreement had been reached on civil and political equality, equality within the family remained a contentious issue.

Along with the principle of equality, the women's movement was committed to universal adult franchise as a means of securing political participation and representation not only of women, but other dispossessed groups within Indian society. The nationalists, for their part, accepted these two key principles of gender equality and universal adult suffrage, and they were incorporated in the 1928 *Report of the Indian National Congress*. At the Karachi session in 1931 the Congress party formally adopted these principles.[105] The nationalists however were ambivalent with regard to accepting the principle of gender equality in family law.

Although there was relatively little opposition to the idea of extending equality to women in terms of suffrage and political representation, the struggle for equal rights within the family proved to be far more difficult. The challenge to gender hierarchy through reform of personal law was one that the male elite among the nationalists found unpalatable. Thus, the legal regulation of women within the family became the site of intense struggle, as the women's movement fought to extend the ideal of equality to the family. Although Indian nationalist leaders were supportive of the movement for women's suffrage and increased civil and political rights, they fiercely resisted the attempt to introduce the idea of equality within the private sphere.[106] The issue of personal law reform brought out the contradictory approach within the nationalist movement to women's equality.[107]

---

105 Kapur and Cossman, *Subversive Sites*, 54–5; Everett, *supra* note 29 at 101–40.
106 Kapur and Cossman, *ibid.* at 56, 57.
107 Everett, *supra* note 29 at 94–5.

Interestingly, during this period when Hindu family law was being reviewed by the Rau Committee and the nationalists were pursuing a policy of non-cooperation with the British, in 1939 the Congress party set up its own National Planning Committee (NPC) subcommittee composed of women to examine the changes necessary for the reform of the social, economic, and legal status of women. In addition, the party initiated the establishment of a Women's Department.[108] While women leaders continued to petition the British and the Indian political elite in the legislatures for law reform, the setting-up of the NPC and the Women's Department gave them another forum in which to advocate the cause of law reform. In fact, the membership of the subcommittee of the NPC on women's role was made up primarily of women leaders from women's organizations and from the Congress.

By the 1940s the co-option of the feminist agenda by the nationalists meant that women were divided in their struggle. A number of women leaders chose to pursue nationalist goals and withdrew from the feminist cause. Others who remained committed to a feminist agenda found themselves working for legal change with depleted ranks, as many of their sisters were engaged fully in the nationalist struggle.[109] The mandate of the Women's Department, as revealed in 'The Aims of the Women's Department of the AICC,' was telling: it was to determine how best to harness 'women's genius and peculiar gifts for the revolutionary purposes of achieving independence and then making a contribution in national life.'[110] This document made it clear that women's first obligation was to nation, and it was only after the goal of national liberation had been achieved that women's liberation from oppressive custom and practice could occur. Clearly, the national good was prioritized over women's interests, and a hierarchy of causes was explicit. The Women's Department was given the task of ensuring that the national women's organizations functioned under the guidance of the Congress party and identified its goals and struggles in consonance with Congress priorities.[111]

Yet, at the same time, it is interesting to compare the report of the women's subcommittee with the report of the NPC itself, as it reveals

---

108   Forbes, *supra* note 7 at 117, 199. National Planning Committee, subcommittee on Women's Role in the Planned Economy, AICC, file no. G-23 (1940).

109   *Ibid.* at 209

110   AICC, File no. WD-7, 1.

111   Forbes, *supra* note 7 at 208.

the attitudes of Congress leaders to women's rights.[112] Although the NPC reports were never utilized, because of the arrest of Congress leaders before they could be completed, this comparison is interesting for what it reveals about attitudes to women's rights. Both the NPC report and that of the women's subcommittee called for a uniform civil code to replace the personal law, which was to be optional in the initial stage. One Muslim member of the NPC objected to this recommendation. Yet in other resolutions passed by both groups the suggestion seemed to be that such a uniform code was a practical impossibility. Whereas the subcommittee report called for the setting up of a committee of experts to draft such a code, the NPC report did not mention doing so. The subcommittee report made several recommendations on inheritance based on equality between men and women. However, the NPC report included only one general recommendation proposing equality in property laws, while three Muslim members categorically rejected any interference with Muslim personal law.

Arguably, this may be seen as evidence that by 1940 the Congress party was committed to personal law reform. Women leaders had been able to build links with both nationalists and the British authorities through their interaction with sympathetic liberals in the Assembly. However, it must be remembered that among the Indian elite was a small group of liberals who historically had been sympathetic to the women's cause and themselves had initiated social reform. What is significant is that the intense campaign of the women's movement signalled to the political authorities, as well as to the nationalists, that women were demanding change.

In light of the Congress party's commitment to gender equality outlined at the Karachi Conference, there was little opposition to clauses relating to civil and political rights. Nevertheless, there was bitter opposition to extending these rights of equality to the sphere of family law. The reform of Hindu personal law was not discussed until later, when the Indian Constituent Assembly became the Parliament. After Independence, the proposed changes in Hindu law continued to divide national opinion and the law minister resigned in protest against the lack of implementation of the Code as originally envisaged. The first president of independent India, Rajendra Prasad, wholly opposed these changes and threatened to refuse to give his assent. It

---

112   Everett, *supra* note 29 at 150.

was only after Jawaharlal Nehru won an overwhelming mandate in the first national election that he was able to railroad a Parliament into passing the Code, but again only piecemeal, not as a single legislation as had originally been envisaged.[113]

With regard to Muslim personal law, the conflict primarily arose over the perceived opposition between religious freedom and the right to religious personal law and the reform of personal law to include women's equality. Minority members especially opposed the proposed change in personal law. In 1947, although Congress leaders appeared to sympathize with AIWC demands, they also displayed a greater unwillingness to offend religious sensibilities by reform of personal law. Ultimately, AIWC leaders were unable to persuade Congress leaders otherwise.[114] The idea of a uniform civil code based on the principle of gender equality, to eventually replace discriminatory personal law, was ultimately included in the new *Constitution* as a directive principle rather than as an enforceable fundamental right.

The Position of Muslim Women

By the 1930s communalism had become a serious issue that had to be confronted. The emphasis on communal representation, reiterated by the British through the Communal Award and the *Government of India Act* of 1935, meant that religious identity had become a sharply divisive political force.[115] As religious groups vied for a share of government benefits and political power upon the Independence of India, religion was used to consolidate group boundaries, to delineate groups, and to increase cohesiveness of religious groups. Inevitably, the strengthening of community boundaries resulted in the sharpening of difference in an effort to forward group claims and to increase political power. Religious antagonism, especially between Hindus and Muslims, increased sharply.

The women's movement had to contend with the politicization of religious identity and the adverse impact it had on women's unity within the movement. Trying to maintain a united front, the movement recruited Muslim women and sought to include their perspective

---

113   Parashar, *Women and Family Law Reform*, 86.
114   Shiva Rao, *Framing of India's Constitution*, 205.
115   Ray, *supra* note 44 at 95; Forbes, *supra* note 7 at 191.

and represent their interests.[116] Just as the Congress party claimed to speak for all Indians, the women's movement, too, claimed to represent all Indian women. However, the reality of communal politics could not be ignored, and its members had difficulty in responding to this issue.

The women's movement had opposed the Communal Award and argued against special representation. Women's organizations held that, whereas community differences affected men, women were united in experiencing the same difficulties in a patriarchal society, irrespective of religion.[117] The women's movement saw itself as a unifying force in the face of increasing communalism.[118] Women's organizations argued that even if religious group differences were important to men, they were not important to women, who were united in their struggle against male privilege. Despite the efforts of the movement to present a united front in the face of communal divisions, this was more wishful thinking than concrete reality. The communal question was a constant thorn in its side, challenging its unity.[119] The questions of legal reform, *purdah*, and communal representation were critical issues, which challenged the unity of the national women's movement. The AIWC was strongly opposed to the Communal Award, rejecting differentiation on the basis of gender and religious identity. Yet not all Muslim members of the AIWC agreed, and Begum Shah Nawaz was outspoken in her support of communal representation for Muslims as a way to safeguard their rights.[120]

The communalization of politics inevitably complicated the response of Muslim women to the issue of women's rights. Nonetheless, there were several Muslim women leaders who were prominent participants in the national women's movement as well as in nationalist politics and who remained committed to a secular politics.[121] Inevitably, however, the articulation of a progressive politics eschewing community and religious differences was particularly hard for Muslim women. To articulate a nationalist feminist agenda different from the agenda of the Muslim League presented something of a

---

116 Forbes, *supra* note 7 at 202,
117 Chaudhuri, *supra* note 77 at 9, 6.
118 *Ibid*. at 155.
119 *Ibid*. at 137.
120 *Ibid*. at 155.
121 Forbes, *supra* note 7 at 196–7.

moral dilemma for Muslim women, who felt unable or unwilling to forward a feminist Muslim agenda at the imagined expense of betraying the agenda of the Muslim League and in fear of causing communal antagonism.

The critical importance of religious identity at this point made the articulation of gender identity oppositional to the articulation of a Muslim identity. Thus, Muslim women leaders, who had hitherto worked closely with the AIWC now found themselves compelled by the exigencies of identity politics to support Muslim men through support of the Muslim League's political agenda as the only way to ensure communal harmony. Similar issues face women activists today where the threat of communalism is very real and poses a special problem for the women's movement, impacting the manner in which the national coalition of women's organizations defines its agenda and priorities.

The centrality of religious identity to furthering political aims resulted in an emphasis on the status of women as central to identity politics. The emphasis on women as symbols of community culture and the importance of women as the discursive site upon which culture and tradition were contested and constructed meant that women were crucial to the political agenda of the Muslim League. As a consequence, the All India Muslim Women's League was established.[122] The Indian women's movement was now forced by the reality of communal politics to acknowledge the divergence of interests between it and Muslim women leaders, who had hitherto joined the AIWC in consensus on key issues.[123]

Muslim women were confronted with a similar dilemma with respect to nationalist politics. The nationalist movement articulated as its goal an independent India, free of divisions of caste, religion, and gender. Accordingly, for the nationalists, the goal of nation preceded the goal of community. In this prioritizing of goals, the secular nation became the only legitimate expression of group aspirations.[124] As the nationalist movement co-opted the woman question, nationalist leaders declared that the question of women's freedom was the question of the freedom of the nation. In other words, women's freedom

---

122   *Ibid.* at 197.
123   *Ibid.*
124   Chaudhuri, *supra* note 77 at 104.

would follow national liberation, the goal of national liberation being the prior objective. To this end, nationalist leaders put forth the notion of a unified India, a unity that would transcend caste, class, and gender distinctions.

Secularism was the national credo in the context of the widening gulf of religious antagonism, the struggle to gain political access in terms of religious groupings. Communalism thus was constructed as the Other of nationalism, and it followed that the only legitimate assertion of nationalism was secular rather than communal. In these circumstances, any other articulation of community was seen as antithetical to the idea of a united India. Yet, as Gyan Pandey points out, notions of communalism were implicated far more deeply in the idea of nation than nationalist leaders allowed for.[125] For Muslim women in particular, it was all the more difficult to participate in nationalist politics when doing so meant a repudiation of the goals of Muslim separatist politics. Especially with the rise of the Muslim League, claiming to represent specifically Muslim interests in the face of Hindu dominance, this issue was particularly delicate for Muslim women, who had to face not simply the choice Hindu women faced between feminism and nationalism, but indeed a choice between feminism, community, and nation. The communal question was a persistent strand of the dominant discourse on the national question and the woman's question, not least because of the British policy of communal representation.

Although the women's movement claimed to represent all Indian women, in reality it was not so. Quite apart from the vast regional differences, 'The ideology of the women's organizations was too Hindu, too middle-class and too urban to appeal to or to adequately represent all Indian women.'[126] Gandhi did alter his message, using the symbols and terms of Islam when facing a Muslim audience, as he did in his speeches regarding the Khilafat movement, which in fact united both Hindus and Muslims. Ultimately, however, it is arguable that his overtly Hindu ideological basis alienated a great many Muslim women, who further felt neglected by Congress organizers.[127] For

---

125 *Construction of Communalism*, 241.
126 Forbes, *supra* note 7 at 189.
127 *Ibid.* at 154–5.

example, the NPC constituted by the Congress party had only one Muslim woman on its women's subcommittee.[128]

In the context of the politicization of religious identity as a means to secure political gain, whereas the primary self definition of the women's movement had been in relation to a colonialist Other, increasingly now the categories were becoming more complicated with the parallel enunciation of the 'self' and Other in relation not only to an imperialist Other, but also to the Other in terms of religious group.[129] Necessarily, this complicated the unity of the national women's movement, whether or not it was acknowledged. Divisions based on religious identity began to appear in terms of political alliances and articulation of goals. Most critically, in terms of nationalist politics, the communalization of politics fostered the development of the Hindu self as the true national self in opposition to the Muslim other. This 'othering' based on religious antagonism continues to pose a serious threat to progressive politics for women's empowerment today.

Victim Subject

The status of women was central both to the imperialist mission and to the nationalist project. Both colonial and nationalist discourse framed Indian women as victims, in need of rescuing, although necessarily with opposing political agendas. Indian women today continue be portrayed as victims in need of rescuing or, alternatively, as heroines who don't need saving at all because they have an exalted status in Indian society as women. In either scenario, women's actual voices are erased, and women are denied both agency and complex personalities.[130] In addition, the question of the status of women is further implicated in the national question in terms of positionality, context, and location in the historiography of Indian women.

---

128   Lateef, *Muslim Women in India*, 94; Forbes, *supra* note 7 at 199. Sharifah Hamid Ali was conscious of being sidelined by women's politics when her suggestion regarding a review of Muslim law based on a Muslim authority was ignored. The draft report of this subcommittee was challenged by Ms Hamid Ali as displaying a lack of awareness of Muslim law.

129   Chaudhuri, *supra* note 77 at 4.

130   Forbes, *supra* note 7 at 12; Lata Mani, 'Contentious Traditions: The Debate on Sati in Colonial India,' in Sangari and Vaid, *supra* note 12, 88 at 117–18.

In this section, I focus on the framing of women as victims and its implications for the struggle for women's rights. I refer to the victim subject status that has been accorded to Indian women, not by themselves but by others: by the British colonial masters, who used this as a legitimization of their colonial beneficence; by the Indian nationalists, who saw this as a way to challenge the imperial plan and to save Indian women from British interference; by, indeed, the post-colonial state, which uses this very language to absolve itself of culpability and responsibility for change; by India's Supreme Court, which continues to see women as victims in need of paternal protection of the court; by Muslim men, who are trying to save their women from the hegemony of the state and from the hostility of the Hindus; and, finally, by the Hindu right, which uses this rhetoric to justify the undermining of minority rights.

The rhetoric of victimhood appears in the discourse of the state, which sees itself as a benevolent, paternalistic actor. Its focus on women as victims compels a protectionist response from the state. In turn, this is liable to encourage the framing of women as victims by feminist politics as a strategy to obtain concessions from the state.[131] Such a focus also has served to reinforce gender essentialism together with cultural essentialism, resulting in the reification of the First World / Third World divide.[132] Continuing to focus on women as victims results both in reifying the 'native' subject as well as, more important, in justifying imperialist interventions. Therefore, it is imperative to displace this understanding of women as victims, and to problematize notions of cultural and gender essentialism.[133] It is imperative to understand feminist politics as bringing those in the margins to the centre, as containing the transformatory potential to achieve a just society based on the inclusion of voices hitherto marginalized. Focusing on the transformative potential and on the emancipatory political value of such an understanding engenders the identification of the margins as locations of resistance in comprehending gender inequality. Such a focus on the peripheral subject brings with it the understanding that new sites of resistance mean new adversaries, not merely state-actors, in the struggle for women's equality.

---

131 Kapur, 'The Tragedy of Victimization Rhetoric,' 2.
132 *Ibid.*
133 *Ibid.* at 3.

Framing women primarily as victims is problematic. On the one hand, it suggests a sort of perpetual helplessness. On the other hand, rejecting the notion of the victimization of women might lead to blaming women themselves for their powerlessness.[134] As Martha Minow points out, 'It may lead to a sense of futility and political passivity for just those people.'[135] In the context of women in India, I refer to the perception by the state of women as victims, which has resulted in a protectionist attitude towards women, who are seen as in need of special protection. To focus on women as victims is to reify the unidimensional understanding of Indian women as always dispossessed, marginalized, and without agency. It inevitably attracts strategies, choices, and goals that reinforce the protectionist attitudes of the state and reinforce an understanding of Indian women not far removed from the colonial perception of Indian women as civilizationally backward and in need of imperialist intervention. Such an attitude towards women's rights cannot produce an emancipatory, liberatory politics for Indian women, as it ultimately denies women their voice and the power to challenge oppressions. It leads to the infantilization of women, rather than to an acknowledgment of women's rights or of women's agency, or, ultimately, of women's claims to equality. On the contrary, it may well be used to justify the imposition of greater restrictions and control over women in the name of 'protection,' as we witnessed during the *Shah Bano* controversy. While this might be seen as a useful way to gain certain short-term objectives – a calculated judgment, for example, to get more stringent domestic violence laws passed by the state – in the long term, such an understanding takes away from the political challenge presented to the state to address gender disadvantage in a meaningful, contextual way. Moving away from a focus on women as victims frees women's rights activists to give attention instead to alternative strategies, and it impacts as well the articulation of goals in order to forward women's equality.

The focus on women as victims is detrimental to women's rights and to an analysis of the struggle and strategies, because it obfuscates the degrees both of harm and of responsibility of individuals as well as of

---

134   Martha Minow, 'Surviving Victim Talk,' 1413. Although Minow's article is about the self-description of victims as a means to greater entitlements, I draw from her work on 'victim talk' and apply it to the context of India, where women have been given an overarching identity of 'victim.'

135   *Ibid.* at 1420.

the state and the larger social structures.[136] In the context of Muslim women, seeing them primarily as victims would result in masking the degree to which the leaders of the community and the larger structures of society are responsible for the endemic disadvantage of women. Further, as Martha Minow argues, 'uncritical acceptance of victim rhetoric can derail political efforts to challenge oppression.'[137] A primary focus on women as victims also may weaken the sense of possibility and power, which are crucial to challenge oppression.[138]

The discourse of victimhood serves to isolate women, disconnecting them from the larger social structures while at the same time masking the role of these structures in perpetuating women's subordination. Consequently, women are forced to seek paternal protection from the court as individuals, rather than to challenge the root of gender oppression as systemic and based on GROUP disadvantage.[139] Often this forces women to blame themselves for their troubles and, further, to abstain from bringing a complaint in order to demonstrate strength of character. In the Indian context, this is precisely what happened to Shah Bano. She was forced to approach the court as an individual, victimized woman seeking protection from her husband. In turn, the Supreme Court, while deciding in her favour, couched its response in protectionist terms, reifying in the process the understanding of women, especially Muslim women, as helpless victims of male patriarchy and casting itself in the role of benevolent rescuer. Finally, Shah Bano was forced to reject the Supreme Court judgment in her favour, declaring that as a true Muslim woman she must recant her testimony. Additionally, for Muslim women, the reluctance to challenge Muslim men along with traditional practices of keeping family matters behind closed doors are exacerbated by their reluctance to be seen as undermining group unity.[140]

Certainly, the dilemma of framing women primarily as victims is very real. Whereas, on the one hand, understanding women primarily in terms of victimhood challenges their ability to exercise agency, at the same time, focusing on women's capacity to make choices and take action may result in negating the fact of victimization and disadvan-

---

136   *Ibid.* at 1413.
137   *Ibid.*
138   *Ibid.* at 1420.
139   *Ibid.* at 1421.
140   *Ibid.* at 1424.

tage of women.[141] Drawing from Minow's insights, we can argue that the portrayal of Indian women alternately as heroic figures or as victims minimizes the very real costs of oppression and absolves the state from the responsibility of real action in dismantling discriminatory social structures and going to the root of oppression.[142]

In colonial India, women were marginalized and silenced, and arguably this has not materially changed in the post-colonial state. Gayatri Spivak in her powerful essay, 'Can the Subaltern Speak?' argues that because Indian women were seen not as subjects but rather as objects of colonial interventions, they were silenced, not because they did not speak, but because they did not have a position from which to articulate their voice. Women became, for the colonizers as well as for indigenous patriarchies, objects of rescue.[143] To understand colonial history, subaltern studies scholars Douglas Haynes and Gyan Prakash suggest that we need to pay attention not only to the 'extraordinary moments of collective protest' but also to a 'variety of non-confrontational resistances and contestory behaviour.'[144] They believe we should look at everyday acts of resistance of subordinated groups to better grasp how the social relations of daily existence are inextricably linked with and impacted by resistance, both 'extraordinary' and 'everyday.'[145] For Muslim women in India, such consideration can lead to an appreciation that the state should pay close attention not only to the meta-narrative of women's movement campaigns, but equally to the everyday acts of resistance, which ought to signal to the state that Muslim women are demanding change in the gender status quo. It can lead to an understanding that women exercise agency even while participating in a patriarchal society.[146]

Feminist theory is built upon relating the experience of the individual to the larger social and political context. However, Minow warns that the asserted authority of a subjective experience is hard to evaluate and even harder to rank in a priority of oppressions. She suggests

---

141   *Ibid.* at 1427.
142   *Ibid.*
143   Paul B. Courtright, and Namita Goswami, 'Who Was Roop Kanwar? Sati, Law, Religion and Postcolonial Feminism,' in Larson, *Religion and Personal Law*, 200 at 211.
144   Haynes and Prakash, 'Introduction,' 1–2.
145   *Ibid.* at 2.
146   Forbes, *supra* note 7 at 4.

that 'the way out of this inconsistency ... is to insist upon connecting personal stories with larger understanding of social structures in which those stories arise.'[147] Minow's argument that meta-narratives must be paid attention to if the subjectivity of individual narratives is to have any contextual meaning is compelling. Indeed, for women's particular individualized accounts of oppression to have any real impact, they have to be interpreted within the larger social and political context. Without this contextual understanding, we would not be able to situate women's suffering or to come up with an analysis of liberation and how it is to be achieved. Thus, we must be wary of a simplistic rejection of the meta-narrative. Rather, we must pay close attention both to the personal, as well as to the wider social context of interpretation if women's personal experience is to have any wider impact on a feminist formulation of law reform and public policy.

In colonial and post-colonial discourse, women's helplessness justifies, even demands, imperialist/state intervention. For colonial authorities, while they condemn Indian patriarchy, the focus is on the poor, degraded, helpless Indian woman, whose rescue by the beneficial impact of imperialism is deemed a necessity *for her own good*. Similarly, in the post-colonial continuity of the discourse of protection and the paternal state, Shah Bano is an example. Since she was a victim of Muslim law and of male patriarchy, the court was left with no choice but to offer her protection. To justify its actions, imposing greater patriarchal control over Muslim women and denying them previously held rights, the post-colonial state also couched its new retrograde act in those terms, ironically calling it the *Muslim Women's (Protection of Rights on Divorce) Act*. Arguably, there is an uncanny continuity in the portrayal of woman as victim in post-colonial India, with similar results – albeit intervention by a national government.

It is important to understand the impact of the historiography of women on the oppression of women – in other words, how the manner in which (Indian) women are written about reifies their victim subject status. Who can legitimately speak for Indian women; indeed, can there be any generalized truths about Indian women; and in what circumstances may an outsider speak out or criticize what may be defended as an 'internal matter'?[148] Is there, or can there be, a univer-

---

147 Minow, *supra* note 134 at 1437.
148 Jayawardena, *supra* note 3 at 10.

salist discourse on women's rights that transcends differences of class, race, and religion? On the other hand, should we fall back on an inclusive agenda of cultural difference, paying close attention to women's differences? Or would this cultural relativism lead to inaction, or paralysis of action, and the inability to confront inequality and oppression on the basis of the cultural defence? These are complex issues that defy any easy solution. Yet these questions are crucial to an understanding of what direction the struggle for women's rights must take, to an understanding, also, of the choices to be made and the goals to be identified in order to forward women's claims to equality. I seek to advocate a perspective that combines universalist discourse with a respect for difference, what Nira Yuval Davis has called universality in diversity.[149] Such a perspective retains an appreciation of the universal condition of women's subordination, recognizing the right to speak out against oppression everywhere, while retaining the understanding that we have to pay close attention to differences in class, caste, race, and other situated differences that mediate women's understanding of, and response to, their disadvantage.[150]

In the context of colonialism and nationalism, the woman question was further implicated in the political struggle for freedom by the way in which contemporary feminists wrote about women and by contemporary understandings of women as victims.[151] This raises the issue of the 'reciprocal relationship between political and textual practices.'[152] Edward Said has written insightfully about cultural imperialism and the manner in which the production of knowledge has to be understood as being linked to the political context.[153] Arguably, the production of knowledge goes hand in hand with the imperial project, serving the colonial purpose of legitimizing political domination. Writing about empire was closely linked with contemporary understandings of the imperial project, and the production of culture and knowledge and contemporary narratives have to be understood as being closely linked with the political and social institutions of British rule and an appreciation of the moral responsibility of imperial domination.[154] The ques-

---

149   *Gender and Nation*, 4, 5.
150   *Ibid.*
151   Liddle and Joshi, *supra* note 8 at 31.
152   David, *Rule Britannia*, 4.
153   Said, *Culture and Imperialism*; *Orientalism*.
154   David, *supra* note 152 at 8.

tion of political reform for the colony was implicated in writings about the status of women that were used to defend imperialism and to forward the notion that Indians, owing to their abysmal treatment of women, were unfit for home rule.

The questions of speaking for others, positionality, and location of the speaker are fraught with tension, especially in the context of colonialism and nationalism.[155] In the Indian nationalist imagination, the private sphere and, most centrally, the status of women were cast as pure, autonomous, and free from imperial hegemony. Excluded from any significant participation in colonial politics, the notion of the private sphere was fiercely defended against colonial interference, as the family became the only arena in which Indian males could preserve their power. Colonial authorities encouraged this perception, arguably as a way to divert the attention of indigenous elites from their lack of political power in the public sphere.

In this context, criticism by a foreigner was invariably received with hostility. The book *Mother India*, published in 1927 by American feminist Katherine Mayo, illustrates the difficulties inherent in speaking out against women's subordination as an outsider.[156] Most particularly, Mayo's book demonstrates the difficulty of critiquing a society from the outside without a nuanced understanding of either the political or the social context. It was against this background that Indian feminists and nationalists harshly condemned *Mother India*. The book fiercely critiqued Indian male patriarchy. Mayo condemned Hindu civilization in broad strokes, blaming it, or rather lack of it, for the ills that plagued India, especially poverty, and she held Indian male patriarchy culpable for the degraded status of women.[157] Mayo used all of these criticisms to argue that India was not ready for political autonomy, and she thus legitimized the colonial power, using her book to endorse and support the imperial project. Her views as a feminist led her to censure male patriarchy, but did not lead her to a more liberal political view. For Mayo, the goal of women's liberation did not include national liberation. Not surprisingly, women's rights advocates and nationalists were appalled. Such a position was unacceptable to Indian feminists,

---

155 Alcoff, 'Cultural Feminism,' 432, 434–5.
156 Mayo, *Mother India*.
157 Jayawardena, *supra* note 3 at 95.

while nationalists denounced the book, which Gandhi characterized as a 'Drain Inspector's Report.'[158]

On the other hand, the British welcomed *Mother India* as a legitimation of their political dominance over India. According to this interesting quote from the *New Statesman and Nation of London*, the book revealed 'the filthy personal habits of even the most highly educated classes in India – which, like the degradation of Hindu women, are unequalled even among the most primitive African or Australian savages.' And it ended, 'Katherine Mayo makes the claims for Swaraj [self-rule] seem nonsense and the will to grant it almost a crime.'[159]

In the colonial context, criticism of Indian culture by a foreigner was received with suspicion, particularly because it challenged the nationalist discourse of the split between home and the world, where the home was the repository of all things pure and untouched by colonial hegemony. The nationalist discourse was a discursive projection of an identity and culture constructed as ancient and ideal, in contrast to the current state of Indian society. Nationalist discourse constructed the myth of a golden age, which was contrasted with the current ills plaguing India, which were now attributed to the evils of imperialism. Thus, nationalism was a conscious assertion of national pride and an exercise in identity, and any criticism of Indian culture met with hostility and was seen as an attack on the nation.[160] In keeping with the nationalist construction of home and the world, with the emphasis on the status of women as the marker of culture and community, legislative interventions by the colonizers were seen as an unacceptable intrusion into the private sphere and an interference with gender relations.

Arguably, had Mayo's book been written outside the context of colonial domination and had she paid attention to the political and social contexts, at the very least acknowledging the impact of colonial dominance on the lives of Indians, the rejection of her book may have been understood simply as a rejection of the criticism by male elites. However, the political context of colonialism was all-dominant and naturally impacted any interpretation of her writing by Indians. At the same time, Mayo's book did not advocate liberation for the women of India, but rather made the case for continued British presence. What

---

158 Liddle and Joshi, *supra* note 8 at 31. They included Tagore and Palme Dutt.
159 *Ibid.*
160 Jayawardena, *supra* note 3 at 7.

increased hostility to the book was that it was used by the British to claim legitimacy for their rule over India.

For Indian feminists, in the context of the British ambiguity towards the question of women's rights in India and the difficulties the women's movement had experienced in pushing for legal reform through petitioning the British, combined with the manner in which Indian criticisms of male patriarchy were used to endorse colonialism rather than to forward a women's rights agenda, the situation was all the more complex. The women's movement, not surprisingly, was reluctant to acknowledge Indian men as the main enemy and chose instead to focus on the ending of colonial rule as its main objective. As noted earlier, however, this choice meant that the examination of the causes of women's subordination was never the primary focus; it restricted an analysis of the causes of women's oppression and rendered the movement dependent on nationalist men for the implementation of legal reform.[161]

Yet Mary Daly offers, surprisingly, an endorsement of the views presented in *Mother India*.[162] Perhaps more surprising is Daly's support of the critique of a culture by outsiders, by encouraging feminists not to be afraid of criticizing other cultures. However, she does not qualify this endorsement with a caution as to awareness of location and context of the speaker.[163] Daly decries the manner in which Mayo has been unjustly denounced for what Daly believes is just criticism of Third World patriarchy. Yet Daly neglects to problematize Mayo's motives in this critique, or her support for colonial domination. Certainly, there was a need to fight social evils disadvantaging Indian women. But if Mayo had been serious about reforming the status of Indian women, her method left much to be desired – continued imperial domination with the justification of British rule was ultimately unhelpful to Indian women and to nationalists, all of whom were committed to the goal of national liberation.[164] Daly, while condemning patriarchal oppression in the western world, suggests that the worst patriarchy is that of Third World men, once again placing Indian women squarely in victim subject position, thus ultimately silencing

---

161 Liddle and Joshi, *supra* note 8 at 32.
162 Daly, *Gyn/ecology*, 127–9.
163 Jayawardena, *supra* note 3 at 8.
164 *Ibid*. at 99.

them through her understanding of Third World male patriarchy as completely suppressing women's agency.[165]

The continued hostility in India today towards what are considered 'western' ideas manifests itself in attacks on feminism as western and on Indian feminists as not being 'true' Indian women. As Kumari Jayawardena observes, 'The concept of feminism has ... been the cause of much confusion in Third World countries. It has variously been alleged by traditionalists, political conservatives and even certain leftists, that feminism is a product of "decadent" Western capitalism; that it is based on a foreign culture of no relevance to women in the Third World; that it is the ideology of the women of the local bourgeoisie; and that it alienates or diverts women from their culture, religion, and family responsibilities on the one hand, and from the revolutionary struggles for national liberation and socialism on the other.'[166] Those who supported the *Shah Bano* judgment and opposed the fundamentalist construction of the true Muslim woman were denounced as 'western' and as not being true Muslims. Feminists in a Third World context have to contend with anti-feminist attitudes, and the identification of feminism as bourgeois and pro-western.[167] The terms *western* and *bourgeois* are used to denounce women's struggles, with resort to language and arguments that colonialists used to vilify movements of national liberation and still are used today to deny women their rights.

There are many feminists from the Third World who successfully negotiate the delicate balance between extreme universalism, on the one hand, and extreme cultural relativism, on the other.[168] They recognize the cultural chauvinism and male patriarchal privilege protected by a relativist discourse; they reject the universalism of anti-western rhetoric, which denounces Third World feminists and feminism as pro-western and anti-indigenous, as being supportive of structures of gender oppression. Prominent among them is Valentine Moghadam, who has warned against such 'insular thinking' and the 'nativist mentality' of some Third World intellectuals, who denounce 'any concept, practice or institution that originates in the "West" as Orientalism or neocolonialism.'[169] 'What is privileged is "authentic-

---

165 Forbes, *supra* note 7 at 4.
166 Jayawardena, *Feminism and Nationalism*, 2.
167 Jayawardena, *supra* note 3 at 12.
168 *Ibid.*
169 Moghadam. 'Against Eurocentrism and Nativism,' 88.

ity"; what is sought for is "identity,"' she adds, noting that this often leads to a rejection of democracy, socialism, secularism, and feminism as 'alien and culturally inappropriate.'[170] Demystifying received notions of culture and identity unmasks how these arguments are used to serve particular interests. Further, it challenges the credibility of the 'tradition' and 'modernity' binary, which has served to disempower women.[171] This east/west binary and the setting up of a dichotomy between tradition and modernity is a self-serving argument of those opposed to social change, and Indian women invariably have come to recognize that 'the main enemy is within' – the nation state, religious fundamentalisms, and dominant social and cultural institutions.[172]

---

170 *Ibid.*
171 Narain, *supra* note 102 at 96.
172 Jayawardena, *supra* note 3 at 11.

3 The Post-Colonial Predicament: Muslim Women and the Law

The post-colonial Indian state sought to establish a society free from distinctions of caste, religion, and gender. Yet it retained religion, through personal law, as a defining status in an individual's relationship to the state.[1] This seeming contradiction has to be understood in the context of India's partition along religious lines and the anxiety of the post-colonial state to retain Muslim loyalty to its secular, nationalist ideology by safeguarding Muslim group rights. This contradictory embrace of a composite national identity with an ascriptive religious identity, from which there can be no exit, has had critical consequences for Muslim women, to whom the state has simultaneously granted and denied an equal national identity. The impact is felt primarily in the continuing disadvantage of women through the denial of gender equality within the family, the sphere in which Indian women continue to experience the sharpest discrimination.[2]

Despite a formal commitment to gender equality, the post-colonial state continues to sanction inequality for Muslim women by perpetuating the personal law system and by making no effort to reform Muslim family law to address women's legal disadvantage. This parallel coexistence of formal guarantees of equality with the reality of discriminatory personal law highlights 'the complex, contradictory nature of the structures of domination and the possibilities of resistance.'[3] It is critical to recognize that the subordination of women under

---

1 Lateef, *Muslim Women in India*, 5.
2 Kapur and Cossman, *Subversive Sites*, 13.
3 Amrita Basu, 'Resisting the Sacred and the Secular,' in Jeffery and Basu, eds, *Resisting the Sacred and the Secular*, 3 at 5.

personal law not only structures the position of women within the patriarchal family, but also impacts the relationship between Muslim women and the state. Personal law reform is critical to addressing the social and economic vulnerability of Muslim women in India. Proactive state action is essential to enforce the principle of gender equality, and the state must formulate public policy to ensure the full participation of Muslim women in the political mainstream as equal citizens of the nation.[4]

The (mis)treatment of Muslim women in the law reflects the political arrangements of the post-colonial state. The reluctance of the state to reform personal law to address gender discrimination should be understood as being inextricably linked with the state's political agenda of governing a pluralist, multi-religious nation.[5] Primarily, considerations of political expediency and national development, rather than a commitment to women's rights, shape state policy towards personal law reform.[6] The state casts itself as protector of women and agent of social change, while at the same time forming political alliances with conservative leaders of the community that contradict its proclaimed objectives of equal citizenship and gender equality. The *Muslim Women's (Protection of Rights on Divorce) Act* is an example of this contradiction.[7]

Impelled by a desire to maintain control over groups constituting the nation, the state seeks to retain power over and restrict the authority of religious leaders. As a consequence, state and community leaders are locked in a relationship that is both conflicting and mutually constituting. This ambivalent alliance, reflecting and reinforcing traditional patriarchal forms of control, has had a profound impact on Muslim women. Simultaneously championed and abandoned by the state and controlled and neglected by religious fundamentalist leaders, Muslim women quickly become no more than metaphors in the power struggle between state and community to retain control over the Muslim collectivity.

In this chapter, I begin by setting out the constitutional context of the legal status of Muslim women. I analyse constitutional challenges to discrimination under the personal law, examining whether the

---

4 Kazi, *Muslim Women in India*, 3, 4.
5 Parashar, *Women and Family Law Reform*, 144.
6 *Ibid.* at 20–1.
7 See 'Statutes' in the Bibliography.

response of the judiciary to such challenges has served to undermine or to uphold women's rights. I consider judicial decisions exploring the promise of law as a site from which to challenge gender discrimination. I discuss the potential of a constitutional rights litigation strategy to forward women's rights. Understanding the realm of constitutional law as a critical discursive site, I seek to evaluate its potential as a space from which women can challenge the contradiction between formally guaranteed equality rights and the discriminatory personal law system.

The Constitutional Context

Articles 14 and 15 of the Indian *Constitution* guarantee equality before the law and freedom from discrimination, and Article 25 guarantees religious freedom.[8] In addition to these fundamental rights, Article 44 directs the state to enact a uniform civil code (UCC) of family laws for all citizens of India.[9] However, this is not an enforceable fundamental right but a directive principle that is nevertheless intended to be fun-

---

8   The *Constitution of India*, 1950 (hereinafter the *Constitution*). The fundamental rights are provided in Part III of the *Constitution* in Articles 12 through 35. Article 14: 'Equality before law. – The State shall not deny to any person equality before the law or equal protection of the laws within the territory of India.' The relevant provisions of Article 15 are: 'A. 15. – Prohibition of discrimination on the grounds of religion, race, caste, sex, or place of birth. – (1) The State shall not discriminate against any citizens on grounds only of religion, race, caste, sex, place of birth or any of them. (3) Nothing in this article shall prevent the State from making any special provision for women and children. (4) Nothing in this article or in clause (2) of article 29 shall prevent the State from making any special provision for the advancement of any socially or educationally backward classes of citizens or for Scheduled Castes and Scheduled Tribes.' Article 25: 'Freedom of conscience and free profession, practice and propagation of religion. – (1) Subject to public order, morality and health and to other provisions of this Part [the fundamental rights chapter] all persons are equally entitled to freedom of conscience and the right freely to profess, practice and propagate religion. – (2) Nothing in this article shall affect the operation of any existing law or prevent the State from making any law – (a) regulating or restricting any economic, financial, political or other secular activity which may be associated with religious practice; (b) providing for social welfare and reform or the throwing open of Hindu religious institutions of a public character to all classes and sections of Hindus.'

9   Article 44: 'Uniform Civil Code for the citizens. – The State shall endeavor to secure for the citizens a uniform civil code throughout the territory of India.'

damental to the state's governing policy.[10] The *Constitution* directs the state to apply the principle of Article 44 in formulating new laws. For Muslim women, the right to gender equality and the right to freedom from discrimination are invariably denied by both community leaders and the state, citing the right to religious freedom and the preservation of minority rights as the justification. In such a situation, regimes of competing rights are set up, and false dichotomies are constructed between group rights and women's rights.

As Lloyd and Susanne Rudolph point out, the personal law system that sanctions inequality and the directive principle to enact a uniform civil code 'confronts the nation with an unfinished agenda.'[11] Together, the question of the constitutional validity of personal law and the state's obligation to comply with the constitutional directive to initiate a UCC are matters of some controversy and debate. The focus of the discussion has remained the implications for minority rights, rather than the potential for gender justice.[12] Paradoxically, the secular state must both reform the worst excesses of religion in terms of the status of lower castes and of women, and at the same time safeguard the religious beliefs of minorities.[13] It is this conundrum that constitutes India's post-colonial predicament, with far-reaching implications for Muslim women's rights.

It is questionable whether it is constitutionally permissible for the state to retain the personal law system, which is based explicitly on differences of religion and gender.[14] Indeed, Article 13(1) of the Indian *Constitution* provides that all laws in force, insofar as they are inconsistent with the fundamental rights shall be

---

10 Directive Principles of State Policy are not enforceable. They lay down the aims of state policy and are recommendatory rather than mandatory. Article 37: 'Application of the principles contained in this Part [Directive Principles of State Policy]. – The Provisions contained in this Part shall not be enforceable by any court, but the principles therein laid down are nevertheless fundamental in the governance of the country and it shall be the duty of the State to apply these principles in making laws.'

11 Rudolph and Rudolph, *The Modernity of Tradition*, 123.

12 Parashar, *supra* note 5 at 202, 203.

13 Donald E. Smith, 'India As a Secular State,' in Rajeev Bhargava, ed., *Secularism and its Critics*, 177 at 227.

14 John H. Mansfield, 'The Personal Laws or a Uniform Civil Code,' in Baird, *Religion and Law*, 139 at 153.

void.[15] Ironically, Article 44 has been used both to argue that the constitution makers intended to phase out personal law and introduce a UCC, as well as to argue the opposite, that Article 44 by its very presence indicates that personal law was to be continued.[16] Donald E. Smith argues that Article 44 is far-reaching in its implications, as it calls upon the state to reform personal law while at the same time affirming the concept of secularism. Arguably, the fundamental right to equality casts the duty on the state to reform personal law to bring it into conformity with national constitutional principles. The UCC provision should be seen as evidence that the constitution makers were aware of the contradiction between equality guarantees and discriminatory personal law, and its inclusion ought to be understood as a way they envisaged of negotiating this complex question.[17]

The *Constitution* in itself was a charter for social change and reform. It explicitly sets out that the state, and through it the judiciary, must reform the worst excesses of oppressive religious customs to bring about much needed social change. Specific provisions abolish untouchability and open up public temples to all Hindus irrespective of caste. Article 25, guaranteeing religious freedom, begins from the explicit premise that the state has the authority to reform and regulate religion. Ameliorative provisions for women and children and affirmative action for disadvantaged groups are specifically permitted.[18] It was the

---

15 Article 13: 'Laws inconsistent with or in derogation of the fundamental rights. – (1) All laws in force in the territory of India immediately before the commencement of this Constitution, in so far as they are inconsistent with the provisions of this Part, [the Fundamental Rights Chapter] shall, to the extent of such inconsistency, be void.'

16 Mansfield, *supra* note 14 at 148.

17 Bhattacharjee, *Matrimonial Laws and the Constitution*, 4.

18 Articles 17, 15(3) and (4), and 25(2) (b), *Constitution of India*. Article 17: 'Abolition of Untouchability. – "Untouchability" is abolished and its practice in any form is forbidden. The enforcement of any disability arising out of "Untouchability" shall be an offence punishable in accordance with law.' Article 15(3): 'Nothing ... shall prevent the State from making any special provision for women and children.' 15(4): 'Nothing ... shall prevent the State from making any special provision for the advancement of any socially and educationally backward classes of citizens or for the Scheduled Castes and the Scheduled Tribes.' Article 25(2)(b): 'Freedom of Conscience and free profession, practice and propagation of religion. – Nothing in this article shall affect the operation of any existing law or prevent the State from making any law providing for social welfare and reform or the throwing open of Hindu religious institutions of a public character to all classes and sections of Hindus.'

recognition of the *Constitution* makers that personal law was unjust to women as well as to other disadvantaged groups, including the lower castes, that led to the inclusion of Article 44, which directed the state to introduce a uniform civil code of family laws for all citizens of India.

The *Constitution* predominantly safeguards the rights of individuals rather than the rights of groups. Its makers were conscious of the dangers involved in reinforcing group identities on the basis of religion.[19] However, in recognition of the entrenched nature of communal, sectarian identities in India, they sought to provide space for cultural and religious diversity.[20] The right to religious freedom explicitly recognizes the critical role of religion in Indian life, and as such, points to a recognition of the potential incommensurability of judicial decisions with religious beliefs. Clearly, there are non-constitutional reasons for preserving personal law. The state's decision to retain the discriminatory personal law system is inevitably based on its own ideology and the need to strengthen minority allegiance to the state. Whereas the *Constitution* drafters understood the UCC as a means of strengthening national unity, increasingly in the contemporary context it is seen as a violation of the secular minority rights arrangements of the post-colonial state and as a threat to political stability, rather than as an instrument of integration.[21] Arguably, judicial intervention by itself might be unsuccessful in solving problems of such intricacy and complicated scope.

The *Constitution* is a complex document, reflecting the complexity of social relations in the reality of life in India and also the conflicting impulses of Indian nationalism.[22] Whereas the inconsistencies in the *Constitution's* contradictory embrace of individual rights and group rights have been resolved in specific settings, such as in programs of affirmative action and in the opening of temples to Hindus of all castes, as far as Muslim women's rights under personal law are concerned, this dichotomy remains unresolved. With regard to the state's authority to regulate religion through reform of personal law, the law minister emphasized that the state retained the right to reform and regulate the personal law of any community.[23] This statement made it

---

19 Parashar, *supra* note 5 at 195.
20 Jacobsohn, *The Wheel of Law*, 92.
21 Mansfield, *supra* note 14 at 157.
22 Dhavan, 'Religious Freedom in India,' 230.
23 B.R. Ambedkar, *Parliamentary Debates* 20. Ix. 51, cols 2950–1.

clear that personal law was not beyond the regulating power of the state, as determined by the *Constitution*. Indeed, the state pushed through the reform of Hindu law on the grounds that all laws must conform to *Constitutional* principles.[24]

As well, the Supreme Court of India has established the state's authority to reform religion, through a series of decisions on religious freedom. The courts have interpreted this provision of the *Constitution* to largely restrict the operation of religious freedom to permit state regulation in most areas of religious life, with the notable exception of challenges to the personal law system.[25] This modern reformism adopted by the courts resonates with the constitutional mandate to accommodate the need for social welfare and reform and speaks to 'the transformative dimension of Indian nationalism.'[26] However, the idea of modernist secularism, which conflated the imperatives of reform with those of secularism, was not intended to erase India's diversity; rather, it was a charter for the state to embark on a course of social reform that necessarily included the reform of religion, and it was for the courts to decide the extent, nature, and pace of such change.[27]

The state is committed to reform as an aspect of state policy. Yet the state has studiously avoided addressing both the issue of gender inequality in Muslim personal law, as well as the enactment of a UCC.[28] Whereas state regulation of religious institutions, such as charitable endowments (*Wakfs*), has been a large part of the state agenda, Muslim personal law has been left unreformed in return for the political support of traditional male leaders of the community. Consequently, women's equality rights have been overlooked. To a great extent then, the state has been complicit in increasing the influence of traditional leadership to buttress its own position, playing off community against gender. As *Shah Bano* shows, the state has legitimized the authority of religious leaders over the community, especially over the women of the community, to forward its own political agenda.

---

24 Parashar, *supra* note 5 at 97.
25 Rajeev Dhavan, 'The Road to Xanadu: India's Quest for Secularism,' in Larson, *Religion and Personal Law in India*, 301 at 310, 311.
26 Jacobsohn, *supra* note 20 at 93.
27 Rajeev Dhavan and Fali S. Nariman, 'The Supreme Court and Group Life: Religious Freedom, Minority Groups, and Disadvantaged Communities,' in Kirpal, et al., *Supreme But Not Infallible*, 256 at 270.
28 Parashar, *supra* note 5 at 18, 204.

Indeed, the state has the option to enact a UCC to address the problem of discriminatory personal law. Alternatively, the choice before the state to address discrimination under personal law is the fundamental rights solution. Arguably, in accordance with the provisions of Article 13 of the *Constitution*, personal law must be tested against the principles guaranteed in the fundamental rights, invalidating all those provisions to the extent that they are inconsistent with the fundamental rights. Thus, if certain provisions of personal law are found to be discriminatory against women on the basis of gender and religion, they would have to be struck down as *ultra vires* the *Constitution* – a strong constitutional argument in favour of personal law reform. Such a solution, however, is primarily judicial, leaving it to the courts to decide whether and which aspects of personal law violate constitutionally guaranteed fundamental rights. The courts, despite embracing a reformist zeal with respect to other aspects of the reform of religion, have backed away from this fundamental rights solution. As Rajeev Dhavan argues, 'Finding technical refuge in the impossible distinction that "personal laws" were not like other "customary laws" and therefore outside the ambit of the Fundamental Rights chapter, the courts shied away from being lumbered with the responsibility of making personal laws fair, just, and non-discriminatory.'[29] The third option available to the state is the legislative reform of personal law. This option has been eschewed for the Muslim community. Dhavan contends that the politically sensitive nature of such legislative reform is what prompted the *Constitution* makers to address the issue of personal law reform by inserting the neutral wording of Article 44 directing the state to enact, eventually, a UCC.[30]

Archana Parashar questions the state's failure to subject discriminatory provisions of personal law to the test of constitutional principles of gender equality and freedom from discrimination.[31] She argues that in light of the fact that the principle of gender equality has been accepted in the *Constitution*, those provisions of personal law that discriminate against women can no longer be permitted.[32] A.M. Bhattacharjee states that not only the discriminatory provisions in the various personal laws but, in fact, the entire personal law system

---

29 Dhavan, *supra* note 25 at 316.
30 *Ibid*.
31 Parashar, *supra* note 5 at 20.
32 *Ibid*. at 21.

based on religious affiliation 'are open to serious challenges on the ground of constitutionality.'[33] According to him, the replacement of these laws by a uniform code of secular family law is not merely a constitutional objective as envisaged by Article 44, but 'an imperative constitutional necessity.'[34]

Although Independence liberated Indian women within the public sphere, this freedom in public life was not permitted to encroach on women's private realities such as inequitable family laws. Political liberation was acceptable as long as it did not dictate, most especially to minority communities, how to address women's inequality. Significantly, in the nationalist project, a distinction was made between emancipation and national liberation. In turn, a further distinction was drawn between community and state, where social emancipation was understood as the exclusive sphere of the community, fiercely protected against state hegemony. It was in this manner that the public/private distinction was posited on the discourse of emancipation-independence with profound results for women, which were, arguably, ideologically opposed to the professed fundamental organizing principles of the post-colonial state. The state entered into Faustian bargains with community leaders to iterate that social reform must be initiated from within the community itself, with the state assuming a selective hands-off policy towards reform of Muslim personal law. This stance permitted and legitimized the deep-rooted traditional understanding of women's rights, as demonstrated in the *Shah Bano* controversy.

The granting of formal equality in the public sphere meant that, in theory, Muslim women were freed from disabilities in civil society, but the continuance of personal law and the state's refusal to intervene has led to a complex array of continuing disadvantages for Muslim women.[35] Ambiguity in the constitutional provisions permits contradictory claims and enables the state to act inconsistently with respect to essentially similar claims of different communities with regard to law reform.[36] Whenever the state's political goal of retaining minority

---

33 Bhattacharjee, *supra* note 17 at 8–9.
34 *Ibid*.
35 Galanter, *Competing Equalities*, 22.
36 Parashar, *supra* note 5 at 19. In view of Article 15, which invalidates discrimination on the basis of religion, the authority of the state to reform only certain personal laws and not others has been questioned.

allegiance to the ideology of nationalism appears to be threatened, the state has shown its readiness to abandon any efforts to enforce the principle of gender equality, invariably seeking refuge in the contention that the religious nature of personal law prevents state intervention.[37] Yet, significantly, personal law as it exists today is the result both of state legislative initiatives and of political negotiations by religious communities themselves and is reflective of political and social hegemonies.[38]

Personal law has been accepted by the state as the private sphere of Muslim autonomy, although, in fact, the state has not hesitated to interfere with it whenever such interference coincided with its political agenda. Maintaining such a system of differentiated personal law, and preserving the myth of the autonomy of the Muslim community with regard to personal law have impacted Muslim women. Their inequality has been neither challenged nor addressed either by the state or by community leaders. The question of socio-legal reform for the Muslim community was thus abandoned to the traditional male leadership of that community, who were disinclined to accept women's claiming their rights as equal, independent interrogators of hegemonic definitions of religion, tradition, and group interest.[39] In so doing, the state has effectively legitimized and granted the group the right to preserve practices that disproportionately discriminate against women. In these circumstances, women's citizenship rights are severely impaired by a constitutional system that defers to the exclusive jurisdiction of the Muslim community with respect to family law, including marriage and divorce, guardianship, custody, inheritance, and succession, among others, which systematically disadvantage women.[40] The status of women as citizens is rendered ambiguous by the dual legal structure upheld by the state. From this critical perspective it is quickly apparent that the state has created a system of differentiated citizenship wherein the state has differing rights and obligations to its citizens based not only on gender but also on religious affiliation.

---

37 *Ibid.* at 21.
38 Basu, 'Shading the Secular,' 132.
39 See also *Itwari* v. *Asghari*, AIR 1960 All 680.
40 Ran Hirschl and Ayelet Shachar, 'Constitutional Transformation, Gender Equality, and Religious/National Conflict in Israel,' in Baines and Rubio-Marin, *Gender of Constitutional Jurisprudence*, 205 at 222.

The state has accepted the equation of personal law with group identity and has not questioned this definition of group accommodation or of group interest. By allowing Muslim leaders to continue to exercise authority over women of the community by refusing to reform the personal law, together with the state's policy of reinforcing the public/private split by claiming that no change is possible in the personal law unless the call for change comes from the community itself, the state has abandoned Muslim women to patriarchal interpretations of personal law and has legitimized their continued subordination. By giving the conservative, powerful, articulate sections of the community the legal backing to control the women of the community, the state has allowed the traditional male leaders of that community to define not only what constitutes a good Muslim, but also who belongs to the community and to control entry into and exit from the group. In addition, while simultaneously adding to the advantage of male members of the Muslim community, patriarchal control over women in the community has in fact been reinforced by state policy. As a result, women's voices have been effectively excluded not only from the discourse and debate around their daily life but also from plans for future reform.[41]

The struggle between the state and patriarchal community leaders over the status of women is enmeshed in the problematic of 'protection.' The discourse of women's rights is subsumed under that of protection, displacing issues of women's rights onto discussions of what women may be privileged to have for the moment, within the rhetoric of 'community interest.'[42] Discourses of both state and community leadership deploy the notion of women in need of rescue to justify their respective agendas of controlling electoral politics, buttressing patriarchal structures of authority, and reasserting male privilege and control over gender roles and women's rights. The *Shah Bano* controversy illustrates the convergence of these narratives and the discursive treatment of women as essentially without agency and without voice. Both discourses, of state and of community leaders, though emanating from differing concerns regarding gender and community, ultimately result in the erasure of Muslim women as unified legal subjects, permitting and perpetuating discursive displacements that result in denying the gendered subjectivity of Muslim women.

---

41 Dhavan, 'Introduction,' i at lxxx.
42 Pathak and Sunder Rajan, 'Shahbano,' 569.

   Community leaders have resisted any calls for change on the basis that personal law is the primary signifier of group identity, and further that the right to religious freedom prevents the state from interfering in personal law, and finally, that as religious law, it is immutable. The right to religious freedom is used to shield personal law against state scrutiny, and the state has not questioned the givenness of this link between personal law, religious freedom, group identity, and women's status. Inevitably, the issue becomes one of group rights versus women's rights. Calls for change from Muslim women themselves are viewed by community leaders as a challenge to the community, as a betrayal of the group, and as an assault on religion. Dissent within the group is suppressed, and personal law sanctioning gender discrimination is upheld as a measure of group autonomy. The characterization of women as weak and helpless is used to defend their continued subordination under personal law.

   The equation of women with group identity and status has impacted the framing of the debate on personal law reform. Rather than an examination of the legal disadvantage of Muslim women, there is invariably a discursive displacement of the question of gender equality onto issues of Muslim minority rights.[43] Community leaders have displaced the question of gender inequality under the personal law, replacing it with questions of threats to community identity and group autonomy. Any proposed reform of personal law, even when it comes from within the community, is fraught with political tension and is perceived as a threat to group identity.[44] Fundamentalist leaders have presented their massive campaign against the *Shah Bano* judgment in terms of the protection of the community, and of the women of the community, from the dangers of assimilation. Community leaders have invoked the notion of 'protection' to justify the renewed patriarchal community control over women. Muslim women are made to conform to a narrow interpretation of their rights under personal law. The 'true' Muslim woman is constructed in opposition to the westernized feminist.

   The narrative of protection by the community denies the possibility of progressive change, it suppresses the politics of subalternity, and it frames Muslim women narrowly. The protection of the community became the key plank of the argument as the protection of women was

---

43 Mukhopadhyay, *Legally Dispossessed*, 23.
44 Sunder Rajan, *The Scandal of the State*, 148.

subsumed under this larger narrative of group integrity and identity. The two issues were conflated, and Muslim women's protection was understood essentially as protection of the community. Muslim women, indeed, Shah Bano herself, became little more than a metaphor for group identity, a symbol of collective identity. The question of women's rights received scant attention. The real person of Shah Bano and her real predicament of economic and social vulnerability were erased from the discourse, replaced by an imagined 'true' Muslim woman represented and signified solely through community identity. The *Shah Bano* case became for the fundamentalists essentially a political struggle to re-establish control over the community, and over the women of the community, to consolidate group boundaries, and to create a greater political space for themselves as leaders of the community. Not surprisingly, as the more politically articulate and powerful section within the Muslim community, the reality of democratic politics, so crucially dependent on votes, meant that the state was paying attention to these self-appointed leaders. This focus was especially marked after the ruling party's electoral loss in a state by-election, largely attributable to its initial support of the Supreme Court's *Shah Bano* judgment.[45]

The state assumed the homogeneity of the Muslim community and refused to acknowledge dissent within the group.[46] The acceptance of the religious leadership as the sole legitimate representatives of the group highlights the symbiotic relationship between the state and religious leaders, each seeking to reinforce existing patterns of privilege and power, with profound consequences for women. The state thus reinforced patriarchal structures of oppression and authority over the women of the community. It not only undermined Muslim women's claims to equality but also refused to acknowledge the economic and social vulnerability of Muslim women in situations of family breakdown.[47] This attitude was highlighted in *Shah Bano*, where the state's political dependence on the religious leadership of the Muslim community meant that it was unwilling to defend either the secular project

---

45 The ruling Congress (I) party's candidate lost a by-election in Kishenganj, Bihar, to Syed Shahabuddin, a leader of the anti-*Shah Bano* campaign. Kumar, *History of Doing*, 165.

46 Zoya Hasan, 'Gender Politics, Legal Reform, and the Muslim Community in India,' in Jeffery and Basu, *supra* note 3, 71 at 75–6.

47 Jayal, *Democracy and the State*, 243.

or women's rights.[48] Throughout this controversy the state insisted that change could not be imposed from outside, yet the voices privileged by the state were, and continue to be, those of the male elite; women's voices are silenced, even as they demand change, as did Shah Bano.[49] Muslim women were assumed to be passive onlookers without agency, yet the reality of their voices and their exercise of agency demanding their rights went unacknowledged by the state.[50]

Despite the fact that there have been many calls for change from moderate reformists and women's groups, the state has privileged instead the voice of the politically more influential traditional male leadership.[51] Moderate and reformist Muslims together with women's groups have demanded the reform of marriage and divorce laws and have called upon the All India Muslim Personal Law Board (AIMPLB) to address women's disadvantage, especially in these areas.[52] Most significantly, in February 2005 Muslim women's organizations, frustrated with the lack of response from their traditional community

---

48 *Ibid*. at 244.
49 Arguments of protecting Muslim personal law by the Congress party echoed Muslim Personal Law Board arguments. The idea of vote banks, the manipulation of religious identity for political gain, was ignored by the state; in fact, the state, in order to secure political loyalty of the Muslim conservative leadership, joined with the anti-reform, fundamentalist, Muslim Personal Law Board to promulgate a new Act. The debate on the *Muslim Women's Act* was similar to earlier debates in the Constituent Assembly on the UCC and Hindu law reform. Hasan, *supra* note 46 at 74.
50 Muslim women fiercely battled this effort to take away their rights; they mobilized in great numbers, and their opposition to the proposed bill was significant. As Zoya Hasan points out, 'Muslim women's opposition was a significant feature of the protest against the Muslim Women's Bill in Kerala, West Bengal, Bombay and Delhi, where the rights of indigent women were reaffirmed in public meetings and *mullas* (Muslim teachers or interpreters of Muslim law) were derided for turning religious law into an instrument of injustice. In Delhi, fifteen hundred Muslim women participated in a rally organized by the All India Democratic Women's Association. For the first time Muslim women came out into the streets to fight for their rights in the face of opposition from family, neighbourhood, community, and religious leadership.' Hasan, *supra* note 46 at 84.
51 Kazi, *supra* note 4 at 27.
52 The All India Muslim Personal Law Board, the self-appointed arbiter of Muslim personal law, was founded in 1973 specifically to safeguard that law against any reform, to protect what the members deemed the true Shariat. The Board was an intervenor in the *Shah Bano* case on behalf of the ex-husband, Mohammed Ahmed Khan.

leaders and the AIMPLB, in a remarkable exercise of agency have established their own Personal Law Board, stating that they were forced to do so to address Muslim women's issues, which the AIMPLB had shown reluctance to deal with. This imporant development signals the determination of Muslim women to challenge existing laws and to renegotiate their rights.[53] Certainly, it is linked to current debates on gender and Islam. The significance of this participation is that it highlights not only the diversity of voices among Muslim women themselves, but, just as important, it shows that Muslim women are speaking out against gender discrimination in the law and are calling for change.

In discussions of personal law reform, Muslim women are framed by state discourse in terms of the notion of protection. In *Shah Bano*, the state claimed to be safeguarding the rights of Muslim women. This discourse of protection, arguably, is used by the state to suit its own political agenda rather than to address the systemic disadvantage of women. It serves to emphasize the state's portrayal of itself as proactively enforcing the principle of gender equality, permitting the state to make dubious claims of serving women's interests. In reality, the state enacted a new retrogressive law that took away the rights available to Muslim women under the general criminal law and circumscribed their right to spousal support. On the other hand, it strengthened male control over the women of the community; it safeguarded Muslim men's privilege under the law, absolving them of the duty of spousal support; and it reiterated their unfettered right to unregulated, extrajudicial divorce.

In the political battle over the *Muslim Women's Act*, neither the state nor the community leaders addressed the reality of Muslim women's vulnerability or the issue of Muslim women's rights.[54] Although both community leaders and the state cloaked their arguments in terms of the protection of women, the focus of the debate was on the minority rights and the importance of retaining personal law as a separate sphere of authority free from the constitutional and juridical requirements of the larger society, rather than on the severe systemic disad-

---

53 See the discussion in chapter 4, below. See also Kazi, *supra* note 4 and chapter 4, note 195.
54 Shahida Lateef 'Defining Women through Legislation,' in Hasan, *Forging Identities*, 38 at 57.

vantage of Muslim women.[55] In both these discourses, women were displaced as the primary subjects of debate to objects in the power struggle between community and state. In what was purportedly a discussion of Muslim women's rights, the outstanding feature of both discourses was the marginalization of Muslim women's voices and the trivialization of their rights.[56]

The focus of the debate remained fixed on the comparative rights of religious communities, as the question of Muslim women's rights became subsumed under the larger question of the rights of the Muslim collectivity. The question of legal reform was assessed in terms of the relationship between state and community and the political negotiation of these boundaries, rather than the intrinsic value of reform to address women's inequality within personal law. The state framed the discussion around the issue of personal law, emphasizing a notion of citizenship in which ascriptive group identity was given precedence over constitutional guarantees of equality before the law and equal protection under the law. This approach illustrates the post-colonial predicament, wherein the recognition of religious difference through the preservation of discriminatory personal law violates the formal rights granted by the *Constitution*, and, at the same time, the denial of group rights might lead to a violation of the state's obligation to preserve minority rights. This suggests that we must reconceptualize the frameworks within which we debate notions of difference and discrimination. Further, we must interrogate any accommodation of difference that is premised on the subordination of women's rights.

Any efforts to forward gender equality in India must necessarily interrogate the binary of either state or society as a force to forward women's equality. The situation arguably is more complex than such a binary understanding suggests, as the nature of political and social change is complex. As Niraja Jayal argues, 'to exclusively privilege either the state or society is to ignore the internal complexity of both these categories, of the realities they describe, and often disguise, and, of course, the irreducibility of this reality to two arbitrarily defined and mutually exclusive conceptual categories.'[57] The post-colonial state has an ambivalent policy towards women. We must be careful, however, not to essentialize the state and to recognize that the state

---

55 *Ibid*. at 39.
56 Hasan, *supra* note 46 at 83.
57 Jayal, *supra* note 47 at 141.

itself is not monolithic, but comprises various institutions that do not always work in conjunction with each other. We must understand the state as itself constituted of competing interests and open to differing influences. Moreover, relations between state and society are constantly being renegotiated.[58]

In India, the state is central to transformative change, and women's rights advocates recognize the importance of engaging the state in any attempt to forward those rights, notwithstanding the state's frequent reinforcement of the gender status quo. Power is located in the state, and, despite ambivalence, efforts to secure women's rights necessarily have to continue to address the state in the effort to reclaim citizenship. Yet we have to acknowledge that the state alone cannot be the focus of struggles for women's rights. Indeed, women's organizations have criticized the state for its failure to make the constitutional equality guarantees meaningful for women. Arguably, 'State intervention often complements, upholds and reinforces the interests of patriarchal communities by disregarding or denigrating women's attempts to free themselves from community sanctions.'[59] As Mary John argues, 'It was thus possible, and considered necessary, to question the state, expose the hollowness of its claims or the vested interests it harboured, while at the same time demanding a certain accountability through the rights of citizenship. However critical the institution of patriarchy was to become in the self-understanding of the women's movement, especially among autonomous groups, the Indian state has been the movement's most constitutive site of contestation, or so I would like to contend.'[60]

The *Shah Bano* controversy highlights the ambivalence of the state towards enforcing the principle of gender equality, particularly where it conflicts with the state's perceived political interest. The rights claims of Muslim women emphasize the failed promise of the nationalist struggle, the compromise with the formal guarantees of the *Constitution*, and the continued disadvantage of Muslim women.[61] The law is implicated in contradictory ways in the oppression of women, yet law is a site where gendered roles and identities have been chal-

---

58 Jan Jindy Pettman, 'Globalisation and the Gendered Politics of Citizenship,' in Yuval-Davis and Werbner, *Women, Citizenship and Difference*, 207 at 211.

59 Basu, *supra* note 3 at 6.

60 Mary E. John, 'Gender, Development and the Women's Movement,' in Sunder Rajan, *Signposts*, 101 at 108.

61 Jayal, *supra* note 47 at 258.

lenged by social reformers and feminists.[62] Moving towards a nuanced understanding of the complexity of the law, rather than seeing it simplistically as either an instrument of patriarchal oppression or as an instrument of social change, emphasizes the fact that the law itself holds out a contradictory promise. It is both an emancipatory ally as well as an emissary of the state.[63]

Law's Contradictory Promise

As a self-conscious project of modernization, the post-colonial Indian state and the independent judiciary that was established embraced a reformist ideology. This nationalist project included both the emphatic discursive creation of nationalism, secularism, and freedom from discrimination and the recreation of re-imagined traditions in opposition to the colonial devaluation of things 'native.' Returning the imperial gaze meant that women's legal status was an important aspect of the construction of the nationalist project. It was no accident that women's bodies were the terrain on which these resurrected traditions and values of modernity, equality, and liberty were renegotiated and contested. Women's rights are at the centre of these debates and are 'a hotly contested ideological terrain where women were used to symbolize the progressive aspirations of a secularist elite or a hankering for cultural authenticity expressed in Islamic terms.'[64]

The continued centrality of women's issues to national politics is demonstrated by the tremendous impact of women's legal challenges to the gender status quo. Shah Bano's attempts to claim her rights by turning to the courts shattered the complacency of the secular democratic consensus in post-colonial India and precipitated a national crisis. Yet, together with the success of the legal challenges posed by Shah Bano and others, which highlight the emancipatory possibilities of the law, there have been other legal encounters, which have been more ambivalent in upholding women's rights.

Judicial decisions in challenges to discrimination under personal law reveal the liberatory potential of the law and of constitutional

---

62 Kapur and Cossman, *supra* note 2 at 12.
63 Baxi, 'The State's Emissary,' 253.
64 Deniz Kandiyoti, 'Introduction,' in Kandiyoti, *Women, Islam and the State*, 1 at 3.

guarantees of equality and freedom from discrimination. At the same time, they also emphasize the way in which traditional understandings of women's rights are reified and the hegemony of patriarchal privilege is buttressed. As Srimati Basu argues, 'The figure of "Woman" is refracted in numerous competing and contradictory ways within the legal system of a post-colonial nation; individual women get represented as empowered agents, invisible presences, signifiers of sexual, family and property relations, while law in relation to women gets coded as arbitration, protection, conservation, or liberation.'[65] In this section, looking at key judicial decisions, I consider whether the response of the judiciary to challenges to personal law has served to undermine women's equality in the family or to uphold it. Not all of the cases considered specifically refer to Muslim women, but they are equally important for all Indian women, as these decisions reflect how judges view women's rights, the tropes employed, and the ideologies that inform their decisions. As well, a consideration of judicial decisions allows us to more definitively understand possibilities for future action in the struggle to forward women's rights. The convergence of issues of gender equality, personal law reform, and the enactment of a UCC, in challenges to the personal law, means that all these linked issues are implicated in and affected by such challenges. As such, it is difficult to separate and categorize these cases as either Muslim personal law cases, gender discrimination cases, or constitutional challenges. Necessarily then, in the following discussion, there is a considerable imbrication of these issues and cases.

Fundamental rights challenges to the personal law system have been decided in a manner that often re-inscribes and reifies women's difference rather than challenging familial and legal discourse that frames women as subordinate and needing protection.[66] Women's challenges to personal law, most notably, the *Shah Bano* case, see the judges depicting themselves as modern and concerned about women's rights.[67] Courts have emphasized the need for the judiciary to step in where the state did not, to protect helpless women. However, judicial opinion, although in many cases seeking to distance and distinguish

---

65 Srimati Basu, 'Cutting to Size: Gender and Identity in the Indian Higher Courts,' in Sunder Rajan, *supra* note 60, 248 at 248.

66 Kapur and Cossman, *supra* note 2 at 16–17; Brenda Cossman and Ratna Kapur, 'Women, Familial Ideology and the Constitution: Challenging Equality Rights,' in Kapur, *Feminist Terrains*, 61 at 61.

67 Basu, *supra* note 65 at 265.

itself from prevailing executive state authority and state administration, invariably reflects prevailing notions of women's rights in which
sex equality is understood as a matter of women's protection rather
than as their inalienable right as equal citizens of the nation.

Shah Bano and other decisions reveal that the law has treated women
in a manner that, while it may be empowering in individual instances,
may also serve to reinforce existing familial ideology that supports
gender inequalities. Framing women as helpless and weak, judicial decisions often support women's rights, as such a perception of women is
compatible with traditional understandings of gender roles that allow
for an uncomplicated support of their rights through the law.[68] Yet law
is a site where hegemonic discourses of identity and gender roles have
been challenged, as women's rights advocates seek to renegotiate
women's roles and entitlements as equal citizens.[69]

An important issue is the extent to which constitutional rights can be
used to pursue women's equality claims. Judicial decisions demonstrate how women's rights are created or undermined, revealing the
extent to which constitutional rights further or detract from progress
towards equality and giving us the material and political context in
which these rights are situated.[70] To forward women's rights using a
constitutional framework, we need to relate these formal guarantees to
the material reality of women's experiences in their attempts to claim
their rights. It is imperative to understand the *Constitution* not simply
as the locus of women's rights, but, just as important, as a framework
within which women's rights and the rights of other disadvantaged
groups can be articulated.[71]

In India, the *Constitution* makers gave the judiciary the task of being
the conscience of the nascent state and the custodian of fundamental
rights. In this context, the issues of personal law reform and social
reform through the reform of oppressive customs and religious practices became the responsibility of the independent judiciary. In today's

---

68 *Ibid.* at 267.
69 Kapur and Cossman, *supra* note 2 at 12.
70 Isabel Karpin and Karen O'Connell, 'Speaking into a Silence: Embedded Constitu-
    tionalism, the Australian Constitution, and the Rights of Women,' in Baines and
    Rubio-Marin, *supra* note 40, 22 at 24, 39.
71 *Ibid.* at 22.

political context of Hindu right-wing ascent and the threat this poses to constitutional secularism, the role of the judiciary is even more crucial. Reform measures, such as the abolition of untouchability, have been relatively free from challenge, and the courts have been able to enforce these constitutional rights. The Supreme Court has proactively enforced the rights of disadvantaged groups, most particularly with regard to bonded labour, children, as well as issues such as the protection of the environment and government corruption, but it has not, with rare exceptions, meaningfully addressed the issue of gender discrimination in the personal law system.[72]

In the matter of personal law reform and the enactment of a uniform civil code, the judiciary has been less insistent on pursuing a social reform agenda.[73] Although the Supreme Court has been enthusiastic about the reform of laws with respect to sex equality challenges in the workplace and sexual assault, the judiciary has been less eager to embrace equality challenges brought against discriminatory family law provisions, seeking instead to decide such challenges in other technical terms wherever possible. Its reluctance to address directly gender discrimination in personal law and its failure to pursue aggressively a social reform agenda with respect to gender equality in the private sphere of the family, falling within what is arguably its reform mandate as outlined in the fundamental rights, have been criticized by scholars.[74]

Constitutional challenges to the personal law system and to specific discriminatory features of these laws have been rejected on the grounds that personal law is not subject to the fundamental rights

---

72 Marc Galanter and Jayanth Krishnan, 'Personal Law Systems and Religious Conflict: A Comparison of India and Israel,' in Larson, *supra* note 25, 270 at 284.

73 Dhavan and Nariman, *supra* note 27 at 270.

74 *Ibid.* at 274. B. Sivarammayya argues that the court has a duty to address the question of gender justice in personal laws. According to him, the court has two options: 'either to declare all gender discrimination as void under the Constitution in tune with contemporary international conventions and human rights. But this requires courage and craft on the part of the court and not least a confrontation with the political system, Judged by experience, Parliament will strive to undo what the court attempts to do, by constitutional amendments, and try to curb the powers of the court.' The other option, which he calls the soft option, is to 'swim with the legislative currents and not against them and to declare personal laws as being outside the purview of the Constitution and anti-discrimination provisions. It is a please-all option.' 'Gender Justice,' in Varma and Kusum, *Fifty Years*, 290 at 312, 313.

guaranteed in the *Constitution*.[75] In the absence of an authoritative Supreme Court decision on the impact of fundamental rights on personal law, the focal point of discussion continues to be the *Narasu Appa* case, decided by the Bombay High Court in 1952.[76] *Narasu Appa* held that personal law was not subject to fundamental rights, as personal law was not included in the Article 13 definition of laws in force.[77] Arguably, this decision must be rejected as being an incorrect interpretation of the constitutional status of personal law.

Indeed, there are other, later High Court decisions that hold that personal law is subject to the fundamental rights. In *Abdullah Khan* v. *Chandni Bi*, the Bhopal High Court ruled that different alimony provisions for Hindu and Muslim women violated the equality provisions of the *Constitution*.[78] The court held that personal law must conform to the fundamental rights guaranteed in the *Constitution*. In *Gurdial Kaur* v. *Manghal Singh*, although the Punjab High Court did not make an explicit ruling on the impact of the fundamental right to equality on personal law, by testing the validity of discriminatory inheritance rules under customary law, it implied acceptance that personal law must be governed by the fundamental rights.[79] Yet later, in the 1980 case, *Krishna Singh* v. *Mathura Ahir*, the Supreme Court reiterated the view expressed in *Narasu Appa* to hold that 'Part III [the Fundamental Rights chapter] of the Constitution does not touch upon the personal law of the parties.'[80] Although this was *obiter dicta*, it has been accepted by some as a binding decision on the relationship between fundamental rights and personal law.

---

75 Mansfield, *supra* note 14 at 154. The discussion turns on whether personal law is included in the expression 'laws in force' within the meaning of the *Constitution* and must therefore conform to the fundamental rights. Article 13 stipulates that all laws must conform to the fundamental rights guaranteed in the *Constitution*. It provides that 'all laws in force in the territory of India immediately before the commencement of this Constitution, in so far as they are inconsistent with this part [the fundamental rights], shall to the extent of such inconsistency, be void.' If personal law is within the definition of 'laws in force,' then it must be understood as being governed by the fundamental rights chapter of the *Constitution*.

76 *State of Bombay* v. *Narasu Appa Mali* AIR 1952 Bom 84. This was the first time that judges were called upon to examine the relationship between fundamental rights and personal law. Owing to the eminence of the deciding judges and the fact that until a 1992 High Court decision (*Amina, infra* note 81) *Narasu Appa* had not been specifically rejected, this decision has been regarded as authoritative.

77 *Ibid.* at 88–9.

78 *Abdullah Khan* v. *Chandni Bi* AIR 1956 Bhopal 71.

79 *Gurdial Kaur* v. *Manghal Singh* AIR 1968 Punjab 396.

80 *Krishna Singh* v. *Mathura Ahir*, AIR 1980 SC 707.

In yet another turn, in a 1992 decision, *In re Amina*, the Bombay High Court chose to disregard this *Krishna Singh obiter* to rule that indeed all personal laws are governed by the fundamental rights.[81] The specific questions before the court were whether personal law was subject to the fundamental rights and whether the Muslim personal law of inheritance, whereby a daughter is entitled only to one-half of the share of a son, violates the equality provisions of the *Constitution*. The judge in *Amina* specifically ruled on the constitutionality of personal law, and whether, in case of a conflict with the fundamental right to equality, personal law must be declared void to the extent of this inconsistency. Categorically rejecting *Narasu Appa*, the *Amina* court held that personal law must conform to the fundamental rights.[82] Several subsequent Supreme Court decisions, though not dealing specifically with personal law, arguably lead to the conclusion that *Narasu Appa* was decided incorrectly. However, we must keep in mind the political and social context of law reform in newly independent India. Indeed, in the political and social context of judicial reformism, it was unlikely that the *Narasu Appa* court would reach a conclusion that would undo the social reform measures undertaken by the state, in this case with respect to prohibiting bigamy for Hindus.

The courts have attempted to introduce small-scale legislative changes in personal law. They have made changes in disparate personal laws by claiming that the equal protection clause of the *Constitution* does not apply to changes in individual personal laws, as these laws are not laws for the purposes of fundamental rights protection. Although this contention itself is disputed, using this logic, the courts have sanctioned the prohibition of bigamy for Hindus, but not for Muslims, as shown in the *Narasu Appa* case. They have attempted to decide cases while being sensitive to secularism and the reform imperative without disrespecting traditional religious law.[83]

Rajeev Dhavan and Fali Nariman argue that the logical extension of the state's social reform mandate articulated in the *Constitution* would inevitably lead to the reform of those provisions in personal law that are inequitable.[84] It is doubtful, however, whether such reform could be undertaken by judicial action alone, and it would have to be supported

---

81 *In re Amina*, AIR 1992 Bombay 214 at 219.
82 *Ibid*. at 216–17.
83 William D. Popkin, 'Some Continuing Issues,' in Larson, *supra* note 25, 330 at 334–6.
84 Dhavan and Nariman, *supra* note 27 at 273.

as well by the legislative enactment of a UCC. To address this situation, the *Constitution* drafters provided Article 44 in the form of a Directive Principle, obviously suggesting to the state that this was a way out of the dilemma. Nevertheless, the fact that the *Constitution* does provide the state with the mandate to legislatively enact a uniform family law that is equitable and conforms to constitutional principles does not prevent the courts from holding that personal law is indeed subject to Article 13 of the *Constitution* and therefore would be unconstitutional to the extent that it violated the fundamental rights. Yet by refusing to explicitly test discriminatory provisions of personal law against the touchstone of the *Constitution*, the Supreme Court has shown its reluctance to be drawn into controversy over the critical need to reform personal law.

The noted constitutional scholar, H.M. Seervai argues that personal law must be understood as being subject to the fundamental rights guaranteed in the *Constitution*.[85] However, the judges have, by a convoluted logic held that personal law was not subject to fundamental rights. The Supreme Court affirmed this in *obiter dicta* in 1980 and more comprehensively in 1997.[86] The judiciary thus emphasized its unwillingness to take on what it considered to be the role of the legislature. According to Dhavan, 'for wholly inexplicable and unacceptable reasons, the high courts rejected the "Article 13 solution" to inequality in the personal law, refusing to test personal laws on the touchstone of the fundamental rights.'[87]

India's *Constitution* recognized equality as a fundamental organizing principle of the post-colonial state.[88] The concept of equality was understood to be critically important in combating discrimination and invidious classification based on religion, caste, and gender.[89] In the *Constitution*, the substantive model of equality was articulated from the very outset.[90] It was explicitly understood that the state must pursue substantive equality for previously subordinated groups.[91]

---

85 Seervai, *Constitutional Law of India*, 401, 402.
86 Dhavan and Nariman, *supra* note 84. See *Ahmedabad Women's Action Group (AWAG)* v. *Union of India* (1997) 3 SCC 573.
87 Dhavan and Nariman, *supra* note 84. See *Narasu Appa*, *supra* note 76 and *Srinivasa Aiyar* v. *Saraswathi Ammal*, AIR 1952 Madras 193.
88 Articles 14 through 18, *Constitution*.
89 Dhagamwar, *Uniform Civil Code*, 56.
90 Galanter, *Law and Society*, 260–1.
91 Martha C. Nussbaum, 'India, Sex Equality and Constitutional Law,' in Baines and Rubio-Marin, *supra* note 40, 174 at 179.

However, although the text of the *Constitution* with regard to gender discrimination is in many ways exemplary, traditions of interpretation have varied.

Challenges to gender discrimination have met with an uneven success.[92] Indeed, there is considerable disarray and lack of coherence in the area of equality jurisprudence.[93] Indian judicial discourse is characterized by the prevalence of both the formal model of equality and the substantive model.[94] Despite a substantive understanding of equality, the persistence of traditional notions of gender roles often work to prevent a consistent application of this understanding of equality.[95] Judicial decisions highlight the contradictory impulses of the courts regarding family ideology and the notion of the protection of the family and reveal the uneven application of equality principles. Such an untidy approach to deciding constitutional challenges to women's inequality in the family is perhaps reflective of the lack of unified policy within the judiciary and the often contradictory and conflicting views held by the judges themselves.

Thus it is not surprising that the 'family continues to be constructed as a private sphere, sometimes beyond the legitimate intervention of the law, sometimes requiring the law to protect its privacy. Efforts to challenge the public/private distinction are resisted in and through the very familial ideology on which the distinction is based and reinforced.'[96] An example is the 1984 case, *Harvinder Kaur* v. *Harmander Singh Choudhary*, which concerned a challenge by a wife to the constitutionality of the provision for the restitution of conjugal rights in the *Hindu Marriage Act*.[97] Rejecting this challenge, the court held: 'Introduction of Constitutional Law in the home is most inappropriate. It is like introducing a bull in a china shop. It will prove to be a ruthless destroyer of the marriage institution and all that it stands for. In the privacy of the home and the married life, neither Article 21 nor Article 14 have [*sic*] any place. In a sensitive sphere which is at once most intimate and delicate, the introduction of the cold principles of Constitu-

---

92 *Ibid.* at 174.
93 Galanter, *supra* note 90 at 271.
94 Kapur and Cossman, *supra* note 2 at 175–6.
95 Nussbaum, *supra* note 91 at 185.
96 Kapur and Cossman, *supra* note 2 at 118.
97 *Harvinder Kaur* v. *Harmandar Singh Choudhary* AIR 1984 Delhi 66.

tional Law will have the effect of weakening the marriage bond.'[98] The decision in *Harvinder Kaur* demonstrates how the operation of the public/private distinction serves to keep the family and its existing inequalities shielded from the scrutiny of public law. The family is seen as private and immune from the rights and freedoms that apply to the larger society. Further, it reveals how this understanding reinforces gender stereotypes by emphasizing that women cannot challenge discrimination within the family by appealing to their larger rights as citizens.

Nevertheless, despite the persistence of a formal understanding of equality, most particularly in constitutional challenges to the personal law, the Indian Supreme Court has also moved steadily towards implementing a substantive notion of equality, wherein it has established the judicial view that constitutionality is determined by the effect of the law on the fundamental rights of a citizen, not only on the purported object of the law. The landmark Supreme Court case, *State of Kerala* v. *N.M. Thomas*, is the culmination of this doctrinal shift.[99] This case concerned the state's affirmative action policy in the employment of constitutionally recognized disadvantaged (caste) groups. The court ruled that the state has a positive duty to pursue substantive equality and equality of result, not merely formal equality, declaring that 'the government has an affirmative duty to eliminate inequalities and to provide opportunities for the exercise of human rights and claims.'[100]

The *Thomas* decision has been criticized on the grounds that in a society of endemic shortage, lack of resources, and dependence on government patronage and benefits the emphasis on substantive equality might reduce this notion of equality to an unworkable, diffuse concept.[101] Another criticism is that it has enlarged state power while reinforcing the dependent status of disadvantaged groups. Notwithstanding these concerns, the true import of the *Thomas* decision lies in the emphatic declaration that the state has a duty to pursue substantive equality.[102] *Thomas*'s explicit recognition that formal equality in itself is insufficient to address historic disadvantage is of critical importance to constitutional challenges to discrimination in personal

---

98   *Ibid.* at 75.
99   *State of Kerala* v. *N.M. Thomas* AIR 1976 SC 490. See Galanter, *supra* note 90 at 112.
100   *Thomas, supra* note 99 at 518, 529, 516.
101   Galanter, *supra* note 35 at 391, 393.
102   *Ibid.* at 394.

law. This has a great significance for disadvantaged groups, who can, as a result of this understanding, compel the state to proactively fulfil its responsibilities. Specifically for Muslim women, it signifies that the state can be held accountable to women as a group to address their systemic disadvantage under the personal law system. It provides a doctrinal justification for the argument that the state has the positive duty to pursue equality for all marginalized groups, and that this accountability can be mediated through the courts.[103]

India's complex system of affirmative action is juxtaposed with the theme of formal equality. The constitutional provisions for affirmative action are included in the right to equality as exceptions within a framework of enforceable fundamental rights, with the purpose of curtailing the significance of ascriptive groups and guaranteeing equal treatment to the individual.[104] Indeed, affirmative action for women is one of the exceptions to the fundamental rights to equality. This exception is not a deviation from the general principle of equality; on the contrary, it is an expression of the commitment to implement the general principle. It represents the power of the state to pursue substantive equality to address systemic disadvantage.[105] Marc Galanter asserts, 'The constitutional embrace of the antagonistic principles of equal treatment and compensatory discrimination [affirmative action], individual rights and group rights, confronts both government and courts with the problem of reconciling them in specific settings.'[106] This understanding of substantive equality and affirmative action is particularly relevant to the issue of personal law reform and Muslim women's rights. In the final analysis, a decision must be based on the state's own policy, not on that embodied in either of the relevant

---

103 See *Indra Sawhney* v. *Union of India* AIR 1993 SC 477, where the Supreme Court reiterates the substantive notion of equality and the understanding that affirmative action is necessary to address substantive, historic disadvantage. Galanter, *supra* note 35 at 394.

104 Article 15(3), *Constitution*: 'Prohibition of discrimination on grounds of religion race, caste, sex, place of birth. Nothing in this article shall prevent the State from making any special provision for women and children. (4) Nothing in this article ... Shall prevent the State from making any special provision for the advancement of any socially and educationally backward classes of citizens or for the Scheduled Castes and the Scheduled Tribes.' See Galanter, *supra* note 35 at 364.

105 *Ibid.* at 378.

106 *Ibid.* at 381.

personal laws.[107] Drawing from Galanter's theoretical insights, in the context of Muslim women's rights, arguably this aspect of constitutional guarantees must be extended to cover the rights of Muslim women, indeed, all Indian women as a group, which is systemically discriminated against despite constitutional guarantees of equality.[108]

Another important equality case is *C.B. Muthamma* v. *Union of India*, which concerned a challenge to sex discrimination in government employment policies.[109] The Supreme Court emphatically stated that discrimination on the grounds of any inability, disability, or incapacity of women resulting from distinctions of their gender would amount to discrimination on the grounds of gender alone.[110] Interestingly, Krishna Iyer, J., noted that the struggle for gender equality had been an integral part of the nationalist movement for independence, and, especially in this context, he deplored the continued resistance to women's equality, noting the gap between the formally guaranteed constitutional rights and the 'Law in action.'[111] Despite this ruling in favour of gender equity in employment, the Supreme Court cast women as 'the gentler of the species,' demonstrating the continuance of a formal model of equality and reinforcing an understanding of women as passive victims.[112] Nonetheless, although it was not a challenge to personal law, *Muthamma* is significant because it reaffirmed the Supreme Court's commitment to the substantive notion of equality, and it has been used in subsequent judicial decisions concerning challenges to gender discrimination in personal law.[113]

When dealing with challenges to personal laws, however, the Supreme Court has invariably sidestepped equality issues, choosing to decide these cases on legal and procedural technicalities rather than on the question of the constitutionality of discriminatory personal laws. An example is the *Mary Roy* case, which was decided in favour of

---

107 John Mansfield, 'Religious and Charitable Endowments and a Uniform Civil Code' in Larson, *supra* note 25, 69 at 71.
108 Galanter, *supra* note 35 at 167, 169. Indeed, the Backward Classes Commission, set up in 1953 to determine which groups could be thus classified, recommended that all women in India made up a Backward Class.
109 *C.B. Muthamma* v. *Union of India* AIR 1979 SC 1868.
110 *Ibid.* at 1869–70.
111 *Ibid.* at 1870.
112 *Ibid.* Nussbaum, *supra* note 91 at 185.
113 See, for example, in *Swapna Ghosh* v. *Sadananda Ghosh* AIR 1989 Cal 1.

women, not on the basis of an examination of women's constitutional right to equality, but rather on a technicality of the applicability of a particular law.[114] Mary Roy explicitly challenged the discriminatory inheritance provisions of the *Travancore Christian Succession Act* whereby a daughter's share of inheritance was one-third of the son's share or Rs. 5,000, whichever amount was less.[115]

The Supreme Court, rather than ruling on the constitutional challenge under Article 14, instead based its decision on a legal technicality whereby it held that the *Travancore Act* was no longer valid. The court observed that it would be unnecessary 'to examine this challenge to the constitutional validity of the rules laid down by the *Travancore Christian Succession Act* ... as that would be a futile exercise and would unnecessarily burden the judgment.'[116] The *Mary Roy* decision was hailed as a victory for women's rights, yet the court itself evaded the responsibility of articulating its position on gender discrimination under personal law, or on the constitutional validity of those provisions of personal law that conflict with the fundamental rights.

Demonstrating the application of constitutional principles to personal law challenges, the Calcutta High Court, in *Swapna Ghosh*, relying on the *C.B. Muthamma* decision, held that the *Indian Divorce Act* was discriminatory against women.[117] However, although it granted the petitioner the right to divorce, the court was not altogether progressive in the way it arrived at its decision. Though the court found that the divorce provisions were discriminatory to women, it did not go so far as to strike down the law, deciding the case on facts without going into the constitutionality of the law. The court stated that its 'only endeavour is to draw the attention of our concerned legislature to this anachronistic incongruities [*sic*] and the provisions of Article 15 of the Constitution forbidding all discrimination on the ground of

---

114 *Mary Roy* v. *State of Kerala* AIR 1986 SC 1011.

115 See 'Statutes' in the Bibliography.

116 *Mary Roy, supra* note 14 at 1013. The Supreme Court invalidated the *Travancore Christian Succession Act* on the grounds that it was the law of the former princely state of Travancore, which, when it merged with the Union of India, was now obliged to follow the *Indian Succession Act*, which granted equal intestate inheritance rights to men and women.

117 The *Indian Divorce Act*, governing Indian Christians, was subsequently reformed in 2001. The grounds of divorce available to women have been amended to give women the same grounds for divorce as men have.

Religion or Sex and also to Article 44 staring at our face for four decades with its solemn directive to frame a UCC.'[118]

In the subsequent 1992 Bombay High Court case noted above, *In Re Amina*, the court specifically rejected the *Narasu Appa* view that gender discrimination under personal law did not violate Article 15. The court emphatically stated that Muslim personal law discriminates against women solely on the basis of sex and that gender discrimination under personal law was unconstitutional, but it did not go so far as to strike down the personal law system.[119]

In *Githa Hariharan* v. *Reserve Bank of India*,[120] a constitutional challenge to guardianship rules in Hindu personal law, the Supreme Court had to consider the gender discriminatory aspects of the *Hindu Minority and Guardians Act*, 1956, which appeared to stipulate that the mother can be the legal guardian of a child only after the lifetime of the father.[121] Although the chief justice stated that 'the section has to be struck down as unconstitutional as it undoubtedly violates gender equality, one of the basic principles of our Constitution,' he did not, in fact, strike it down.[122] Instead, the Supreme Court held that the *Hindu Minority and Guardians Act* must be interpreted in conformity with constitutional guarantees of equal rights of women to conclude that mothers and fathers have the right to custody of minor children. Once again, the court evaded the opportunity to explicitly rule on the impact of the fundamental right to equality and freedom from discrimination on women's rights under personal law.[123] Despite the positive aspects of this decision, *Githa Hariharan* demonstrates the continued reluctance of the court to address squarely the constitutional question of gender discrimination in personal law.

Nonetheless, recent judicial decisions reveal the success that the women's movement has had in using the constitutional rights strategy to forward women's claims. Martha Nussbaum notes that, although gender-based violence continues to be a major problem in India, the courts have demonstrated their willingness to take a more proactive

---

118 *Swapna Ghosh, supra* note 113 at 4.
119 *Amina, supra* note 81 at 218.
120 *Githa Hariharan* v. *Reserve Bank* (1999) 2 SCC 228.
121 According to Section 6(a) of the *Hindu Guardianship and Adoption Act*, the guardian of a minor is the father and after him the mother.
122 *Githa Hariharan, supra* note 120 at 235.
123 Indira Jaising, 'Gender Justice and the Supreme Court,' in Kirpal, *supra* note 27, 288 at 301.

role. This attitude underscores the importance of the constitutional strategy to successfully enforce women's rights.[124] Significantly, Indian courts have recognized the need to interpret women's constitutional rights in conformity with relevant international law and international conventions. Recent cases demonstrate the courts' willingness to invoke international norms and to hold the state to internationally recognized norms of gender equality. That national courts are ready and willing to favourably receive international law and incorporate it in their own interpretation of the Indian *Constitution* is significant for women's rights. This is an important step forward, giving women yet another authority to which they can hold the state accountable.[125] It is interesting to note that the courts have upheld this view with regard to both women's civil and political rights as well as personal law challenges.

The importance of international human rights law as an intrinsic part of the constitutional strategy to forward women's rights is demonstrated by the decision in *Vishaka* v. *State of Rajasthan*.[126] *Vishaka* was a case brought by a writ petition under Article 32 of the *Constitution* that allows citizens to appeal directly to the Supreme Court for the enforcement of constitutional rights.[127] This remedy has proved invaluable to women as a tool to enforce equality rights.[128] The case was brought by a network of women's groups and NGOs after the rape of a woman community worker and the subsequent refusal by local officials to institute a case investigation. They petitioned the Supreme Court to rule on the issue of sexual harassment of women in the workplace. Arguing on the basis that such sexual harassment violates the constitutionally guaranteed rights to equality, as well as to life and liberty, they also made a case based on the Convention on the Elimination of All Forms of Discrimination against Women (CEDAW),

---

124 Nussbaum, *supra* note 91 at 200.
125 Beverley Baines and Ruth Rubio-Marin, 'Introduction: Towards a Feminist Constitutional Agenda' in Baines and Rubio-Marin, *supra* note 40, 1 at 11.
126 *Vishaka* v. *State of Rajasthan* AIR 1997 SC 3011.
127 Article 32, *Constitution*: 'Remedies for enforcement of rights conferred by this Part [the Fundamental Rights]. – (1) The right to move the Supreme Court by proceedings for the enforcement of the rights conferred by this Part is guaranteed. (2) The Supreme Court shall have the power to issue directions or orders or writs, including writs of the nature of habeas corpus, mandamus, prohibition quo warranto and certiorari, whichever may be appropriate, for the enforcement of any of the rights conferred by this Part.'
128 Nussbaum, *supra* note 91 at 197.

which India had ratified, arguing that the state was bound to enforce women's rights in the workplace in compliance with its international obligations under CEDAW. They contended that the principles of gender equality outlined in the convention must be applied to the constitutional guarantee of gender equality in India, through Article 51(c) of the Indian *Constitution*, which calls on the state to 'foster respect for international law and treaty obligations in the dealings of organized people with one another.'[129]

The Supreme Court accepted this argument of the petitioners and applied fundamental rights to the question of sexual harassment, observing that 'the meaning and content of the fundamental rights guaranteed in the Constitution of India are of sufficient amplitude to encompass all the facets of gender equality including prevention of sexual harassment or abuse.'[130] It further ruled that the relevant constitutional provisions must be read in consonance with the CEDAW provisions. The court turned to CEDAW to elaborate and give further meaning to Indian constitutional guarantees against sexual discrimination. In the absence of legislative action, a resultant set of guidelines and norms, binding private and public employers, was drafted, and it included a definition of sexual harassment modelled on CEDAW's General Recommendation No. 19.[131]

A further significant feature of this decision was the court's readiness to step in where the legislature had not. The court declared that until the legislature enacted a law consistent with CEDAW, which India was obliged to do as a signatory, the guidelines set out by the court in *Vishaka*, adopting the convention, would be enforceable.[132] The importance of the *Vishaka* case lies in the court's ruling that international conventions and human rights law must be read in conjunc-

---

129 Article 51(c), *Constitution*, is a Directive Principle of State Policy, as is Article 44 calling for a UCC. Article 51: 'Promotion of international peace and security. – The State shall endeavour to (c) foster respect for international law and treaty obligations in the dealings of organised people with one another.'

130 *Vishaka, supra* note 126 at 3015.

131 U.N. General Recommendation No. 19, Violence Against Women, U.N. CEDAW Comm., 11th Sess., U.N. Doc. A/47/38 (1992) provides that discrimination against women includes gender-based violence, that is, violence directed against a woman because she is a woman, or violence that affects women disproportionately. It further states that gender-based violence is a form of discrimination that inhibits a woman's ability to enjoy rights and freedoms on an equal basis.

132 Ashok H. Desai and S. Muralidhar, 'Public Interest Litigation: Potential and Problems,' in Kirpal, *supra* note 27, 159 at 177–8.

tion with national law to ensure that the state meets its obligations to enforce the principle of gender equality. *Vishaka* demonstrates both the concrete impact of international law in the domestic arena and its normative function. It emphasizes how international human rights law may forward the domestic agenda and enlarge the scope of the fundamental rights in the Indian *Constitution*, as international human rights standards were incorporated in domestic law.[133] Thus, international law has emerged as an important aspect of the domestic constitutional protection of Indian women's rights by the courts themselves.

The Supreme Court has shown an increasing sensitivity to violence against women. In *Chairman, Railway Board v. Mrs. Chandrima Das*, a Bangladeshi woman was gang-raped by railway employees together with men posing as railway employees as she waited at the station to board a train.[134] In this landmark 2000 decision, it was held that rape was a violation of women's constitutional right to life with dignity, as well as a violation of the Universal Declaration of Human Rights, which was binding on India. The court ruled that fundamental rights under the Indian *Constitution* must be interpreted in accordance with the Universal Declaration of Human Rights.[135]

The Supreme Court has vacillated on the question of the state's obligation to reform gender discriminatory aspects of personal law and to enact a uniform family code, changing its position from case to case. It has shifted from explicitly exhorting the state to enact a UCC to ensure gender equality to refusing to address the issue on the grounds that it is a matter for the legislature, not the judiciary.[136] In sharp contrast to its activist intervention with regard to affirmative action, the Supreme Court has sought to avoid involvement in the issue of personal law reform and the enactment of a UCC.[137]

The convergence of issues of personal law reform, gender justice, and the enactment of a UCC is dramatically highlighted in the *Shah Bano* case. In *Shah Bano*, the Supreme Court called emphatically for a UCC, which was seen as necessary both to promote the cause of

---

133 This ruling of the court was reiterated in the *Apparel Export Promotion Council v. A. K. Chopra* AIR 1999 SC 625 at 634.
134 *Chairman, Railway Board v. Mrs. Chandrima Das* AIR 2000 SC 988.
135 Nussbaum, *supra* note 91 at 199.
136 Desai and Muralidhar, *supra* note 132 at 178.
137 Dhavan and Nariman, *supra* note 27 at 273.

national unity as well as to address women's legal disadvantage under personal law. *Shah Bano* emphasized the duty of the state to enact a UCC, reiterating that religious freedom did not prevent the state from progressive social reform of oppressive customs and practices.[138] According to the court, it would 'help the cause of national integration by removing disparate loyalties to laws which have conflicting ideologies.'[139] Significantly, the court made the connection between women's continuing legal disadvantage and the state's failure to enact a UCC. Assuming the role of protector, the court stated, 'Inevitably, the role of reformer has to be assumed by the courts because it is beyond the endurance of sensitive minds to allow injustice when it is so palpable. But piecemeal attempts of courts to bridge the gap between personal laws cannot take the place of a Common Civil Code. Justice to all is a far more satisfactory way of dispensing justice than justice from case to case.'[140] Yet here, too, the court avoided directly addressing the issue of women's inequality under personal law in terms of constitutional entitlements.[141] Nonetheless, this is a landmark decision, because through it the Supreme Court signalled its understanding that adjudicating individual problems was not sufficient to address the systemic gender disadvantage of women in India, and that a far broader perspective and a substantive notion of equality were imperative.

In *Jorden Diengdeh* v. *S.S. Chopra*, which followed soon after *Shah Bano*, the Supreme Court re-emphasized its position in *Shah Bano* and called again for a UCC. This case involved a constitutional challenge to the discriminatory aspects of the *Indian Divorce Act* (governing Indian Christians), which did not permit irretrievable breakdown of marriage or mutual consent as grounds for divorce. The wife petitioned for nullity because she had no other choice under the law.[142] The court observed, in this context, 'It is thus seen that the law relating to judicial separation, divorce and nullity of marriage is far from uniform. Surely the time has now come for a complete reform of the law of marriage and make a uniform law applicable to all people irrespective of religion or caste ... We suggest that the time has come for the intervention of the legislature in these matters to provide for a

---

138 *Mohammed Ahmed Khan* v. *Shah Bano Begum* AIR 1985 SC 945 at 954–5.
139 *Ibid.*
140 *Ibid.* at 955.
141 Jaising, *supra* note 123 at 300.
142 *Jorden Diengdeh* v. *S. S. Chopra* AIR 1985 SC 935.

uniform code of marriage and divorce and to provide by law a way out of the unhappy situations in which couples like the present have found themselves.'[143]

In *Sarla Mudgal*, the Supreme Court emphatically called upon the state to enact a UCC.[144] The questions before the Supreme Court here were whether conversion by a Hindu husband to Islam solely for the purpose of entering into a bigamous marriage was valid, and further, whether he was liable for prosecution for the offence of bigamy. Kuldip Singh, J., made a statement directing the state to enact a UCC, which was generally accepted as a mandatory injunction from the Supreme Court to the government to take positive action.[145] Sahai, J., concurred, emphasizing the human rights aspect of a UCC for women: 'therefore a unified code is imperative both for the protection of the oppressed and promotion of national unity and solidarity ... The government would be well advised to entrust the responsibility to the Law Commission which may in consultation with the Minorities Commission examine the matter and bring about a comprehensive legislation in keeping with the modern-day concept of human rights for women.'[146]

The *Sarla Mudgal* decision drew strong criticism for its apparent criticism of the Muslim community for refusing to introduce progressive change in personal law, thereby fuelling the anti-Muslim agenda of the Hindu right.[147] It was criticized by Muslim leaders, who saw it as a threat to the Muslim community and as an indictment of Muslim personal law. Women's groups, too, objected to this decision for its reference to the recalcitrance of the Muslim community in reforming its family law. Indeed, the court made unnecessary references to Muslim identity, the community's commitment to the ideology of nationalism, and the lack of reform in Muslim personal law.[148] It gratuitously singled out Muslim personal law as in need of reform, which served

---

143 *Ibid.* at 940–1.
144 *Sarla Mudgal (Smt.) President, Kalyani and Others* v. *Union of India and Others*, 1995 3 SCC 635.
145 *Ibid.* at 649–50. Dhavan and Nariman, *supra* note 27. See *Matthew* v. *UOI* (1999) 1 Ker LJ, 824); see also Bhattacharjee, *supra* note 17, criticizing the approach of the High Courts and the Supreme Court.
146 *Sarla Mudgal, supra* note 144 at 652.
147 Kapur and Cossman, *supra* note 2 at 259, 260.
148 *Sarla Mudgal, supra* note 144 at 650.

simultaneously to draw attention away from the lack of gender equality in the personal law of other groups, most notably Hindu law.

Nevertheless, despite these controversial and unfortunate aspects of the *Sarla Mudgal* decision, the essential point remains that it was a decision that sought to apply principles of constitutional law to gender discrimination in personal law, ruling that conversion to Islam cannot be used as a way of circumventing the prohibition of bigamy.[149] Going beyond *Shah Bano* and *Jorden Diengdeh*, *Sarla Mudgal* emphasized the need for a UCC and directed the state to enact a UCC.[150] Significantly, the court made explicit the link between the lack of a UCC and the denial of women's rights, although it reiterated that a UCC was essential both for promoting national unity as well as for protecting women's rights.[151]

However, the Supreme Court, soon after making this bold statement in *Sarla Mudgal* putting the state on notice that it had to address gender inequality, retreated from this position. In *Ahmedabad Women's Action Group (AWAG) and Others* v. *Union of India*, the Supreme Court stated that it was the legislature's duty to step in and make changes in discriminatory personal laws. Further, it clarified that the direction issued in *Sarla Mudgal* was not mandatory.[152] *Ahmedabad Women's Action Group* was a writ petition, filed together with other writ petitions, challenging personal law as violating fundamental rights. The petitions sought a declaration by the court that polygamy and triple *talaq* permitted by Muslim personal law violated the fundamental right to gender equality guaranteed by the *Constitution*, and that the *Muslim Women's Act* violated equality guarantees. Further, the petitions challenged gender discriminatory aspects of Hindu and Christian personal laws, and, finally, they asked the court to direct that a UCC be enacted.

These writ petitions were dismissed on the grounds that the issues raised concerned the legislature rather than the judiciary and therefore could not be heard on merits by the Supreme Court. The court emphasized that the removal of gender discrimination in personal laws involved 'issues of State policies with which the Court will not ordinarily have any concern'[153] and declined to entertain the writ petitions

---

149 *Ibid.* at 649–50.
150 *Ibid.* at 651.
151 *Ibid.* at 652.
152 *AWAG, supra* note 86 at 3614.
153 *Ibid.*

for the enactment of a UCC.[154] Further, the court declined to rule on the constitutionality of the *Muslim Women's Act*, as a challenge to that law was already pending before it.[155]

The Supreme Court has not spoken with one voice, and its decisions have been conflicting. Whereas in *AWAG*, one bench of the court categorically stated that the personal laws were beyond the reach of the fundamental rights, thus adding to the doctrinal disarray, at the same time another bench of the Supreme Court in *C. Masilamani Mudaliar* v. *Idol of Sri S.S. Thirukoil*,[156] observed: 'The personal laws conferring inferior status on women are anathema to equality. Personal laws are derived not from the Constitution but from religious scriptures. The laws thus derived must be consistent with the Constitution lest they become void [under the recognition clause] if they violate fundamental rights.'[157] However, these words were simply *obiter dicta* and, ultimately, the Supreme Court has refused to test the personal law against the fundamental rights to equality.[158]

Nonetheless, some progress has been made with regard to internal reform of Christian personal law. In a 1982 case, *Reynolds Rajamani*, which challenged the *Indian Divorce Act* applicable to Christians, the court held that including a provision for divorce by mutual consent was a matter to be decided by the legislature, not the court, thus showing its reluctance to interfere not only with Muslim personal law, but indeed with all personal laws.[159] However, by the late 1990s there were increasing challenges in the High Courts to the discriminatory provisions of divorce under the *Divorce Act*. In *Ammini E.J.* v. *Union of India*, and *Mary Sonia Zachariah* v. *Union of India*, the Kerala High Court ruled that those provisions of Christian law that laid out discriminatory grounds for divorce were unconstitutional. Christian groups initiated a lengthy reform process, which culminated finally in the reform of Christian laws concerning marriage and divorce.[160] This reform now equalizes and liberalizes the grounds for divorce for men and

---

154   Sivarammaya, *supra* note 74 at 313.
155   *Danial Latifi v. Union of India* (2001) 7 SCC 740.
156   *C. Masilamani Mudaliar v. Idol of Sri S. S. Thirukoil*, (1996) 8 SCC 525.
157   *Ibid.* at 531.
158   Jaising, *supra* note 123 at 300.
159   *Reynolds Rajamani v. Union of India* (1982) 2 SCC 474 at 478–9.
160   *Ammini E.J.* v. *Union of India*, AIR 1995 Kerala 252; *Mary Sonia Zachariah* v. *Union of India*, (1990) (I) KLT 130.

women alike and also includes a provision for divorce by mutual consent, which previously had not been allowed.[161] This reform of Christian personal law is a demonstration of the normative effect of constitutional litigation as a strategy to forward women's rights.

Yet the Supreme Court has shown its reluctance to rule on matters relating to challenges to the *Muslim Women's Act* and the enactment of a UCC in Public Interest Litigation brought before it. In *Maharishi Avadesh*, the writ petition seeking a directive from the Supreme Court on the enactment of a UCC was dismissed.[162] In *Pannalal Bansilal Pitti*, the court appeared to be backing down from earlier calls to enact a UCC: 'A uniform law, though is highly desirable, enactment thereof in one go perhaps may be counter-productive to the unity and integrity of the nation.'[163] No mention was made of the need for a UCC to address women's rights within the family.

In the 2000 decision *Lily Thomas* v. *Union of India*,[164] which discussed at length the decision in *Sarla Mudgal*, the court clarified that the *Sarla Mudgal* court had not issued a directive to the government to enact a UCC,[165] but had merely expressed the view of the deciding judges based on the particular facts and circumstances of that case.[166] The *Lily Thomas* court favourably cited the *Maharishi Avadesh*[167] decision in which 'this Court had specifically declined to issue a writ directing the respondents to consider the question of enacting a Common Civil Code for all citizens of India holding that the issue raised being a matter of policy, it was for the Legislature to take effective steps as the Court cannot legislate.'[168]

In dealing with cases concerning women's experience of disadvantage under personal law, the Supreme Court recognized the critical need for a UCC to address women's inequality within the family.

---

161 *The Indian Divorce (Amendment) Act* and *The Christian Marriage (Amendment) Act*. See 'Statutes' in Bibliography. Section 10 of the *Indian Divorce Act* has been amended to provide equal grounds for divorce for men and women, and under section 10(A), divorce by mutual consent is now permitted.

162 *Maharishi Avadesh* v. *Union of India* 1994 Supp 1 SCC 713 at 714.

163 *Pannalal Bansilal Pitti* v. *State of A.P.* (1996) 2 SCC 498 at 510.

164 *Lily Thomas* v. *Union of India*, AIR 2000 SC 1650.

165 *Ibid.* at 1660–1.

166 *Ibid.* at 1669.

167 *Maharishi Avadesh*, *supra* note 162.

168 *Lily Thomas*, *supra* note 164 at 1668.

Despite this sensitivity to women's disadvantage under the personal law system, however, these decisions demonstrate that the question of a UCC continues to be debated within the parameters of minority identity and national integration, rather than gender justice, thereby erasing women's subjectivity. In a discourse that so thoroughly implicates women's rights, even decisions welcomed as pro-women see the erasure of women as free-standing interrogators of the status quo. Notwithstanding the Supreme Court's powerful injunctions in several cases to the state to enact a UCC, the state itself has made no effort to comply with the court's directives. Although Christian personal law was amended to give Christian women enlarged grounds for divorce, personal laws have been left unreformed, and regarding Muslim personal law, there has been instead a regressive curtailment of women's rights through the enactment of the *Muslim Women's Act* in 1986.

This vacillation and lack of consensus within the Supreme Court on the complex question of the enactment of a UCC has complicated the response of those seeking to forward women's rights.[169] The Supreme Court has been reluctant to use its constituent power to strike down even explicitly discriminatory personal law and has not evolved a consistent doctrine of gender justice.[170] Despite its constitutional mandate to proactively enforce the principle of equality, challenges have been either avoided or subsumed under 'a larger politics of pragmatism.'[171] Notwithstanding the acknowledgment that gender discrimination was inherent in the personal law system and in specific aspects of personal law, no court has gone so far as to declare the personal law system void.[172]

Specifically with regard to Muslim personal law, there have been, nevertheless, some significant decisions. *Shah Bano* was a landmark decision seeking to uphold Muslim women's rights and to apply a substantive understanding of equality to address Muslim divorcees'

---

169 *Maharishi Avadesh, supra* note 162 at 714; *Reynolds Rajamani, supra* note 159 at 478–9; *Pannalal, supra* note 163; *Madhu Kishwar* v. *State of Bihar* (1996) 5 SCC 125; *AWAG, supra* note 86 at 575–801. The court was reluctant to pronounce on matters that were declared to be within the exclusive domain of the legislature. See *Sarla Mudgal, supra* note 144 at 649–50, in which a plea was made for a uniform civil code by Kuldip Singh, J.; this was generally understood as an injunction to the government to change the law.
170 Jaising, *supra* note 123 at 288–9.
171 *Ibid.* at 290, 294.
172 See, for example, *Shah Bano, supra* note 138; *Jorden Diengdeh, supra* note 142; *In re Amina, supra* note 81.

economic vulnerability. However, *Shah Bano* was not technically a case brought under Muslim law, but in fact a case brought under section 125 of the *Indian Criminal Procedure Code*, which had hitherto applied to all Indian women irrespective of religious affiliation to enable them to seek spousal support. It was Shah Bano's ex-husband's defence, that under Muslim personal law applicable to him, he had no obligation to support Shah Bano, which raised the question of Muslim law. In recent rulings, specifically on points of Muslim personal law, courts have sought to safeguard Muslim women's rights and have departed from the long-held judicial opinion that the right to divorce can be exercised by men unilaterally and for any reason, or for no reason at all, to hold that the right to triple *talaq* must be subject to procedural requirements and judicial regulation.[173]

In a 1994 case concerning the legality of the triple *talaq*, an Allahabad High Court judge, Hari Nath Tilhari, ruled that the practice of triple *talaq* was unconstitutional, as it violated both Muslim law and the Indian *Constitution*.[174] The response to this decision came primarily from the Muslim community and it was divided. Religious and political leaders condemned the ruling as an intrusion into the private sphere of personal law, while scholars like Tahir Mahmood welcomed it as a long-overdue examination of the *talaq* process, which had been reformed in many Muslim states but not in India. Muslim women welcomed the decision and declared that they were going to ask the Muslim Personal Law Board to consider the matter of reforming *talaq* procedures. The Hindu right, too, welcomed the decision for completely different reasons. They used it to fuel their agenda of undermining Muslim personal law as being discriminatory to women and resisting much needed reform. The judge himself was a supporter of Hindu majoritarian politics, and although he used the notions of secularism and constitutionality, it is more than plausible, as Srimati Basu argues, that he was impelled by anti-Muslim prejudice, including ideas of the backwardness of the Muslim community and their intran-

---

173 Triple *talaq* is the unilateral right to divorce exercised by men, whereby divorce is pronounced thrice in a single sitting; it is not judicially regulated.

174 *Rahmat Ullah v. State of U.P.*, Writ Petition no. 45 of 1993 and *Khatoon Nisa v. State of U.P.*, Writ Petition no. 57 of 1993, unreported. For an insightful discussion of this decision, see Kapur and Cossman, *supra* note 2 at 257; Agnes, *Law and Gender Inequality*, 111–16; and Basu, *supra* note 38 at 143.

sigence in reforming their personal law, rather than by a specific empathy for the vulnerability of Muslim women.[175] This case illustrates the way in which the discourse of protection may be subverted to the agendas of the judiciary, anti-progressive forces of Hindu right-wing politics, and the community itself. Just as important, it highlights the ways in which judges themselves are imbricated in contemporary meta-narratives and often reinforce hegemonic discourses.

The question of triple *talaq* came up again in the *Dagdu Pathan* case, brought by a Muslim woman claiming maintenance for herself and her children from her husband.[176] The husband denied any liability for maintenance under Muslim law, alleging in his written statement to the court that he had divorced his wife.[177] In a decision that has changed the current understanding of *talaq* in India, the court ruled that 'mere pronouncement of talaq by the husband or merely declaring his intentions or his acts of having pronounced the talaq [*sic*] are not sufficient and does not meet the requirement of law. In every such exercise of the right to talaq the husband is required to satisfy the preconditions of arbitration for reconciliation and reasons for talaq.'[178] The court held that, even under Muslim law, a husband cannot divorce his wife at his will alone; that a mere assertion to the court that he has divorced his wife is insufficient, and he must prove the divorce by leading evidence before the court; and, most important, that certain conditions are applicable and must be fulfilled for the divorce to be valid.[179]

The case of *Dagdu Pathan* demonstrates how the judiciary has felt compelled to step in to address state inaction in reforming the law, as they did in *Shah Bano*, exhorting the state to address discrimination under the personal law by enacting a UCC. The triple *talaq* is a significant source of oppression for Muslim women. Yet the state has refused to take the initiative to reform or regulate the *talaq* procedure in Muslim personal law.[180] Community leaders, too, have refused to

---

175 Basu, *supra* note 38 at 145.
176 *Dagdu* v. *Rahimbi Dagdu Pathan and Others*, II (2002) Divorce and Matrimonial Cases 315 (FB), Bombay High Court.
177 Under Muslim law, a divorced wife is entitled to spousal support for a period of only three months, known as the *iddat* period.
178 *Dagdu*, *supra* note 176 at 342.
179 *Ibid.* at 338, 341, 344.
180 Although in other Muslim states divorce law has been reformed and is moderated and regulated by the state, in India the use of triple *talaq* proceeds unchecked by any state legislative action or community regulation.

address Muslim women's demands for a change in divorce laws that would curtail Muslim men's unfettered, unregulated right to extra-judicial divorce. This decision is critically important for Muslim women, who have long been demanding regulation of men's right to the triple divorce. It is in this context that the court's decision in *Dagdu* is significant; the court favourably cited the *Danial Latifi* case: 'In inter-preting the provisions where matrimonial relationship is involved, we have to consider the social conditions prevalent in our society. In our society, whether they belong to the majority or the minority group, what is apparent is that there exists a great disparity in the matter of economic resourcefulness between a man and a woman. Our society is male dominated, both economically and socially and women are assigned, invariably, a dependent role, irrespective of the class of society to which she belongs.'[181]

The significance of this ruling is the recognition of the systemic gender bias in Indian society and, further, the recognition that the courts must interpret the law contextually and purposively, thus sig-nalling their understanding of a substantive notion of equality. Further, it points to the courts' appreciation that it is not religion alone that defines women's status. Most recently, the Supreme Court in *Shamimara Begum* reaffirmed the decision in *Dagdu* that the right to divorce can no longer be understood as an unregulated right without following certain legal requirements, and that it can no longer be understood, as previously held, that divorce could be for any reason or for no reason at all, on the mere whim or caprice of the husband.[182]

Under the *Muslim Women's Act*, enacted consequent upon the *Shah Bano* decision, the maintenance rights of divorced Muslim women were curtailed, and they were no longer permitted to use the general law of maintenance. Under this law Muslim women, upon divorce, are entitled to the repayment of their dower (*mehr*), a one-time provision as provided in the Koran, and maintenance for a period of three months (the *iddat* period). Despite this statutory enactment, there has been a wide variation in the way cases have been decided. Some

---

181   *Dagdu, supra* note 176 at 338.
182   *Ahmed Kasim Molla* v. *Khatun Bibi* ILR Calcutta 833. *Shamim Ara* v. *State of U.P. and Another*, 2002 SOL Case no. 514.

judges have interpreted the new law as broadening the scope of Muslim women's rights to maintenance, while others have held that, indeed, the *Muslim Women's Act* correctly applies the Islamic principle of restricting maintenance for a period of three months only.

The most celebrated decision under this law was, in fact, the first one made under the new law, by Rekha Dixit, the district magistrate of the city of Lucknow. She interpreted the *Muslim Women's Act* to give a Muslim woman claimant an amount of maintenance far greater than she might have been awarded under the secular law of maintenance. She interpreted the rule of fair and reasonable provision to award the divorced wife a total payment of Rs. 80,000. Of this amount, Rs. 60,000 was the one-time lump-sum payment, the repayment of the dower, and maintenance for three months.[183] However, the fact that an individual judge granted an individual woman a generous maintenance amount does not mitigate the regressive nature of the law. Such a decision could not change the fact that this new law has severely curtailed Muslim women's maintenance rights and their rights as equal citizens, while at the same time reaffirming Muslim men's right to deny spousal support to divorced wives, without addressing the issue of Muslim women's pervasive disadvantage.

In contrast, in *Usman Khan Bahamani*, the judge emphasized the protective aspect of the *Muslim Women's Act* as giving Muslim women a speedier remedy, avoiding the time constraints involved in the secular law of maintenance.[184] The judge, a Muslim himself, reiterated the need for the *Muslim Women's Act* in the face of the controversial *Shah Bano* judgment, presenting the Act as a correction by the state of the Supreme Court's misinterpretation of Quranic injunctions. Further, he reiterated the authority of an essentialized ahistoric notion of Islam and of Muslim women's rights, reaffirming the provisions of the Act that restrict maintenance for divorced Muslim women to one lump-sum payment and the three-month *iddat* period. Such decisions highlight the use of the *Muslim Women's Act* to absolve husbands of the duty of spousal support, with disastrous consequences for Muslim women.

Interestingly, both those courts that applied a restrictive interpretation of the *Muslim Women's Act* and those that applied a wider interpretation used the discourse of protection to justify their decisions. On

---

183 Engineer, 'Maintenance for Muslim Women.'
184 *Usman Khan Bahamani* v. *Fathimunnisa Begum* AIR 1990 AP 225.

the other hand, certain judges have sought to interpret the Act as an addition to the rights under the existing secular law by making judgments that go well beyond the legislative intent of the *Muslim Women's Act*, which was, in fact, a law designed to curtail Muslim women's rights and to calm the concerns of fundamentalists in an election year that Muslim personal law not be reformed in a way that would upset the gender status quo. These judges have interpreted 'protection' literally, granting women sums that would not have been possible under the secular law now denied to them.[185] They interpreted and applied the law in what amounted to a subversion of its original intent.[186] Both these protectionist discourses are part of the larger negotiation of regulating Muslim women's rights and the tension between the hegemony of patriarchal understandings and resistance by modernizing groups.[187] As these decisions show, the law and the courts proved to be both subversive sites as well as sites for the reaffirmation of hegemonic discourses of women's rights.

The uncertainty and varied interpretation and application of Muslim divorcees' maintenance rights was recently settled in the 2001 *Danial Latifi* decision.[188] This was a crucial sex equality case in which Shah Bano's lawyer in the Supreme Court, Danial Latifi, and others filed a writ petition in the Supreme Court challenging the constitutionality of the *Muslim Women's Act*. This case completes the circle from *Shah Bano* on. It implicates the constitutionality of personal law, the impact of fundamental rights on discriminatory personal law, and, equally important, the question of sex equality. Significantly, although this decision reaffirmed the *Shah Bano* decision and interpreted the *Muslim Women's Act* broadly to bring divorced Muslim women's spousal support entitlements in line with those available to other Indian women – a clear contradiction to the fundamentalist interpretation of Muslim women's rights – there was little public outrage and no orchestrated campaign against the decision, as happened in the wake of *Shah Bano*.[189]

---

185 Amrita Chachhi, 'Forced Identities: The State, Communalism, Fundamentalism and Women in India,' in Kandiyoti, *supra* note 64, 144 at 167.

186 Basu, *supra* note 38 at 142–43.

187 *Ibid*. at 143.

188 *Danial Latifi, supra* note 155.

189 Nussbaum, *supra* note 91 at 175. In contrast to *Shah Bano*, however, this decision passed unnoticed by the general public and was notable for the lack of controversy it generated, despite the boldness of the declaration sought by Latifi to declare the *Muslim Women's Act* unconstitutional.

The Supreme Court tried to maintain a balancing act, attempting to uphold Muslim women's rights without addressing the constitutionality of gender and religious discrimination in personal law. The *Danial Latifi* court reiterated the validity of the *Shah Bano* judgment. Once again, in this case, as in *Shah Bano*, the Personal Law Board was an intervenor in the case, presenting arguments supporting the constitutionality of the *Muslim Women's Act* based on a fundamentalist interpretation of Muslim law. The Law Board questioned the authority of the court to interpret religious texts. It also contended that the provisions for maintenance under the *Muslim Women's Act* were adequate, and that, indeed, under Muslim law the husband did not have an extended liability to support his ex-wife. However, the court declined to go into theological questions or interpretation of religious texts, emphasizing that it relied on the exposition of religious law as interpreted and settled by *Shah Bano*. The court considered only the constitutionality of the Act and upheld it.

Following a process of reading down and interpretation, the court held that the *Muslim Women's Act* does not, in fact, preclude maintenance for divorced Muslim women, and that Muslim men must pay spousal support until such time as the divorced wife remarries. Whereas on the one hand, the court held that if, indeed, the *Muslim Women's Act* accorded Muslim divorcees unequal rights to spousal support compared with the provisions of the secular law under section 125 of the *Indian Criminal Procedure Code*, then the law would, in fact, be unconstitutional. However, the Supreme Court was reluctant to find the *Muslim Women's Act* unconstitutional and ruled, through a strained application of the principles of interpretation, that the law was not unconstitutional, as it could be interpreted in a manner that gave Muslim women equal rights with other Indian women.[190]

In so doing, the court introduced two additional, critically important interpretive principles. First, it insisted that any decision regarding marital disputes must be made in the context of prevailing social conditions. These conditions were understood to include, in contemporary India, the systemic disadvantage of women within the patriarchal

---

190   *Danial Latifi, supra* note 155 at 757–8, 764.

family. Second, the court held that decisions involving 'basic human rights, culture, dignity and decency of life and dictates of necessity in the pursuit of social justice should invariably be left to be decided on considerations other than religion or religious faith or beliefs or national, sectarian, racial or communal constraints.'[191] Although to this extent it is indeed a vindication of the rights of Muslim women, the manner in which the court arrived at this decision reflects the judiciary's continued reluctance to address expressly the constitutionality of the personal law system and the gender discrimination that is so emphatically a part of it.

Most recently, in 2003 in *John Vallamattom* v. *Union of India*, a constitutional challenge to the provisions of the *Indian Succession Act* applicable to Indian Christians, the court held that it was forbidden under both the Indian *Constitution* and international law, to discriminate on the basis of gender.[192] Here, too, the court invoked international law in conjunction with Indian constitutional principles to uphold women's right to inherit property and to make wills. The court went on to say, 'It is a matter of regret that Article 44 of the Constitution has not been given effect to. Parliament is still to step in for framing a common civil code in the country.'[193] But similar to other Supreme Court decisions, this judgment goes on to frame the UCC as a way of ensuring national unity rather than for its gender equality value: 'A common civil code will help the cause of national integration by removing the contradictions based on ideologies.'[194]

The *John Vallamattom* decision is significant in several respects. One, it calls for a UCC, rebuking Parliament for so far not enacting one. Second, it subjects personal law to constitutional scrutiny, ruling that the law in question violates the equality article, and therefore it strikes it down as *ultra vires* the *Constitution*. This is significant in the struggle for women's rights and points to the possibility of using constitutional law to forward claims of gender equality within the family. Further, the court specifically held that it is the duty of the court to 'remedy violation of fundamental rights' and that, being in violation of the equality articles of the *Constitution* as well as the freedom of religion provisions, this law restricting the testamentary disposition of property by

---

191 *Ibid*. at 757–8.
192 *John Vallamattom* v. *Union of India*, AIR 2003 SC 384 at 387.
193 *Ibid*. at 397.
194 *Ibid*.

Christians must be struck down. Significantly, the argument of fundamental rights violations was used to decide the validity of a discriminatory personal law. Finally, *John Vallammattom* is important because it
held that discrimination between members of one religious group and
members of other religious groups solely on the basis of religion was
unconstitutional. This logic can be extended to the provisions of Muslim personal law, which explicitly discriminate between Muslims and
non-Muslims, especially with respect to women's rights.

Muslim Women and the Law

Women's interests are diverse, as are the interests of Muslim women.
Indeed, we need to be wary of drawing too simplistic an assessment of
what constitutes the interests not only of women, but also specifically
of Muslim women. At the same time, we need to recognize that the
interests that oppose women's rights are similarly diverse. As Isabel
Karpin and Karen O'Connell argue, 'The Constitution both actively
constitutes and is constituted by those interests.'[195] It is critical to
understand the *Constitution* as implicated, and embedded, in existing
hierarchies of power, with the possibility and the ability to respond
and resist differently at different times to the various pressures of
power and politics. Such an understanding of the material context of
the *Constitution* makes it significant for feminists to identify the frameworks in which the *Constitution* operates, as well as to engage with the
discursive frame of constitutional law.[196]

The judicial decisions considered here reveal that constitutional
rights litigation does indeed have the potential to advance women's
rights. This is truer, however, of those rights that fall within the public
sphere, such as harassment in the workplace, rape by governmental
actors, and employment equity.[197] Recent judicial opinion has shown
the courts to be receptive to the idea of sex equality, despite a reluctance to step into the area of family law. With regard to challenges to
discriminatory personal law that seek to revise oppressive structures
of patriarchal authority within the private sphere, the courts have been
less enthusiastic, showing a limited indulgence towards women's
equality rights in this area.

---

195 Karpin and O'Connell, *supra* note 70 at 46.
196 *Ibid.*
197 For example, *C.B. Muthamma*, *supra* note 109; *Vishaka* v. *State of Rajasthan*, *supra*
      note 126.

Nonetheless, the *Shah Bano* case and others show that courts do broadly recognize women's rights within the family, demonstrating that the law is not an inhospitable site to women pursuing legal equality. However, in many of these cases the judges portray themselves as protectors of helpless women or as secular champions of the post-colonial state, drawing attention to a reformed Hindu law while simultaneously decrying the lack of reform in Muslim personal law. Not surprisingly, this attitude has been interpreted by many as an indictment of the lack of support within the Muslim community for law reform and, however inadvertent, as a reification of the othering of the minority community, thus reinforcing both gender and religious hierarchies while protecting women through law.[198]

The coding of women as in need of protection often operates to reinforce patriarchal structures of authority and the gender status quo, implicitly or explicitly, in both 'progressive' and 'reactionary' legislation. The notion of benevolent patronage, so evident in the *Shah Bano* decision, shows how judges have appropriated to themselves the roles of protectors of helpless women and extenders of benevolent patronage, appropriating to themselves, in this sense, the ambivalent nature of the discourse of protection to control women's behaviour and bodies. Those women who do not fit gender role stereotypes are subject to the authoritarian wrath of the judiciary for transgressing traditional notions of 'the good woman.' In this way, Courts serve to reinforce male power structures within the family.[199]

Law is a contested site where hegemonic norms are reaffirmed and also where they are primarily challenged. This aspect of the law is revealed by a consideration of decided cases in which judges seek to enforce constitutional norms of gender equality and freedom from discrimination and where they also have reinforced stereotypical notions of gender roles. Judicial interpretation of constitutional law works 'simultaneously to disturb and preserve traditional gender arrangements.'[200] This often ambiguous attitude reflects the reality that courts operate within a certain political, social, and ideological context. Although in India the judiciary is entrusted with social

---

198 Basu, *supra* note 65 at 279.
199 *Ibid.*
200 Reva B. Siegel, 'Gender and the United States Constitution,' in Baines and Rubio-Marin, *supra* note 40, 306 at 328.

reform, it is inevitable that it reflects as well prevailing notions of gender roles in the family while also being a catalyst for change.[201] Courts are inevitably influenced by 'national meta-narratives, prevailing ideological and cultural propensities, and the policy preferences of hegemonic elites.'[202] Court decisions show the tension between dominant hegemonic discourses of gender and the social reformist impulse of the judiciary. In the process of deciding cases, judges are reinventing the gendered legal subject, sometimes reaffirming and sometimes subverting dominant understandings of women's equality in the family.

Nonetheless, the use of constitutionally guaranteed fundamental rights is of critical importance in forwarding the women's rights agenda. Although in some cases the courts have explicitly stated that constitutional law has no place within the personal sphere of the family, increasingly we see judicial opinions invoking constitutional guarantees as well as international conventions of gender equality in order to apply them to the situation of Indian women in family law arrangements.[203] It can be hoped that the space of constitutional law will offer women a way of enforcing equality rights by requiring the state either to reform personal laws to make them symmetrical or to confer equality in the family by enacting a gender-just UCC. The constitutional sex equality guarantees, while they are currently being used to hold the state to guarantees of equality in the workplace and in civil and political life, can arguably be extended to the domain of family law.[204] It is critical for women's rights advocates to continue their engagement with the law, mindful always of the law's potential as a subversive site. This insight demonstrates the importance of a continued strategic engagement with challenges to personal law while at the same time seeking to redefine the frameworks in which we discuss questions of gender justice, minority rights, and the reform of family law in India.[205]

Any analysis of the Indian *Constitution* as protector of women's rights must consider that it explicitly guarantees women's equality,

---

201 *Ibid.* at 329.
202 Hirschl and Shachar, *supra* note 40 at 228.
203 *Harvinder Kaur, supra* note 97.
204 Siegel, *supra* note 200 at 329.
205 Basu, *supra* note 38 at 131.

and it further includes the concept of substantive equality. The emphatic recognition in the *Constitution* of gender equality and the right to affirmative action for women, together with the recognition, in the evolution of judicial opinion, that it is the duty of the state to enforce substantive equality, are of critical importance in highlighting the potential of constitutional litigation to forward women's rights. Together they demonstrate an understanding of the group dimension of women's systemic disadvantage, underscoring the recognition that women's disadvantage is linked not only to biology, but, more impor-tant, to social causes. What remains is for the court to extend this understanding equally to the sphere of the family – the private sphere. The challenge for women's rights advocates is to negotiate the dichotomous construction of women's rights and group rights and the inevitable consequence whereby the public/private split is invoked to shield family laws from public scrutiny. To forward Muslim women's rights, it is essential continually to interrogate the public/private dis-tinction from a feminist viewpoint.

Challenges to the gender status quo and changes in the status of women are invariably the most difficult issues to deal with because the family is such a fiercely guarded private sphere, where constitutional norms of gender equality have not been enforced within the 'modern' post-colonial state.[206] The location of Muslim women in India at the intersection of gender, religion, community, and nation means that the struggle for rights has to be carried out in the context of deeply divi-sive religious and communal conflict. Ultimately, what this jurispru-dence reveals is that at one level Muslim women benefit from an emancipatory jurisprudence enlarging women's equality, while at an-other level they must contend with enduring patterns of inequality, thus once again disrupting simple categorization.

The *Shah Bano* case and others highlight the persistence of paternal-ism and the notion of protection in the legal process.[207] Srimati Basu emphasizes that 'even those judgments in favour of women need to be critiqued if the mixed rewards of "protection" are to be decon-structed.'[208] Yet these cases also highlight the fact that women are exer-cising their agency by seeking state support in resolving family dis-

---

206 Basu, *supra* note 65 at 280.
207 Sylvia Vatuk, 'Where Will She Go? What Will She Do?' in Larson, *supra* note 25, 226 at 226.
208 Basu, *supra* note 65 at 280–1.

putes.[209] Thus, despite the social and economic context of systemic gender discrimination in India, women are able to use the law to resist male patriarchy and generally to pursue ends that may be quite incidental to the official purposes for which these institutions were created. This underscores the transformative potential of a subaltern consciousness and the possibility of the law as a subversive site. We have to understand the law as a site of resistance, capable of being used by women to 'negotiate the conditions of their lives, pursue personal goals and to resist hegemonic definitions of selfhood.'[210]

We must recognize the importance of constitutional litigation for forwarding women's rights in the context of state-legitimized legal institutions that contradict formal guarantees of equal citizenship. Although Muslim women have attempted to enlarge the scope of their rights by resorting to the secular law, not many have made use of legislation that was purportedly enacted to protect Muslim women's rights.[211] This avoidance in itself should signal to the state that Muslim women are asking for a reform of their personal law to address their legal vulnerability. Equally important, that they have decided to try to use the law to ameliorate their situation, despite their awareness of the difficulties of pursuing legal remedies, should underscore the fact that Muslim women ought not to be regarded as the passive victims of a patriarchal order, as they are so often assumed to be.[212]

There is, of course, a tremendous gap between what the law says and what it actually does for women who seek to use it.[213] Indeed, the harsh reality of India's traditional patriarchal society is such that, despite their exercise of agency in turning to the law, women can hope for only limited success.[214] Nevertheless, as Carol Smart argues, despite 'inadequate interventions' of law in transforming feminist policy, 'achievements, opportunities and possible developments' are also associated with the legal realm, and she emphasizes the importance of an active feminist engagement with the law, 'a commitment to treating law as a site of struggle.'[215] Other solutions involve a strategic

---

209 Vatuk, *supra* note 207 at 226.
210 *Ibid.*
211 *Ibid.* at 240; for example, the *Muslim Women's Act* or the *Dissolution of Muslim Marriages Act.*
212 *Ibid.* at 242.
213 *Ibid.* at 227–8.
214 *Ibid.* at 242.
215 Smart, *Law, Crime and Sexuality*, 125.

but critical approach to the workings of the law. Brenda Cossman and Ratna Kapur view feminist engagement with the law as a 'discursive struggle, where feminists seek to displace the idea of women's roles and identities.'[216] Despite the formidable tasks involved, it is important to use law as a potential mode of change and a site of negotiation with dominant ideologies.[217]

Arguably, in the Indian context, constitutional law has the potential to forward women's equality in the family. Constitutional challenges to discrimination in personal law are important in forwarding women's rights. The constitutional strategy of forwarding women's rights points to ways in which it is possible to initiate constitutional change, appropriate strategies to reclaim women's equal rights as citizens, and the linking of international protections of gender rights with national constitutional principles.[218] In the case of uneven operation of rights across religions, the task seems relatively straightforward: asking for legal changes, closely monitoring the legislative process, seeking practical ways to make changes in law realistic, and advocating broad socio-economic reform to make a greater empowerment of the legal subject possible.[219]

It becomes apparent that the struggle to forward Muslim women's rights is framed by the power struggle between competing hegemonic discourses. Judicial decisions highlight the dangers of the subversion of a progressive agenda by unlikely champions of Muslim women's rights. At the same time, such decisions complicate the response of Muslim women themselves to the question of legal reform, invariably forcing a choice between forwarding the agenda of the group as a whole or forwarding that of gender rights, in the context of anti-Muslim prejudice and the assimilationist impulse of the larger society.

The *Shah Bano* controversy fuelled the agenda of the Hindu right's anti-Muslim campaign and was used to present the notion of Muslims and of Muslim law as backward. For the Hindu right, reinforcing the notion of 'protecting' Muslim women is a means of emphasizing the lack of progressive reform in Muslim personal law as a signifier of the backwardness of the community as a whole and the consequent need to intervene to save Muslim women from Muslim men. This scenario

---

216 Kapur and Cossman, *supra* note 2 at 15.
217 Basu, *supra* note 65 at 289.
218 Baines and Rubio-Marin, *supra* note 125 at 7.
219 Basu, *supra* note 65 at 280.

unfolds in much the same way as the colonial justification of the civilizing mission, where the British deployed arguments of backwardness and the appalling status of women as justifying, if not necessitating, imperial intervention.[220]

Demystifying what may seem to be, on the face of it, pro-women decisions reveals the complexity of legal remedies and reiterates the dangers of a simplistic notion of protection. The question of legal reform is inextricably bound up with questions of minority identity, cultural dominance, and resistance. Negotiating the boundaries between gender, community, and nation is politically fraught and contingent for Muslim women seeking greater rights. To forward Muslim women's rights, any proposal for the reform of the personal law or for the enactment of a UCC must necessarily be refracted through the multiple identities of Muslim women, the political imperatives of the state, the traditional male leadership's claims to authenticity and representation, and the political manipulation of simplistic categories of religion, culture, and identity.

---

220   Pathak and Sunder Rajan, *supra* note 42 at 567.

4 Reclaiming the Nation

'For,' the outsider will say, 'in fact, as a woman, I have no country. As a woman I want no country. As a woman my country is the whole world.'[1]

In their construction as citizens of independent India, women have been treated as less than equal in the domain of family and community. The post-colonial state has constructed women not as equal citizens, but rather, simultaneously, as gendered citizens and as citizens with a prior religious/cultural identity. The notion of women's citizenship rights has been filtered through the lenses of gender and cultural essentialism, negating constitutional guarantees of equality for women. Such a construction of citizenship underscores the conduct of the state in reinforcing women's political and social personas as being primarily gendered and differentiated according to religious identity, focusing invariably on women's difference with men. It has impacted, most critically, the formulation of personal law specifically and public policy in general, which take into account not only differences between men and women, but also differences between women themselves, based on religious affiliation. This stands in profound contradiction to the rights of equal citizenship.[2]

In contrast to the constitutional guarantee of equality, state-sanctioned inequality within the family persists. Although the nationalist movement was strongly supported by women leaders during the

---

1 Woolf, *Three Guineas*, 197.
2 Sunder Rajan, *Scandal of the State*, 2.

struggle for Independence, the political promise of that cooperation did not result in an aggressive program of social reform to enforce constitutional guarantees of gender equality in family law. Indian women are disadvantaged by the state, which owes duties and responsibilities differently, not only to men and women, but also specifically to women based upon religious identity. The Indian state's discrimination against women in the significant area of personal law, in disregard of the *Constitution*, reifies both gender and cultural essentialism.

The state's failure to enforce women's equality rights was exposed by the landmark feminist document, *Towards Equality*, the Report of the Committee on the Status of Women in India, which was commissioned by the government.[3] The report examined the extent to which constitutionally guaranteed equality rights had not been enforced for women.[4] For the first time, on the publication of this report, the Indian government's failure to ensure equality for women was strongly criticized.[5] *Towards Equality* challenged the state to make equality promises meaningful for women, and the authors expressed disappointment that Indian women were experiencing worsening conditions.[6] This report was a scathing indictment of the state. The authors charged that there had been no visible improvement in the status of women since Independence: 'As members of the pre-Independence generation, we have always been firm believers in equal rights for women. For us the recognition of this principle in the Constitution heralded the beginning of a new era for the women of this country.[7] The review of the disabilities and constraints on women, which stem from sociocultural institutions, indicates that the majority of women are still very far from enjoying the rights and opportunities guaranteed to them by the Constitution ... The social laws that sought to mitigate the problems of women in their family life have remained unknown to a large mass of women in this country, who are as ignorant of their legal rights today as they were before Independence.'[8]

Towards Equality laid bare the dismal record of the post-colonial Indian state, and it galvanized the women's movement into seeking

3 *Towards Equality*; see 'Debates and Reports' in the Bibliography.
4 Forbes, *Cambridge History of India*, 227.
5 *Ibid*. at 226.
6 *Ibid*. at 253.
7 *Towards Equality, supra* note 3 at 355.
8 *Ibid*. at 359.

state accountability.[9] The question of the status of women was now placed prominently on the state's agenda. In the early days of Independence, the new post-colonial state sought to rehabilitate and rescue women in the enthusiasm of nationalism. In continuity with the colonial state's declared mission of establishing civilizational modernity and protecting Indian women, the Indian state saw its role in enforcing women's rights as initiating social reform. Now, women's organizations called upon the state to fulfil its constitutional promise to Indian women as a matter of its accountability as a state and as a member of the international community of nations.[10] The state has been an important site of struggle for women's rights by the Indian women's movement.[11]

In the years following Independence, the women's movement was optimistic that constitutional guarantees of equality and personal law reform would ultimately be addressed by the state. However, the triumph of experience over hope has now led feminists to a more critical understanding of the state's role in enforcing women's equality rights. With the publication of *Towards Equality*, it became clear that the state's inaction in enforcing equality guarantees was something more than simply 'those of the gaps between promises and delivery, progressive laws and their failed implementation, but a betrayal at a deeper level.'[12] The women's movement is divided over the efficacy of legal reform activism to achieve progress, given the state's poor record over the last fifty years. Some members now question the fundamental premise of law reform itself, fearing that state intervention through increased legislation instead may have the effect of increasing patriarchal control over women.

Yet this is not to argue for abandoning of the path of legal reform. To forward women's rights, it is important to pursue legal reform and to engage with the language of rights. As Patricia Williams argues, the symbolic value of a rights claim is of crucial significance to the disadvantaged and the marginalized.[13] Gayatri Spivak states that 'citizenship is indeed the symbolic circuit of the mobilizing of subalternity

---

9 Sunder Rajan, *supra* note 2 at 3.
10 *Ibid.* at 3, 215.
11 Mary E. John, 'Gender, Development and the Women's Movement: Problems for a History of the Present,' in Sunder Rajan, *Signposts*, 101 at 108.
12 Sunder Rajan, *supra* note 2 at 25.
13 Williams, 'Alchemical Notes,' 405.

into hegemony.'[14] At the same time, arguably, the discourse of law has reified gender essentialism, constructing women as in need of protection. This gendered portrayal of women in itself reifies the notion that women are subordinate. Yet women's rights advocates early on used the law to reform the status of women, to challenge the existing status quo, and to reformulate and renegotiate gender roles and identity. The law has been the site of intensive discursive struggle as feminists and social reformers have struggled to establish an understanding of women's rights and women's roles as equal citizens of the nation.[15]

Recognizing the importance of challenging not only the state, but also all aspects of national life that reinforce structures of oppression, the Indian women's movement has sought to expand the sites on which the discursive struggle for women's rights has to be fought. These include individual relations, the family, religious communities, caste relations, and also an understanding of the way all of these sites of struggle relate to the state itself. Further, by challenging the terms of the debate and opening new paradigms within which discussions of women's legal rights in the family and personal law reform are debated to beyond simply a consideration of the competing rights of religious communities and the limits to the state's authority to reform and regulate religion, the women's movement has signalled forcefully to the state that women are indeed proactive subjects demanding change; women are not merely the objects of change but, in fact, the rightful agents of change.[16]

In this concluding chapter, I present the idea of a uniform civil code as a continuing process of negotiation rather than as a one-time enactment of a grand universalizing law. I suggest that we view the struggle for a UCC as a historically contingent process that has signified different things at different times to different groups of people. I argue that the notion of a UCC with its multiple, contested meanings has the possibility of reformulating our conceptions of women's rights, equal citizenship, and the accommodation of group interests, within the legitimacy of a constitutional framework. Inevitably, an exploration of the status of Muslim women raises the question of equal citizenship of the nation

---

14 Spivak, *Critique of Postcolonial Reason*, 309.
15 Kapur and Cossman, *Subversive Sites*, 12.
16 Sunder Rajan, *supra* note 2 at 173.

state. I go on to analyse the construction of citizenship by the post-colonial state, arguing that for Muslim women, the idea of citizenship is mediated by differences of both gender and religious identity. I argue that the state has at once both granted and denied to Muslim women the ideal of equal citizenship rights by its guarantee of formal equality in the public sphere and the simultaneous denial of equality in the private sphere through the perpetuation of discriminatory personal law.

Through the understanding that it is indeed possible to have collective action across difference, I advocate a perspective that seeks to avoid the conundrums of identity politics, while respecting differences among women. The notion of transversal politics is a way of negotiating a progressive politics to forward Muslim women's rights while building coalitions with other disadvantaged groups rather than around an essentialized identity politics. Finally, I conclude that Muslim women's exclusion from equal citizenship has to be challenged if we are to forward gender rights within the family. I suggest that the argument of equal citizenship opens up the space for women to reclaim a selfhood free from essentialist, primordial definitions of gender interests and prescripted identities. I argue that the realm of constitutional law and the notion of citizenship have a counter-hegemonic potential to challenge existing power structures. Drawing on the insights of post-colonial theory, I argue that we need to interrogate dichotomous categories of western/non-western, modern/traditional, Muslim/Other, colonial/post-colonial, in order to emphasize the integration of the colonial past with the post-colonial present. I suggest that we understand the discursive constructedness of these binary categories to underscore the hybridity of culture and the modernity of tradition. Such an understanding is of great significance to the feminist emancipatory project, as it reveals the manner in which oppositional categories of public/private, true Muslim woman / feminist, personal law / uniform law have been used to exclude women from the enjoyment of equal rights.

Contextualizing a Uniform Civil Code

The questions of personal law reform and the enactment of a uniform civil code (UCC) are matters of considerable controversy and debate in contemporary India. After the reform of Hindu personal law in the 1950s the state did little to address the disadvantage of women within the family. The *Shah Bano* case brought these issues back to national attention, pushing the country to the brink of a constitutional crisis as it cast into sharp relief the complex connections between gender justice, personal law reform, and the need for a uniform civil code of family laws. Inevitably, discussions of personal law reform and the enactment of a UCC raise questions of gender justice and equal citizenship for women.[17] The state's refusal either to reform personal law or to introduce a uniform civil code based on the principles of gender equality and anti-discrimination profoundly impacts Muslim women, limiting their autonomy and further legitimizing their role as symbols of the collectivity, without any meaningful examination of their legal, social, and political disadvantage. The perpetuation of discriminatory laws that do not subscribe to the wider constitutional norms of gender equality and freedom from discrimination serves to exclude Muslim women from equal citizenship.

In this section, I briefly contextualize the notion of a UCC, to situate more clearly the discussion that follows later in the chapter. I focus on constructing an understanding of a UCC that emphasizes its multiple and contested meanings and its appropriation to specific political agendas. I argue that to forward Muslim women's claims to equality in family law we need to reformulate the frameworks within which we discuss gender justice and the accommodation of group interests. Doing so necessarily entails a reconceptualization of a uniform civil code as nuanced, historically contingent, and fluid.

The primary focus of discussion on personal law reform and the enactment of a UCC has been the nature of Muslim personal law, whether it is immutable as a divine law or may be subject to modification, and the comparative rights of communities, rather than a serious examination of women's inequality.[18] Hindu law is not subject to the same inquiry, perhaps because it was substantially altered by parliamentary legislation in the 1950s. However, the fact that the changes that were made in Hindu law were far from comprehensive and did not alter family hierarchies in any significant way has been ignored.[19]

---

17 Mukhopadhyay, *Legally Dispossessed*, 204. Although the Constitution calls for the enactment of a uniform civil code of family laws, there is, so far, no legislative initiative to draft such a UCC.

18 Dhagamwar, *Towards the Uniform Civil Code*, 43; Parashar, *Women and Family Law Reform*, 201.

19 For example, by not reforming Hindu law to allow women to be the head of the Hindu joint family and also by exempting agricultural land from Hindu women's intestate inheritance rights.

That all personal laws are discriminatory towards women has been obscured in this discussion. Also excluded is any consideration of constitutional principles that mandate personal law reform and the enactment of a uniform code of family laws. Archana Parashar argues that this focus has served to create the false understanding that a UCC is sought to be enacted solely as a means to reform Muslim personal law.[20]

The state has consistently disregarded demands from women's groups to enact gender-just laws for all women irrespective of religious affiliation. Instead, it has chosen to accept the contention of conservative male leaders of the Muslim community that the reform of personal law or the enactment of a UCC, would violate the right to religious freedom and conflict with the state's commitment to protect minority rights, thereby threatening group integrity and identity.[21] The argument that the initiative to reform personal law must come from within the community and the contention that personal law reform implies a threat to community identity are arguably an oversimplification of a very complex issue.[22] History has shown the extreme reluctance of community leaders to address women's inequality through law reform, despite repeated calls for reform by women's groups and Muslim reformists alike.[23] Further, the claim that the status of women under personal law is a prime signifier of group identity ties Muslim women to an essentialized notion of identity and denies the possibility of internal dissent.[24]

In this paradigm, minority rights and women's rights are set up in a binary opposition.[25] It is important, therefore, conceptually to disentangle the notion of gender justice from the idea of competing minority rights, particularly in a situation where Muslim women's equality rights have been subsumed under the presumed larger interests of the collectivity. In the continued absence of any move by either the state or the community to address discrimination against Muslim women

---

20 Parashar, *supra* note 18 at 240.
21 *Ibid.* at 242, 243.
22 Zoya Hasan, 'Gender Politics, Legal Reform, and the Muslim Community in India,' in Jeffery and Basu, *Resisting the Sacred and the Secular*, 71 at 76.
23 Chhachhi, 'Identity Politics, Secularism, and Women: A South Asian Perspective,' in Hasan, *Forging Identities*, 74 at 82. Asghar Ali Engineer, 'Forces behind the Agitation,' in Engineer, *Shah Bano Controversy*, 35 at 37–41.
24 Narain, *Gender and Community*, 5.
25 Hasan, 'Minority Identity,' *supra* note 23, 59 at 59.

under personal law, the UCC continues to be the site of desire for gender equity, offering women a space that can provide, across differences, the possibility of equal citizenship, free from narrow definitions of what constitutes community identity and what defines a group's interests. The space of secular citizenship offers a site of resistance and the possibility of an emancipatory politics to forward Muslim women's rights. The argument of equal citizenship rights allows Muslim women to challenge their situation under personal law and to confront the contradiction between the state's constitutionally guaranteed rights and the treatment of women under personal law.[26]

The idea of a UCC calling for gender equality as the basis of family laws was a significant aspect of the women's movement's campaign for law reform.[27] Later, the provision for a UCC was debated by the *Constitution* makers in the Constituent Assembly, which had been established by the British and charged with the task of drafting a constitution for India upon independence from Britain. Amrit Kaur and Hansa Mehta, two prominent leaders of the All India Women's Conference (AIWC), were members of the Constituent Assembly Subcommittee on Fundamental Rights, while Amrit Kaur was also a member of the Minorities Subcommittee.[28] These Constituent Assembly debates were an important forum for forwarding the demands of the AIWC and for publicizing its position.[29] The debates reveal the discourses within which the provisions for personal law reform and the UCC were framed. Testifying to the legislative intent of the *Constitution* makers, these debates reveal the rhetoric around the state's authority to define the new post-colonial citizen by regulating those aspects of religion deemed inappropriate to the nationalist modernizing project.[30] At

---

26 Jan Jindy Pettman, 'Globalisation and the Gendered Politics of Citizenship,' in Yuval-Davis and Werbner, *Women, Citizenship and Difference*, 207 at 207.
27 The concept of a UCC was first introduced into the national political debate by leaders of the women's movement in 1940.
28 The All India Women's Conference (AIWC) was a national women's organization founded in 1927; it soon became one of the most prominent women's groups. It was primarily concerned with lobbying government on issues of women's education, suffrage, employment, and personal law reform. See the discussion in chapter 2, above. There were only fifteen women members of the Constituent Assembly. There were no Muslim women represented in the Constituent Assembly. Mukhopadhyay, *supra* note 17 at 191.
29 Constituent Assembly members were chosen from the provincial legislatures in 1946 by indirect election. Everett, *Women and Social Change*, 159–60.
30 Mukhopadhyay, *supra* note 17 at 193.

the same time, they highlight the manner in which the question of women's rights was circumscribed by concerns regarding minority rights.

The idea of a uniform civil code was introduced into the Assembly debates by Minoo Masani on 28 March 1947, at a meeting of the Sub-committee on Fundamental Rights. He proposed that the *Constitution* should provide for a common civil code of family laws applicable to all citizens. However, despite the best efforts of the women represen-tatives to have a uniform civil code included in the *Constitution* as a fundamental right, the proposal was defeated. The majority of the sub-committee, in deference to community leaders, decided that it was beyond the scope of the fundamental rights and belonged instead in the category of the non-justiciable Directive Principles. [31]

The *Constitution* makers framed the UCC as a tool for national inte-gration, to promote the ideal of secular nationalism over the perils of sectarianism. Although in the years preceding Independence leaders of the women's movement had called for a UCC based on gender justice and equal citizenship, their participation in the Constituent Assembly debates reveals that they, too, emphasized the unifying potential of a UCC rather than its gender equality aspect.[32] Neither Hansa Mehta nor Amrit Kaur based their demand for a UCC as a fun-damental right on the basis of women's equality, citing only national unity, and this emphasis was quite different from the women's move-ment's earlier demands for a UCC.[33] In the discussions around the provision of a UCC, there was little mention of its gender justice

---

31 Shiva Rao, *Framing of India's Constitution*, 128. The minority consisted of Mr Minoo Masani, Rajkumari Amrit Kaur, Mrs Hansa Mehta and Dr Ambedkar. The provi-sion for a UCC was included in the *Constitution* in Article 44. Although Directive Principles are not mandatory, they are nonetheless fundamental in the governance of the country. Article 44 is a Directive Principle of state policy, not an enforceable fundamental right. According to the *Constitution*, Directive Principles of state policy are not enforceable. They lay down the aims of state policy and are recommenda-tory rather than mandatory. Article 37: 'Application of the Principles contained in this Part [Directive Principles of State Policy]. – The Provisions contained in this Part shall not be enforceable by any court, but the principles therein laid down are nevertheless fundamental in the governance of the country and it shall be the duty of the State to apply these principles in making laws.' Article 44: 'Uniform Civil Code for the citizens. – The State shall endeavor to secure for the citizens a uniform civil code throughout the territory of India.'

32 *Ibid*. at 122; Everett, *supra* note 29 at 158.

33 Mukhopadhyay, *supra* note 17 at 236.

aspect.[34] The *Constitution* makers did not highlight the connection between a UCC and women's equality.[35] Although they agreed to include a UCC in the *Constitution* as a Directive Principle, arguably doing so signified their acceptance of gender equality as a political principle, but it also testifies to their reluctance to introduce this principle in family law. Despite the Constituent Assembly's support for including clauses guaranteeing sex equality in political and economic spheres, there was strong opposition to sex equality in the private sphere.[36]

The national debate was conflicted and contested. In the Constituent Assembly, concerns regarding minority rights and the right to religious freedom impacted the ultimate shape of the guarantees for gender equality through personal law reform and the provision of a UCC. When the provision of a UCC was discussed in the Assembly, Muslim members strongly objected to its inclusion in the *Constitution*.[37] Claiming that India's cultural diversity prevented the enactment of a UCC, they further argued that such a code would violate the right to religious freedom. They sought to include a proviso explicitly exempting personal laws from state interference.[38] However, the majority of the subcommittee, led by K.M. Munshi, refuted the argument that a UCC would conflict with the right to religious freedom.[39] K.M. Munshi further stated that freedom of religion did not prevent the state from reforming those aspects of religion that were explicitly discriminatory to women, such as inheritance and succession. He argued that to make personal law immune to reform by the state would render the gender equality guarantees in the *Constitution* meaningless.[40]

Parashar notes that perhaps the only time there was an explicit connection made between gender justice, personal law reform, and equal citizenship for women was in the context of debates on the impact of a

---

34 Parashar, *supra* note 18 at 235.
35 *Ibid.* at 236–7.
36 Everett, *supra* note 29 at 161.
37 *Constituent Assembly Debates*, 540; see 'Debates and Reports' in the Bibliography.
38 *Ibid.* at 540–52. These members were Mohammed Ismail Saheb, Naziruddin Ahmed, Mahboob Ali Baig Bahadur, B. Pocker Sahib Bahadur, and Hussain Imam.
39 Vasudha Dhagamwar, 'Women, Children, and the Constitution: Hostages to Religion, Outcaste by Law,' in Baird, *Religion and Law*, 215 at 218–19.
40 *Constituent Assembly Debates, supra* note 37 at 548.

UCC on religious freedom and social reform legislation.[41] During the Assembly debates, some members, including AIWC leaders, Amrit Kaur and Hansa Mehta, expressed the fear that to refuse to allow the state the power to reform religion would conflict with existing legislation that invalidated oppressive customs that have the sanction of religion, such as legislation against child marriage and laws enabling widow remarriage.[42] Furthermore, they were concerned that it might render impossible any future legislation to wipe out social evils practised in the name of religion, including *purdah*, polygamy, unequal laws of inheritance, and prevention of inter-caste marriages.[43] However, as Granville Austin notes, it is surprising that Amrit Kaur and Hansa Mehta, while they were concerned that religious freedom should not be an obstacle in the path of social reform, did not explicitly make the link here between a UCC and its potential for social reform.[44] Amrit Kaur made only a passing reference to women's subordination under the law.[45]

In contrast, members of the Minorities Subcommittee were concerned more with the safeguarding of minority rights through the protection of the right to religious freedom and the preservation of personal law. The rights of women were cast in a dichotomous relation to the rights of groups, as the arguments in the Constituent Assembly pitted the claims of women through social reform legislation against the rights of minorities. The *Constitution* makers overrode the objections of Muslim leaders that the state did not have the authority to regulate and reform religion.[46] Yet the Law minister, B.R. Ambedkar, although strongly rejecting the argument that Muslim law was immutable, in an effort to reassure Muslim leaders, stated that the provision for a UCC, 'merely proposes that the State shall endeavour to secure a civil code for the citizens of the country. It does not say that after the code is framed, the state shall enforce it upon all citizens merely because they are citizens. It is perfectly possible that the future Parliament may make a declaration that the Code shall only apply to

---

41 Mukhopadhyay, *supra* note 17 at 193.
42 Shiva Rao, *supra* note 31 at 146–7. Amrit Kaur sent a letter to B.N. Rau on behalf of Hansa Mehta and herself.
43 Parashar, *supra* note 18 at 223.
44 *Ibid.* at 233.
45 Shiva Rao, *supra* note 31 at 310.
46 Jacobsohn, *The Wheel of Law*, 103.

those who make a declaration that they are prepared to be bound by it, so that in the initial stage, the application of the Code may be purely voluntary.'[47]

Debates around the provision for a UCC retained a focus on the state's authority to regulate religion and the limits of religious freedom in the context of minority rights and personal law. Significantly, the apprehensions of women leaders and reformists of the potential impact of an unrestricted right to religious freedom on social reform legislation were subordinated to minority anxieties. Parashar argues that this focus reflected, as well, the marginality of women's rights in the context of the discussion of religious freedom and personal law reform.[48] Although it was noted in passing that accepting personal law uncritically as an integral part of minority rights and exempting it from social reform legislation would impact women's status, there was little discussion of the link between a UCC and gender equality.[49] Despite the acceptance, in principle, of gender equality, the failure explicitly to link it with a UCC, together with the refusal to make a UCC a fundamental right, has resulted in the continued failure to ensure legal equality within personal law, while simultaneously demonstrating the privileging of group rights over women's rights.[50]

As Granville Austin argues, it was primarily to allay Muslim and Sikh fears that the Subcommittee on Fundamental Rights did not make a UCC clause justiciable.[51] This reluctance to include a UCC as an enforceable fundamental right in the *Constitution* is a reflection of the concern of nationalists, especially in the context of India's violent Partition, to reassure all minorities, but Muslims in particular, that their rights would be safeguarded not only as equal citizens but as a Muslim collectivity. Implicit in this attitude was the understanding that the preservation of personal law was an integral part of minority rights.[52]

By stressing the state's authority to regulate religion, by reforming certain aspects of personal law, by including a UCC in the *Constitution*

---

47 *Constituent Assembly Debates, supra* note 37 at 781.
48 Parashar, *supra* note 18 at 225.
49 *Ibid.* at 235.
50 *Ibid.* at 236.
51 Austin, *Indian Constitution,* 81.
52 Susanne Hoeber Rudolph and Lloyd I. Rudolph, 'Living with Difference in India: Legal Pluralism and Legal Universalism in Historical Context,' in Larson, *Religion and Personal Law,* 36 at 51.

but not as a fundamental right, by not insisting on a timetable for the enactment of a UCC – the state seemed to waver between a strong assertion of the social reform aspect of state power and balancing this with its need to retain minority confidence in the new state. The policy of alternately emphasizing state authority to reform and modernize, on the one hand, and privileging of minority rights over gender rights, on the other, reflects the state's ambivalence towards upholding women's rights. Although a UCC was ultimately included in the *Constitution*, despite Muslim leaders' objections, as an unenforceable Directive Principle rather than as a fundamental right, it failed emphatically to serve women's equality, which was its original intent in the feminist/nationalist struggle.

There are multiple, contested understandings of what a UCC means. In the latter part of the independence struggle and the immediate post-independence years, it was seen as an instrument of national integration bringing together disparate religious communities, uniting them under one common law. The *Constitution* makers envisaged a UCC as eventually replacing discriminatory personal law, which was seen as dividing the nation along communal, sectarian lines. Equally important, a UCC was seen as an integral part of the post-colonial state's modernizing project, where custom and religion were sought to be reformed. Yet members of the minority Muslim community perceived a UCC as a threat to their group identity and as a departure from the promise to minorities that their rights would be safeguarded in independent India. Most striking is the fact that none of these meanings derives from a discourse about gender equality. A UCC was framed primarily as a signifier of the nation's unity, not as an instrument to ensure women's equality. In this context, it becomes apparent that 'these meanings derive from discourses of historically constructed, politicized religious identities locked in a struggle for hegemony in the state.'[53]

However, in the contemporary context, much of this reasoning appears to have come undone as the progress towards a uniform civil code falters in a climate of rising religious fundamentalism and the realpolitik of democratic electoral calculations. The meaning and significance of a UCC has shifted from that of a demonstration of India's secularism to acrimonious debate pitting women's rights against group rights, religion versus secularism and nation versus

---

53 Mukhopadhyay, *supra* note 17 at 197.

community.[54] In contemporary India, the idea of a UCC has been appropriated by the Hindu right as a political tool aimed at undermining Muslim group rights. The notion of a UCC has been transformed from what was once a serious constitutional objective to a trivialized political weapon deployed by the Hindu right to chastise the Muslim community for its reluctance to reform its personal law.[55] Religious fundamentalism, both Hindu and Muslim, and the experience of prejudice and hostility faced by Muslim communities in India have raised the spectre of a UCC that is, in essence, a 'Hindu Code.' As Asghar Ali Engineer, India's foremost Muslim reformist, points out, 'Whatever the merits of a common civil code ... when the demand for it comes from communalist Hindus, it arouses deep suspicion even among the Muslim intelligentsia and they begin to perceive it as a Hindu Code.'[56]

The question of a uniform civil code is complex.[57] The discussion around a UCC has been seriously impacted by and implicated in contemporary events such as the *Shah Bano* controversy, the demolition of the Babri mosque by Hindu right-wing mobs, the 1986 Roop Kanwar Sati and the resultant anti-sati legislation, and, most particularly, by the increased politicization of religion and the rise of religious fundamentalism, both Hindu and Muslim, and the increased sense of anxiety in the Muslim community caused by the rise of Hindu right-wing chauvinism.[58] The fear of Muslims that a UCC would undermine Muslim group rights manifested itself most dramatically in the *Shah Bano* controversy.[59] In this context of Hindu right-wing hostility and Muslim anxiety, Rajeev Dhavan argues that 'the quest for a UCC is laudable. But it can hardly be invoked as policy when it is perceived as a threatening Damocles sword hanging over the future of personal laws. Nor must it be invoked as a constitutional necessity if the exploitative elements complained of in any

---

54 *Ibid.* at 203.
55 Rajeev Dhavan, 'The Road to Xanadu: India's Quest for Secularism' in Larson, *supra* note 52, 301 at 310, 317.
56 Pathak and Sunder Rajan, 'Shahbano,' 558 at 575.
57 Dhavan, *supra* note 55 at 310.
58 John H. Mansfield, 'The Personal Laws or a Uniform Civil Code,' in Baird, *supra* note 39, 139 at 141.
59 Marc Galanter and Jayanth Krishnan, 'Personal Law Systems and Religious Conflict: A Comparison of India and Israel,' in Larson, *supra* note 52, 270 at 275.

religion can be ameliorated by means of the interior tradition of that faith.'[60]

Current debates around a UCC encompass several broad positions that often both conflict and converge. These various positions must be understood within the context of the fundamental contradiction between constitutional guarantees of equality and freedom from discrimination and a system of personal law based explicitly on differences of religion and gender, and they should caution us to be mindful of the speaker's location and politics.[61] Susanne Hoeber Rudolph and Lloyd I. Rudolph emphasize that 'The idea of a uniform civil code carries no single meaning over historical time. Its advocates change, and change sides.'[62] The British implicitly moved towards a uniform civil code when they sought to introduce legal uniformity and certainty in the public law to facilitate the workings of the colonial administration. For nationalist leaders, a UCC is seen as a signifier of national unity. For feminists and social reformers, a UCC signifies an expansion of rights for those hitherto disadvantaged and marginalized. Muslim leaders view a UCC as an attempt to erase their cultural and religious identity by erasing their personal law, which they see as the primary signifier of their group identity. Finally, the Hindu right sees the UCC as a means of assimilating minorities and undermining minority rights.[63]

In a harsh indictment of the state's dismal failure to address women's formalized inequality, the Report of the Committee on the Status of Women declared in 1975, 'The absence of a UCC in the last quarter of the twentieth century, twenty seven years after independence, is an incongruity that cannot be justified with all the emphasis that is placed on secularism, science and modernism. The continuance of various personal laws which accept discrimination between men and women violate the fundamental rights.'[64] Yet here, too, while underscoring the deleterious impact of the continuance of personal laws on women's equality, the committee linked the idea of a UCC with the objective of national unity, going on to state that it was 'against the spirit of national integration and secularism.'[65] Vina

---

60 Dhavan, 'Religious Freedom,' 253.
61 Sunder Rajan, *supra* note 2 at 148.
62 Rudolph and Rudolph, *supra* note 52 at 54–5.
63 *Ibid*.
64 *Towards Equality*, *supra* note 3 at 142.
65 *Ibid*.

Mazumdar, a leading Indian feminist, argues that the great tragedy of the UCC debate is that it has been projected as an instrument for 'national integration,' rather than as a measure to achieve justice for women and other marginalized groups. Further, according to her, the various pronouncements of the Supreme Court exhorting the state to enact a UCC, instead of serving to persuade the state to take action to address systemic gender discrimination, has vitiated a discourse already marked by deep divisions and fundamentalist posturing.[66]

Today, the women's movement has become profoundly divided over the issue of a UCC.[67] Whereas in the earlier years of the women's movement, the pursuit of a UCC was a major feminist goal, in recent years the political confrontation resulting from the rise of communalism and the hijacking of this objective of the women's movement by the Hindu right has caused division and confusion within the movement.[68] Many in the women's movement have moved away from the demand for a UCC in an effort to distance themselves from the politics of the Hindu right, which also demands a UCC, although for very different reasons. The Hindu right has taken over what was historically a major feminist demand, using the language of constitutional rights to set up an opposition between women's rights and minority rights.[69] The issue of a UCC has been used by the Hindu right to challenge India's democratic, secular consensus and to undermine minority rights.[70] Though supported by many liberals and feminists as a crucial instrument for advancing gender justice, the UCC has become a weapon in the hands of fundamentalist Hindus to exhort the Muslims to change their laws just as the Hindus had done in 1955–6.[71]

Mazumdar notes that the failure of the women's movement to prevent the passage of the *Muslim Women's Act* is a demonstration of the movement's lack of influence in national politics. The dilemma for feminists lies in an inadvertent support of the Hindu right by sup-

---

66 Mazumdar, 'Political Ideology,' 9.
67 Rajeswari Sunder Rajan, 'Introduction,' in Sunder Rajan, *supra* note 11, 1 at 4.
68 D.E. Smith defines communalism in the Indian context as the tendency of a socio-religious group 'to attempt to maximize its economic, social, and political strength at the expense of other groups.' 'Emerging Patterns,' 23. Mazumdar, *supra* note 66, 9.
69 Amrita Basu, 'Hindu Women's Activism in India and the Questions It Raises,' in Jeffery and Basu, *supra* note 22, 167 at 171.
70 *Ibid.* at 172.
71 Dhavan, *supra* note 55 at 311, 318.

porting the cause of a UCC. Whereas for feminists the UCC signifies the protection of gender rights in consonance with constitutional prin- ciples and international human rights norms, for the Hindu right it is a means of challenging minority rights. For advocates of Muslim women's rights, the question is how best to forward a progressive fem- inist politics in the context of the anti-Muslim agenda of the Hindu right, which makes it difficult for Muslim women to present a gender justice agenda for fear of serving anti-Muslim interests.[72] Further, the dilemma lies in how best to forward Muslim women's rights claims without undermining group solidarity. Arguably, one way to do so would be to conceptualize a UCC as a continuing process rather than as a rigid universalizing law.[73]

The assertiveness of majoritarian politics has served further to inten- sify the anxieties of Muslim communities. Certainly, the fear of Hindu communalism complicates Muslim women's pursuit of a rights agenda that is seen as undermining group solidarity. Moreover, it forces an alliance between Muslim women and the conservative leaders, the very group opposed to women's rights. It makes the sus- taining of a progressive politics extremely difficult for Muslim women's rights advocates. The *Shah Bano* case emphasizes this predicament. The Supreme Court judgment was supported by femi- nists, Muslim women's groups, liberals, and Muslim reformists, but it was also supported by the Hindu right, who appropriated the contro- versy to forward its anti-Muslim agenda under the pretext of rescuing Muslim women from outdated, unjust laws. Not surprisingly, many Muslim women backed away from opposing the *Muslim Women's Act* and rallied around the fundamentalist slogan of 'Islam in danger.' They felt compelled to support the religious leadership against a majoritarian attack, to defend group integrity against external inter- ference.[74]

Most recently, the Gujarat massacre of 2002, in which 2,000 people, mostly Muslims, lost their lives, is a demonstration of the climate of anti-Muslim prejudice of the Hindu right, and the fragility of India's secularism.[75] It is a stark reminder of the extreme vulnerability, partic-

---

72 Mazumdar, *supra* note 66.
73 Rudolph and Rudolph, *supra* note 52 at 55.
74 Zoya Hasan, 'Introduction: Contextualising Gender and Identity in Contemporary India,' in Hasan, *supra* note 23, vii at viii.
75 Sarkar, 'Semiotics of Terror,' 2873; *Amnesty International Report*, 4.

ularly, of Muslim women. Such events have vitiated an already fraught political atmosphere. In February 2002 Muslims were accused of setting fire to a train killing fifty-nine Hindus who were on their way back from Ayodhya after celebrating the anniversary of the demolition of the Babri mosque. In the retaliatory violence that erupted, Muslim women and children were specifically targeted by organized Hindu right-wing mobs who led the massacres, highlighting the manner in which women are seen as the symbol of collective identity and cultural integrity by those outside the group as well as by the group itself.[76]

This violence should be contextualized within the anti-Muslim agenda of the Hindu right political party in power in the state of Gujarat. There was a complete failure of the state to address the violence. Indeed, the state itself was complicit. Police ignored calls for help and turned a blind eye to violent assaults on Muslims. Appallingly, the judiciary dismissed all complaints brought against Hindu right-wing leaders.[77] Eventually, the Supreme Court of India stepped in and in 2004 ordered that cases be transferred to the state of Maharashtra to be tried in the city of Bombay, as it was apparent that Muslim survivors were being systematically denied justice.[78]

In such a situation, arguably, the best response is to reassert a composite national identity defined within the context of India's *Constitution* and the legitimacy of equality within difference. The response to a renewed communal politics and the reassertion of religious identity can be countered by an understanding of equal citizenship as a secular space. Significantly, as Tanika Sarkar points out, Gujarat survivors are looking to constitutional rights and legal action and the assertion of their rights as equal citizens of the nation. Arguably, 'citizenship is the only ground on which cultural difference can be sustained and asserted. We reject this truth as dated, as an old and therefore unusable brand in the marketplace of ideas, at our peril. The only opposite term to equal citizenship rights is unequal citizenship or the denial of citizenship. That is precisely what happened in Gujarat.'[79]

---

76 Sarkar, *ibid.* at 2875; *Amnesty International Report*, 4.

77 Sarkar, *ibid.* at 2873; *Amnesty International Report*, 4.

78 These cases are significant because they demonstrate the difficulties Muslim women face in seeking justice in the face of anti-Muslim hostility. They were forced several times over to recant their testimony and this real fear of danger to their lives and their families persuaded the Supreme Court to transfer these cases to the Mumbai High Court in the state of Maharashtra. *Amnesty International Report, supra* note 75 at 7.

79 Sarkar, *supra* note 75 at 2876.

For these reasons, it is critical to separate the notion of a UCC both from the idea of national integration and from communalization. In today's climate of politicized religion, it is imperative to have a UCC that allows women to assert a secular identity as equal citizens, an identity that respects women's rights while recognizing their multiple identities.

Feminists have acknowledged the difficulties of choosing either a personal law system or a UCC. Whereas some continue to advocate for a UCC, others are less certain, suggesting that perhaps in the context of communal strife it would be better to have a series of optional family laws rather than a single UCC. There are differences, however, regarding the time frame, content, and manner of implementation of such laws.[80]

In India, the task of negotiating the boundaries between gender, community and nation in the context of constitutionally recognized equality rights and discriminatory personal laws has invariably been left to the judiciary. The Supreme Court took the lead in *Shah Bano* and *Danial Latifi*, emphasizing that the constitutional rights strategy and the use of women's international human rights can be invoked to enforce gender equality and non-discrimination in the national arena. The underlying premise of these decisions was the legitimate claim of Muslim women to equal universal citizenship irrespective of religion.[81] Such decisions that are responsive to India's commitments under international law are a promising move towards accepting women's equality within the family by using constitutional guarantees.

It is necessary to recognize a UCC as the means of translating the constitutional principle of gender equality into actual legal equality for women.[82] Indeed, the substantive content of a UCC must be derived from closing the gap between religious and secular laws, by the internal reform as well of religious laws, and, equally important, by international agreements and conventions. Understanding the UCC through the lens of a constitutional law framework opens up the possibility of recognizing women as equal citizens, freeing them from assertions of religion-based community.

For Muslim women in India, access to citizenship consequent upon the state's policy of multiculturalism has served to be exclusionary on

---

80 Narain, *supra* note 24 at 130.
81 Mullally, 'Feminism and Multicultural Dilemmas,' 673, 674, 684, 685.
82 Parashar, *supra* note 18 at 255.

the basis of their combined gendered and religious identity.[83] So far, UCC debates have been tied to these constraining positions; women's rights are not debated but rather are displaced onto discussions of comparative rights of minorities and the right to religious freedom. It is particularly in this context that an understanding of the UCC as a response to women's inequality under the personal laws is critical to ensuring that the politics of multiculturalism do not obscure the principle of gender justice. Drawing upon Seyla Benhabib's insights, I suggest the idea of a UCC as a normative framework that allows for a discussion of multicultural accommodation and gender equality within a constitutional framework that respects both group rights and women's rights.[84] A UCC can provide a normative framework that combines the importance of legal regulation with an expanded notion of political-cultural dialogue based on the representation and inclusion of all voices. Such an understanding allows for problematizing the status of Muslim women within the context of a differentiated citizenship. Indeed, such an understanding fosters reconciliation and inclusion of Muslim women who have hitherto been disenfranchised by the state in its understanding of minority rights and the accommodation of difference.

Martha Nussbaum proposes that promoting dialogue about norms of sex equality in religious laws might be an effective strategy, relying on international human rights documents that India has ratified. She cites the example of the Indian Supreme Court using CEDAW provisions to draft a sexual harassment policy.[85] However, although the Supreme Court has demonstrated its willingness to address systemic gender discrimination, India's current experience of rising religious tensions, of the continuing refusal of religious leaders to reform the law to address women's disadvantage, and, finally, of the lack of political courage by the state either to reform the personal law system or to enforce constitutional guarantees is not as encouraging.

Particularly significant is the historical experience that communities have rarely altered patriarchal power structures to address women's

---

83 See Ronit Lentin, 'Constitutionally Excluded: Citizenship and (Some) Irish Women,' in Yuval-Davis and Werbner, *supra* note 26, 130 at 131.

84 Seyla Benhabib, *Situating the Self: Gender, Community and Postmodernism in Contemporary Ethics* (Cambridge: Polity Press, 1992) 12; Mullally, *supra* note 81 at 686.

85 Martha C. Nussbaum, 'Religion and Women's Equality: The Case of India,' in Rosenblum, *Obligations of Citizenship*, 335 at 365.

vulnerability.[86] That Muslim women have repeatedly emphatically declared their opposition to the unfettered, unregulated triple *talaq* has been ignored both by the state and by religious leaders, notably the All India Muslim Personal Law Board (AIMPLB). At its meeting in the summer of 2004 the AIMPLB refused to reform triple *talaq* laws, on the grounds that triple *talaq* was permitted by the Shariat. They conceded only to initiating a campaign to publicize its detrimental effect on Muslim women. In response to this continued refusal to address their legal, social, and economic vulnerability, Muslim women, in a historic move, defied the *Ulema* and established their own All India Women's Personal Law Board. Soon after, a Shia Women's Personal Law Board was established specifically to address the rights of Shia women. These women's law boards are committed to the dissemination of knowledge and the redefinition of women's rights under Muslim law. Significantly, the AIMPLB has refused to recognize them, condemning their formation as illegal and declaring that they have no religious authority to interpret the law.[87]

The All India Women's Personal Law Board issued a statement declaring: 'The representation of women, who form about half of the country's Muslim population, on the various Muslim Personal Law Boards, has so far been negligible. This is a serious violation of the [*sic*] democratic principles.'[88] The All India Democratic Women's Association (AIDWA), a national grass-roots women's organization, affiliated with the Communist Party of India (Marxist), submitted a memo to the AIMPLB decrying the lack of reform in Muslim personal law. Specifically, AIDWA demanded that the Board categorically declare the practice of triple divorce illegal and, further, that the Board address the urgent issues of reform in marriage and maintenance laws.[89] Women's groups and Muslim reformists such as Asghar Ali Engineer have expressed their disappointment at the Board's refusal to address what is arguably the greatest source of oppression for Muslim women, the triple *talaq*.[90] They have called upon Muslim leaders to address women's systemic disadvantage and effect much needed reform in Muslim personal law, particularly in the areas of divorce, marriage,

---

86 Chowdhry, 'Communalism, Nationalism and Gender,' at 113.
87 *Times of India*, 3 February 2005.
88 *Deccan Herald*, 3 February 2005.
89 All India Democratic Women's Association (AIDWA), *Memo*.
90 Engineer, 'Triple Divorce.'

and maintenance. Rejecting the assertion of Muslim religious leaders that Muslim law in India is immutable, Engineer calls for reform of personal law. [91]

Nevertheless, this reluctance of religious leaders to address women's disadvantage should not prompt feminists to abandon the struggle for gender justice in family law, but rather should underscore the critical need to disentangle the woman question from particularistic, oppressive, patriarchal interpretations of religious authorities to create gender-just laws. These debates within the women's movement reflect the polarization in the discourse of the UCC and personal law reform, where the two are viewed in an either/or binary. Invariably, the reform of personal law and the continuance of the personal law system are debated as inherently oppositional to a UCC.[92] Whether women's groups call for a UCC explicitly or advocate enacting a series of laws to advance women's rights within the family, it is critical that women's disadvantage in law be addressed. The need to reconceptualize the UCC as a fluid concept that is not unchanging for all time is critical because of the current parameters within which it is debated. The terms of the discourse are so fixed and the discursive space so rigid, that positions have become attenuated and thinking has become contentious. This has led to the reification of false dualities – Indian/western, feminist/true Indian women, Muslim/Other, secular/religious thus disallowing a dynamic reinterpretation of the issues at stake.

Binary constructions of women's rights versus community rights, personal law versus uniform family law, and community versus nation have forced unnecessary oppositions. To pose the question in polarizing terms as either a uniform code or the personal law system is far too harsh a binary. John Mansfield argues that to frame the issue as an either/or choice between a UCC and personal law is unnecessarily dichotomous. Rather than such a sharp opposition between the two, Mansfield suggests that the issue be viewed instead as a process towards greater uniformity, as indeed the British set into motion in 1772. The premises of such an understanding are that it is essential to respect group difference even while moving towards a greater uniformity of rights.[93] This insight engenders the perspective of the UCC as

---

91 Engineer, 'Need for Codification and Reform, 59.
92 Srimati Basu, 'The Personal and the Political: Indian Women and Inheritance Law,' in Larson, *supra* note 52, 163 at 179.
93 Mansfield, *supra* note 58 at 175–6.

a continuing legal process that began over a century ago and that has been continually challenged, and we must set it within constantly changing political and social contexts.[94] It underscores the need to understand the UCC as a process in history rather than as a received notion. As a process, the UCC is subject to continual reconstitution and it is also, as experience has shown, appropriated to suit specific agendas.[95]

We need to reconsider the terms we use to discuss issues of personal law reform, gender justice, Muslim women's rights and a uniform civil code and to reformulate the frameworks within which we debate these issues. When we move away from the rigid perception of a UCC as a means of fostering national unity, we see that it is important to craft a more nuanced understanding of a UCC as ever-changing, constantly in flux in relation to fluid conceptions of gender justice, shifting political coalitions, and political imperatives.[96] We need to view the uniform civil code as contingent and responsive to the contemporary social and political context, and as having different meanings over time to different people. Indeed, the *Shah Bano* case underscores the fact that the notion of a UCC and the struggle for it represent 'a process rather than an enactment, a continual negotiation more than a unilinear progression. Much of that process is likely to consist of the gradual accumulation of court decisions and particular pieces of legislation pointing in contradictory directions.'[97]

As Srimati Basu suggests, it is only by complicating this opposition between personal law and a UCC that we can better understand that the problem lies not merely in the non-existence or even non-implementation of laws, but rather in the cultural configuration of gender and law and their relationship to the state. Law should be viewed as a site of contest, where feminist interventions have the potential to subvert gendered assumptions of legal ideology and state regulation of family relations. 'Feminist interventions can thus lay out the legal nexus and the web of connections between law and state, foreground gender implications of proposed and existing laws, and refuse to answer the question of personal law in binary terms.'[98]

---

94 Rudolph and Rudolph, *supra* note 52 at 51, 52.
95 Griffiths, 'Representation and Production, 23.
96 Partha Chatterjee, 'Secularism and Tolerance,' in Bhargava, *Secularism and Its Critics*, 345 at 370.
97 Rudolph and Rudolph, *supra* note 52 at 53.
98 Basu, *supra* note 68 at 180.

To compromise women's rights on the assumption that to do so would be to respect group integrity is a notion that must be seriously re-examined. Rather than retaining an understanding of women's rights and group rights as competing, we need to move beyond simplistic blanket categories that deny Muslim women voice, that privilege ascriptive identities, and that subject women to an essentialism that, in the final analysis, penalizes them for their membership in a religious group. It is necessary to interrogate hegemonic categories and to rethink our understanding of the legitimate interests of the group if we are to be truly inclusive. The call for a UCC requires taking women's rights out of the protected sphere of the home and subjecting them to public scrutiny; we need to reconceptualize the UCC as gender-conscious, gender-responsive, constitutional civil rights legislation.[99] To forward women's claims to equity in family law, we need to reimagine a UCC not as a grand universalizing law, but rather as a continuation of a dialogue about the rights of women within the context of the *Constitution* and the fundamental rights.

Gender and Citizenship

The state's regulation, through the personal law system, of gender roles and of the construction of family relationships in the private sphere inevitably has determined women's status as citizens in the public sphere. In this context, the notion of citizenship becomes a focus of any exploration of the legal status of Muslim women. The Indian state has constructed citizenship so that it is mediated by differences of both gender and religion. Constructing women as a differentiated category, the state owes dissimilar duties and grants differing rights to women based on their religious affiliation. Consequently, Muslim women do not enjoy the same rights within the family that Muslim men do, while their rights are also dissimilar to those of other Indian women. At the same time, women are also constructed as a unified category and are framed as 'different' from men, such that they require state protection. Emphasizing this contradictory construction, Muslim women are also included in the undifferentiated category of Indian women, thereby granting them the same rights as other Indian women and men in the public domain. This results in an ambiguous location

---

99 Rivera, 'Violence Against Women Act,' 353, 354.

for Muslim women and gives rise to a certain ambivalence regarding their rights.[100]

Inevitably then, for Muslim women, the idea of citizenship is problematic and complex. Whereas the Indian *Constitution* grants all Indian women formal guarantees of equality before the law, the personal law framework that regulates Muslim women's rights and, correspondingly, the duties and obligations of the state towards its female Muslim citizens has meant that the state's address to Muslim women is both gendered and 'religioned.' While, on the one hand, Muslim women are included with all Indian women and men as citizens of the nation, on the other hand, by virtue of the Muslim personal law, they are subject to a different set of laws that relate to them specifically, not simply as Muslims, or as women, but as Muslim women.[101] *Shah Bano* emphasizes the manner in which this overlap of gender and religion results in the disadvantaging of Muslim women as citizens.[102] This construction of Muslim women's difference 'determines their access to entitlements and their capacity to exercise independent agency.'[103]

Women's citizenship, as a consequence of the discriminatory, male-centred personal law, is invariably mediated by male members of the family and even by the state itself, in a hierarchical, dependent relationship. Muslim personal law as it is in force today is framed so that women can never be anything but subordinate citizens in the 'private' sphere through the enforcement of discriminatory laws of marriage, divorce, inheritance, custody, guardianship, inheritance, and succession, among others.[104] Gender discrimination starts within this dual legal structure of 'public' secular law and 'private' religious personal law. This personal law system based on ascriptive religious identity highlights the dual nature of women's citizenship. The dual legal structure and the public/private split are linked, and the separation of private and public is reinforced at every opportunity.

For Muslim women, this dichotomous construction has meant that they are twice abandoned by the state: first, in the construction of per-

---

100 Sunder Rajan, *supra* note 66 at 2.
101 Yuval-Davis, 'Beyond Differences,' 178.
102 Jayal, *Democracy and the State*, 7.
103 Pnina Werbner and Nira Yuval-Davis, 'Women and the New Discourse of Citizenship,' in Yuval-Davis and Werbner, *supra* note 26, 1 at 5.
104 For the provisions of Muslim personal law in India see Bhattacharjee, *Muslim Law and the Constitution*; Diwan, *Muslim Law in Modern India*; Fyzee, *Outlines of Muhammadan Law*.

sonal law as an inherent part of the private sphere and thus theoretically beyond state control, and second, by the culturally specific aspect of such a construction, which has meant that while the state has reformed Hindu law, Muslim law has not been similarly reformed. As Parashar argues, 'the doctrine that personal matters are the rightful domain of regulation by the community is no more than a doctrine that helps keep women disadvantaged.'[105]

In refusing to reform the personal law, the state has abandoned Muslim women to the control of conservative leaders of the community, while simultaneously further tightening state control over Muslim women by insisting that, by virtue of the *Muslim Women's Act*, they are ultimately subject to the state's will in its bargaining with, and support of, Muslim patriarchy. In enacting the *Muslim Women's Act*, the state not only failed to ensure but violated the equal citizenship rights of Muslim women by taking away from them rights available to other Indian women, further removing Muslim women from nationally accepted norms of equality.[106] At the same time, by allowing the regulation of Muslim women's rights by conservative male leaders, the state once again undermined the citizenship rights of Muslim women by abandoning them to the private sphere of group autonomy, where Muslim leaders were permitted to create a set of differentiated rights that contradict constitutional guarantees.

The collusion between the state and the patriarchal community is demonstrated in *Shah Bano*, which highlights the exclusion of Muslim women from equal citizenship through their location on the margins of community and nation. Muslim women's group rights are privileged over their individual rights as equal citizens of the nation; their ascriptive religious identity is emphasized, while their gender identity is explicitly denied. Not permitted a voice in any negotiations over a personal law, Muslim women's demands for change are filtered through community controls and presumed group interests.

The *Shah Bano* controversy emphasizes that the private subjugation of women is very much a part of the public agenda. The division between public and private has often been used to exclude women from freedom and rights.[107] The state's policy of not initiating reform in the personal law 'has resulted in legitimizing discrimination against

---

105 Parashar, *supra* note 18 at 249.
106 Jayal, *supra* note 102 at 250.
107 Yuval-Davis, *Gender and Nation*, 5; Phillips, *Democracy and Difference*, 63.

Muslim women, cutting them off from collective action and state veri-
fication, and abandoning them to conservative, male definitions of
self, family, and community.'[108] Feminist theorists have understood
that, ultimately, the distinction between public and private spheres
is a gendered one delineated along gender lines, the private signifying the location of women – house, home, hearth – and the public
indicating the space of men. Ruth Lister contends: 'The public private
dichotomy and the male-female qualities associated with it, stands
[sic] at the heart of the gendered citizenship relationship. The continued power of this deeply gendered dichotomy has meant that women's admission to citizenship has been on male terms. It has also
meant that much mainstream theorizing about citizenship continues to
discount the relevance of what happens in the private sphere to the
practice of citizenship in the public sphere.'[109]

The situation of Muslim women in India today reflects the importance of traditionalist patriarchy for the conservative understanding of
the Muslim community, imagined as separate from the public sphere
of Indian citizenship as a special symbol of the integrity of the minority Muslim community. Any transgression is seen as a defiance of tradition and such women are subject to greater control.[110] As Maitrayee
Mukhopadhyay notes, the Shah Bano case highlighted the 'difficulty of
asserting women's rights as citizens imbued with rights over and
above their position as markers and symbols of community.'[111]

Women are the cultural symbols of community and of nation. They
are the sites upon which identity and tradition are negotiated and constructed and where the nation is regenerated.[112] Yet, in the discourse of
nation, group and tradition, despite the centrality of women to the
(re)formulation of tradition, women themselves are not the subjects of
this discourse, or the primary participants, and the public/private
dichotomy serves to reinforce their exclusion from the discourse. In
this sense, then, discussions around tradition and the status of women

---

108 Narain, supra note 24 at 115.
109 Lister, 'Feminist Theory.'
110 Zillah Eisenstein, 'Writing Bodies on the Nation for the Globe,' in Ranchod-
     Nilsson and Tetrault, supra note 86, 35 at 43–4.
111 Mukhopadhyay, supra note 17 at 25.
112 Lata Mani, 'Contentious Traditions: The Debate on Sati in Colonial India,' in
     Sangari and Vaid, Recasting Women, 88 at 118; Uma Chakravarti, 'Whatever Hap-
     pened to the Vedic Dasi? Orientalism, Nationalism and a Script for the Past,' in
     Sangari and Vaid, ibid., 27 at 79.

are primarily not about women, but rather about 'authentic' tradition.[113] Women as subjects are absent from the discourse on their rights and on the reform of Muslim personal law. They are merely the ground of the debate that frames women as either abject victims or unworldly heroines.[114] Such a polarized construction of women serves to deny their complex subjectivity even as it erases their agency, making women themselves marginal to the debate around their legal entitlements.[115]

Rarely is the version of cultural difference and how it is to be maintained reflective of the voices of women and other marginalized sections within the group. Muslim women have been denied the power of naming culture, and their voice has been excluded in the discourse of what aspects of difference are to be accommodated by the state and what ought not to be. In such an essentialized notion of cultural difference, the state has not paid sufficient attention to relations of power and relations of force both in the construction of culture and in its representation. As Mary Daly contends, 'We have not been free to use our own power to name ourselves, the world, or God.'[116] This insight is useful for challenging the discourse of the protection of women and of group identity, which has served to deny human agency in the perpetuation and creation of oppressive customs that are sought to be justified as part of culture. Jill McCalla Vickers writes, 'It is clear that categorizing something as custom, rite or whatever explains little of its origins, purposes or whose interests it serves. In fact, it appears to *explain away* just those things we need to understand. This is context stripping on a grand scale.'[117]

It becomes apparent that all these ideas are linked, and, to forward women's rights, notions of culture, representation, and agency must be deconstructed to reveal the power relations, the dynamics, and the dialectics of both the construction of culture and its representatives as the 'authentic voice.'[118] Arguably, an uncomplicated privileging of minority rights through the preservation of the personal law system fails to serve the interests of all members of the group. Specifically in

---

113   Mani, *supra* note 112 at 90.
114   *Ibid*. at 117.
115   *Ibid*. at 118.
116   Daly, *Beyond God the Father*, 8.
117   Vickers, 'Memoirs of an Ontological Exile,' 49. Emphasis in original.
118   Yuval-Davis, *Gender and Nation, supra* note 107 at 57, 58.

the context of discriminatory personal law, the state has essentialized and homogenized Muslim culture, reified the power relations within the group, and discounted the internal contradictions. Such an understanding, unsurprisingly, is supported by the dominant male members of the group, whose position of privilege is reinforced by the acceptance of their claim to speak for the community, of their being the authentic voice of the community. Such an understanding re-emphasizes the delineation between public and private spheres whose construction is both culturally specific and gender specific.[119]

Such constructions of cultural difference do not allow for internal power conflicts. Nor do they provide space for the recognition of difference within the group, such as differences of gender or of class. Furthermore, they serve to rigidify group boundaries as fixed and ahistorical, while conceding no space for growth or change. The difficulty with such an essentialist construction of group difference is that 'When such a perspective becomes translated into social policy, "authenticity" can become an important political resource with which economic and other resources can be claimed from the state by those taken to be the representatives of "the community."'[120]

A very real danger of a simplistic policy of multiculturalism is the possibility that it might reifiy and essentialize cultural communities, constructing an understanding of groups that is homogeneous, rigid, and fixed. A related danger is that the state might concede too much unregulated power and authority over the group to unelected male leaders of the community. *Shah Bano* highlights this danger, raising questions of authenticity, representation, and agency.[121] The state accepts the *Ulema* and the conservative Muslim political leadership as the sole arbiters of Muslim interests.[122] Liberal and progressive opinion within the community is ignored, allowing the *Ulema* to define the overarching concerns and interests of Muslims. It is in this respect that policies of multiculturalism can have a detrimental effect on the position of women, where 'This liberal construction of group voice can therefore collude with fundamentalist leaderships who claim to represent the true "essence" of their collectivity's religion and

---

119 *Ibid*.
120 *Ibid*. at 58.
121 Pnina Werbner, 'The Politics of Multiculturalism,' in Saunders and Haljan, *Whither Multiculturalism*, 47 at 54.
122 Hasan, *supra* note 73 at xiii.

culture, and who have high on their agenda the control of women and their behaviour.'[123]

Moreover, essentialized notions of cultural difference might in themselves constitute 'one of the major modes of contemporary popular racism.'[124] In the context of India, the hegemonic discourse of cultural difference is essentialized to the detriment of difference within the group. Essentialized cultural difference has been practically translated into differential systems of rights, which, in turn, rather than fulfilling the ideal of respecting and accommodating difference, instead has become a way of institutionalizing gender inequality based on a misleading and simplistic notion of difference. It has been used by the state to deny all women the privileges of equal citizenship.

Homi Bhabha has developed an alternative dynamic model of cultural pluralism.[125] Looking to the counter-narratives emerging from the margins, this model emphasizes the constantly changing and contested nature of the constructed borders of the national imagined community and of the narratives that constitute its collective cultural discourses. If we draw from Bhabha's analysis, arguably Muslim women are, in effect, 'hybrids,' as they are situated in the margins of several discourses – of nation, of community, and of gender all at once. Such a hybridity both recalls and removes the constructed boundaries of the imagined community as well as the imagined nation.

The margin is conceptualized by bell hooks as a place of resistance, a site of creativity and power that seeks to erase hegemonic categories of us/them, and colonized/colonizer.[126] bell hooks writes that the margin is also 'the site of radical possibility, a space of resistance.'[127] She names this marginality as 'a central location for the production of a counter-hegemonic discourse.'[128] According to hooks, 'It offers to one the possibility of radical perspective from which to see and create, to imagine alternatives, new worlds.'[129] She emphasizes the significance of 'Understanding marginality as posi-

---

123   Yuval-Davis, *supra* note 107 at 58.
124   *Ibid*. at 40.
125   *Ibid*. at 59. See Bhabha, *Location of Culture* and *Nation and Narration*.
126   bell hooks, 'Choosing the Margin as a Space of Radical Openness,' in Harding, *Feminist Standpoint Theory Reader*, 153 at 159.
127   *Ibid*. at 156.
128   *Ibid*. at 157.
129   *Ibid*.

tion and place of resistance is crucial for oppressed, exploited, colonized people.'[130]

Nevertheless, it is also important to acknowledge that counter-narratives are not necessarily in themselves liberatory or progressive.[131] Rather, we must be careful to situate such counter-narratives within wider negotiations of meaning and of power while simultaneously recognizing local stakes and specificities. However, in the particular case of Muslim women claiming greater legal equity, such a counter-narrative arguably is progressive and seeks a vision of a just society. Yet it is possible that counter-narratives themselves may be essentializing and homogenizing, and we must be wary of too simplistic an understanding of the counter-hegemonic nature of discourse emanating from the margins. We must be wary of valorizing the voice of the oppressed. Indeed, in accordance with feminist critique, we must subject these counter-narratives, too, to notions of constant revision and critical reappraisal and the understanding that culture and identity are fluid and contingent, rather than maintain an unthinking embrace of received notions.

At the same time, we should be careful not to essentialize women and to be aware of the specificities of difference that women experience. We must be careful to avoid universalizing the experience of some women as the experience of all women, being mindful of the dangers of speaking for all women and of obscuring the multiplicity of women's identities and allegiances.[132] As Angela Harris argues, the self is not unitary but rather made up of several selves, conflicting and coexisting simultaneously. Indeed, bell hooks has criticized universalism: 'The vision of sisterhood evoked by women liberationists was based on the idea of common oppression – a false and corrupt platform disguising and mystifying the true nature of women's varied and complex social reality.'[133]

Nevertheless, Harris acknowledges that categories are important to an emancipatory feminist struggle and help to ground feminist strategies. She states that 'even a jurisprudence based on multiple consciousness must categorize,' and that 'without categorization individuals would remain isolated, and there would be neither moral

---

130 *Ibid.*
131 Yuval-Davis, *supra* note 107 at 59.
132 Harris, 'Race and Essentialism,' at 586.
133 hooks, 'Sisterhood,' at 29.

responsibility nor the impetus for social change.'[134] Reiterating the need for categories, while being careful not to speak for all women in a way that obscures diversity of experience and location, Martha Minow notes: 'Cognitively we need simplifying categories, and the unifying category of 'woman' helps to organize experience even at the cost of denying some of it.'[135] Linda Alcoff's concept of positionality is helpful as a way to cope with difference, as a way of recognizing women's subjectivity without falling into the trap of essentialism. Alcoff's analysis enables a contextualized understanding of Muslim women's disadvantage while recognizing that the legal response to it can be neither universal nor frozen in time but subject further to critique and change. [136]

In the context of the rise of politicized religion, it would be unreasonable to argue that contemporary society has seen the end of meta-narratives. At the same time, as Nira Yuval-Davis argues, 'even the most hegemonic naturalized grand narratives in historical societies have never had homogeneous control over the differentially positioned members of those societies.'[137] For Muslim women this understanding underscores the need to pay equal attention to the meta-narrative. Further, it signifies that the state, despite efforts by male representatives of the community to portray the Muslim community as monolithic, must acknowledge the existence of difference within the group and hear the voices of Muslim women.

Being aware of the multiple identities and differences among women could lead all too easily to the deconstructionist conclusion that difference is everywhere and everyone. Such an understanding might, in turn, lead to the undermining of the possibility of collective action against oppression and of the ability to revision the structures of oppression. Indeed, it is argued that differences along group and community lines are among the primary differences among women. However, women's membership in different collectivities must be understood in the context of the power structures with the group. These power structures impact both the status and the power of women within the group and between groups. Furthermore, they determine the manner in which women's group identity is an invol-

134 Harris, *supra* note 132 at 586.
135 Minow, 'Feminist Reason,' 360.
136 Alcoff, 'Cultural Feminism,' 432, 434–5.
137 Yuval-Davis, *supra* note 107 at 4.

untary, forced identity or becomes a postmodernist fluid signifier of identity.[138]

Forwarding Muslim women's rights requires a paradigm that 'respects both the commonalities and the differences women experience.'[139] Nira Yuval-Davis articulates such a model, transversal politics, which avoids the trap of identity politics while taking into account difference among women.[140] Transversal politics, emphasizing unity in diversity, is a way out of the paralysis of action that may result once the differences in women's complex social reality are understood. Such an understanding might lead to inaction, as the logical conclusion of a deconstructionist view of women's differences. Yet rejection of any simplistic assessment of the 'feminist agenda' should include rejection of the idea that collective feminist action is precluded by such an appreciation.

In other words, as these scholars argue, it is indeed possible to have common collective action across identities. Vanaja Dhruvarajan and Jill Vickers argue that difference can be used creatively, so that it is constructed across commonalities and does not reify us/them dichotomies. Paying attention to difference as well as to commonalities, they argue, will result in the creation of new knowledge that can strengthen communication across difference, building not only on how women are different but also on how they are the same.[141] Iris Marion Young argues that communication across differences is possible and essential.[142] By recentring women's advocacy strategies on difference and on the systems of power that construct dominance and oppression based on difference, we stop perceiving minority, marginalized, or Third World women as being without agency, 'passive victims of barbaric and primitive practices.'[143] Thus, a creative use of difference leads us directly to a discussion of commonalities, and of establishing solidarity based on recognition of both difference and commonality.

As Stuart Hall argues, such an appreciation of the boundaries between and within collectivities retains an awareness of constant his-

---

138 *Ibid.* at 11.
139 Vanaja Dhruvarajan and Jill Vickers, 'Introduction, Part II,' in Dhruvarajan and Vickers, *Gender, Race and Nation,* 93 at 93.
140 Yuval-Davis, *supra* note 107 at 4.
141 Jill Vickers and Vanaja Dhruvarajan, 'Gender, Race and Nation,' in Dhruvarajan and Vickers, *supra* note 139, 25 at 49–50.
142 Young, *Inclusion and Democracy.*
143 Waylen, 'Analysing Women,' 9.

toric changes and redrawing of group boundaries, while keeping boundaries and group identities sufficiently flexible so as to allow for coalition building and an inclusive progressive politics. It also allows us to make claims for political change and opens up the possibility for collective action around issues that concern disadvantaged groups within society rather than an exclusionary politics around an essentialist identity.[144]

Further, transversal politics acknowledges the situated knowledge and partiality of perspective based on standpoint, in contrast to an identity politics that homogenizes groups, essentializes group culture, and denies shifting boundaries as well as suppresses internal dissent. In such identity politics, cultures and tradition are recast as fixed and unchanging.[145] Indeed, one of the limitations of identity politics is that individual identity and group identity are conflated, and difference is presented as being between groups while differences within the group are not acknowledged.[146] Some scholars, like Rosalind Brunt, argue for an understanding of identity politics, which calls not for a withdrawal from political collective action but for action built on the understanding that unity in diversity rather than rainbow coalitions are critical to effective action.[147] However, such an all-inclusive embrace of groups, despite its flexible political framework, may be defective simply because it makes no room for the possibility that all groups may not be similarly progressive. Equal validation of all groups based on identity politics may give space to anti-women groups such as fundamentalists.[148]

A critical aspect of transversal politics is dialogue that recognizes the different locations of the participants. Certainly, the issue then becomes how we are to construct such an understanding in terms of public policy. It is here that the concept of a uniform civil code can enter the discourse as reflective of how women can be defined as different and the same. In other words, a UCC ought to be seen as a way to retain an understanding of women's gendered particularities, while understanding the commonality of systemic gender discrimination in the Indian social and political systems. For the situation of Muslim women in India and, in particular, for the reconcepion of a UCC as a

---

144   Hall, 'Minimal Selves,' 44; Yuval-Davis, *supra* note 107 at 126.
145   Yuval-Davis, *supra* note 107 at 131.
146   *Ibid*. at 127.
147   Brunt, 'The Politics of Identity,' 150, 158.
148   Yuval-Davis, *supra* note 107 at 128.

means of ensuring gender justice across communities of difference, this is indeed a crucial point. Such a perspective enables the recognition that, despite differences of community, religion, economic class, and of other situations, the disadvantage of all women under the personal law system remains constant. Such a perspective offers some hope to Muslim women – indeed to all Indian women – seeking to redefine the boundaries of gendered citizenship and equality before the law; it frees advocates of Muslim women's legal rights from the narrow confines and pitfalls of a simplistic identity politics that essentializes difference and gives greater power to the hegemony of dominant members of the community, stifling attempts at dialogue and political change. It offers a way out of the postmodern dilemma of free-floating signifiers while re-emphasizing the very real nature of women's systemic subordination within the personal law system.[149]

In formulating a UCC, we need to pay attention as well to the 'specific political realities that divide women as much as to those that bring women together.'[150] Rather than continuing to define the Muslim woman as a fractured legal subject, I suggest an understanding of a UCC as a site for the construction of a political community of women, based not on primordial ties, but on a considered understanding of the roots of oppression and of systemic discrimination. As Vasuki Nesiah writes, 'such a community will be fraught with instability, but it can be a politically enabling instability if difference is confronted and negotiated.'[151] The tensions of ethnicity, religion, and gender make it imperative that feminists address and contest oppressive structures justified in the name of culture and religion and ensure that cultural relativism does not negate the principle of gender equality.

The hegemonic construction of Muslim identity in India by male leaders of the community, together with the rejection of any demands for change by Muslim women themselves, as exemplified by the *Shah Bano* case, demonstrate that Muslim leadership has failed to speak for the entire community.[152] On the contrary, it has suppressed the politics of subalternity while simultaneously casting its own politics of group

---

149   *Ibid*. at 132.
150   Nesiah, 'Towards a Feminist Internationality: A Critique of U.S. Feminist Legal Scholarship,' in Kapur, *Feminist Terrains in Legal Domains*, 11 at 20.
151   *Ibid*. at 21.
152   R. Radhakrishnan, 'Nationalism, Gender, and the Narrative of Identity,' in Parker et al., *Nationalisms and Sexualities*, 77 at 88.

identity in terms of the marginalized Other. The dichotomous structure upheld and created by both group leaders and national leaders, whereby 'home and the world' is the optic through which group life and the consequent claims and access to state resources are processed, has meant that Muslim male leaders have failed to represent the reality of the group. As such, their representation is highly problematic, partial, and, arguably, exclusionary of women within the group.

The perpetuation of the personal law system leads to the freezing of community identity, and religious identity, as defined by conservative male leadership, and it suppresses the voices that challenge such representation. In this context, arguably, the accommodation of difference through the retention of separate personal laws serves to accommodate a pluralism of oppressions rather than to reinforce an emancipatory, participatory politics. It is further doubtful whether such a policy advances the state's primary objective of retaining minority loyalty to the ideology of the nation state, and it may well result in a reduction of dynamism and pluralism.[153] Ultimately, the enforcement of a rigid pluralism by maintaining retrogressive personal laws in the name of preserving cultural diversity results in the continuing 'Othering' of Muslim women and of the Muslim community. It results in further removing Muslim women both from nationally accepted constitutional principles and from internationally accepted norms of women's human rights.

The difficulty with the Indian state's unquestioned assumption that the retention of discriminatory personal law is a measure of its pluralism and of its commitment to safeguard minority rights has been that the voice of women as a marginalized group within the collectivity has been silenced and that of the powerful male religious leadership has been privileged as the authentic voice of the community. Thus, the Muslim community has been reified, homogenized, and essentialized by the state's simplistic understanding of the accommodation of difference. The state has effectively closed off any space available to women to voice their difference within the group. Instead, the state has privileged the voice of the powerful and suppressed the politics of subalternity, justifying its refusal to enforce constitutional principles on the dubious grounds of cultural relativism.

---

153 Samia Bano, 'Muslim Law and South Asian Women: Customary Law and Citizenship in Britain,' in Yuval-Davis and Werbner, *supra* note 26, 162 at 175.

At the same time, we have to be careful that the emphasis on women's shared oppression does not lead to an uncritical characterization of women as passive victims of male patriarchy or to an abstraction of Muslim women out of their community.[154] While cultural relativism must be acknowledged as masking relations of power and force within a community, so too must we remain sensitive to the context of Hindu hostility, in which the defensive aspects of cultural relativism are situated. Any analysis of Muslim women's struggle for equal rights must, therefore, take into account the complicated response to communal hostility and to the possibilities of negotiating social and political life in the context of a communal agenda.

Muslim women's entry into the realm of citizenship is affected by the immunity granted by the modern Indian state to Muslim personal law as a legitimate expression of community identity. Zoya Hasan calls the emphasis on community identity misplaced, arguing that it adversely affects how Muslim women are then able to negotiate their status within a complex social and political framework.[155] The ambivalent nature of women's citizenship creates an inherent ambivalence within women's politics vis-à-vis their own collectivities, on the one hand, as shown by Shah Bano's experience, and women from other collectivities, on the other hand. Virginia Woolf's famous quotation, 'As a woman I have no country,' emphasizes the realization of many women that they are positioned in a different place from men in relation to their collectivity and that the hegemonic cultural and political projects pursued in the name of their collectivities can be against their interests as women.[156] On the other hand, especially among subordinated groups and minority women, there is a recognition that to fight for their liberation as women is futile as long as their collectivity as a whole is subordinated and oppressed.

Feminist politics are affected by this ambivalence, as demonstrated by the retreat of many women's groups from the long-standing demand for a UCC precisely because of the difficulty of promoting what may inadvertently be an anti-minority agenda in advocating for change in the personal law system. This dilemma is a real problem for the women's movement in India and must be addressed, without backing away from legitimate demands that call for gender equality,

---

154 Nesiah, *supra* note 150 at 22.
155 Hasan, *supra* note 73 at xix, xii.
156 Woolf, *supra* note 1.

but rather, by an interrogation and problematization of hegemonic categories that deny difference within the community and essentialize difference to deny the possibility of internal challenge to tradition and ultimately suppress internal dissent.

The notion of cultural relativism, whereby Muslim men are permitted by the state and by leaders of the community to enjoy far greater rights than women and women exercise far less control over their daily lives and over their bodies, must not be permitted to masquerade as protecting the legitimate cultural expressions of the entire community. As such, the perpetuation of personal law and its political manipulation as the primary signifier of Muslim identity serve to mask the reality of whose interests are being served and whose denied. This is not to make an argument for focusing solely on gender oppression across communities, but rather to make an argument for recognizing the manner in which the unquestioned use of simplistic categories of identity and culture obscures the agency of male elites in the construction of these categories that operate to subordinate women.

Thus, we need a highly contextualized analysis of the situation of Muslim women, not a simplistic understanding of those aspects of culture that most oppress women, such as unilateral divorce and polygamy, in order to situate Muslim women's negotiations along several axes of discrimination and power. We need an analysis that responds to and takes into account this heterogeneity of the trajectories of power, rather than an unreflexive narrative of victimization.[157] A contextual analysis of the situation of Muslim women is critical in preventing a victim narrative while simultaneously acknowledging the complexity of their location. As Nesiah argues, 'Sensitivity to structural privilege and discursive rupture in "women" should not be the re-inscription of an orientalist dichotomy that now, in a call to modernity, appropriates the discourse of feminism to produce a neocolonialist difference.'[158]

The relativism versus universalism debate has a critical impact on the lives of Muslim women in India as they are abandoned by the state and subjected to community control on the argument that internal affairs of a community are a private issue and must not be interfered with. However, when the state supports group demands for autonomy

---

157 Nesiah, *supra* note 150 at 23.
158 *Ibid.* at 25.

based on arguments of cultural specificity, then the state has a duty to ensure that such positions are in keeping with its own policies of anti-discrimination and equality. Certainly, the issue is complex, and arguments of cultural relativism versus universalism must be contextualized to have any meaning.[159]

Relativist conceptions of women's human rights must be understood in the context of the resistance of the minority Muslim community to domination by the majority and the desire to retain group integrity. Yet, with reference to Muslim women's rights, we see how easily these concepts have been manipulated to serve the interests of male patriarchy rather than to address women's disadvantage in any meaningful way. In the context of discriminatory personal law that perpetuates women's disadvantage in the family, subjects them to male and community control in all aspects of family life, and further ensures that they are not equal to men despite formal constitutional guarantees, any criticism of universal conceptions of international human rights must recognize that such rights give Muslim women the space and provide the possibility of envisioning a gender-just society that cultural relativist arguments in this particular context may preclude.[160]

Paradoxically, the protection of Muslim women's right to differ, to challenge internal norms and traditions, 'is best served by articulating and upholding notions of human rights which do not accommodate to the particular.'[161] As Jacqueline Bhabha emphasizes, we need to be wary of extending cultural relativism arguments that become vehicles for perpetuating discrimination and disadvantage by effectively withdrawing the protection human rights and fundamental rights guarantees ought to give Muslim women.

Feminists in India who reject what they see as the abstract universality of a UCC share this rejection of universality with the western feminist critique of abstract universalism. Certainly, the historical context of the feminist critique of abstract universalism is a response to male citizenship claims, which simultaneously excluded different groups on the basis of gender, race, ethnicity, or religion. Universalism was understood as forcing a normative homogeneity and suppressing

---

159 Jacqueline Bhabha, 'Embodied Rights: Gender Persecution, State Sovereignty and Refugees,' in Yuval-Davis and Werbner, *supra* note 26, 178 at 188.
160 *Ibid.* at 189.
161 *Ibid.*

difference and particularism.[162] While one certainly can agree with Young's argument that there can be no 'view from everywhere' or an impartial perspective, yet arguably, the concept is more nuanced, and for Muslim women it must be contextualized within the colonial and post-colonial experience of India.[163] Further, we must retain the understanding that any hegemonic discourse contains within itself the seeds of difference and particularity. In the case of India, democracy is relatively recent, although flourishing, and women's rights are politically contingent; fragile; and fraught with dangers from the forces of increasing religious fundamentalism, the expediencies of governing a pluralist state with conflicting loyalties to caste and community, the enduring tradition of patriarchy, and the lack of political will vigorously to enforce the principle of gender equality.

In these circumstances, as Chantal Mouffe argues, forwarding the cause of women's equality within the family and under the law requires the 'grammar of democratic conduct which [is] embodied in certain abstract universal principles which animate and give procedural structure to concepts such as gender equality and women's international human rights which embody rather than deny abstract universalism.'[164] For an emancipatory politics, not only for women but, indeed, for all oppressed groups, it is this embodiment and existence of universal ground rules that permit and perhaps even nurture the construction of dialogue across difference and that permit coalition building around issues rather than around essentialized identity politics.[165]

At the same time, this understanding of universalism must allow for the public legitimacy of the articulation of difference and cannot be understood as being tolerant of the suppression of difference.[166] That is, it must recognize difference, and one way of doing this is through the insights of transversal politics, which recognizes the partiality of perspectives, the complexity of identity, and aims to construct an egalitarian participatory dialogue.[167] Indeed, 'exclusivist identity politics are not, and cannot be, an alternative to abstract universalism as the

---

162 Werbner and Yuval-Davis, *supra* note 103 at 7.
163 Young, *Justice and the Politics of Difference*, 103.
164 Mouffe, 'Democratic Citizenship,' 238.
165 Werbner and Yuval-Davis, *supra* note 103 at 9.
166 As argued, for example, by Taylor, 'Politics of Recognition,' 25–74; Mouffe, *Return of the Political*; Young, *supra* note 163; Phillips, *supra* note 107; Werbner and Yuval-Davis, *supra* note 103 at 10.
167 Werbner and Yuval-Davis, *supra* note 103 at 10.

basis for democracy.'[168] It is here that Ruth Lister's idea of a 'differentiated universalism' becomes attractive, suggesting a way out, together
with the concept of transversal politics, of the either/or dichotomy. Lister
argues for understanding citizenship as a dialectical process stressing a
differentiated universalism.[169] However, not all minority perspectives
are necessarily emancipatory. Indeed, for Muslim women, where the politics of their rights have been taken over and spoken for by the rights of
the Muslim community as a whole, the claims made for inclusion, participation, and the accommodation of difference by the Muslim community in the struggle for benefits and entitlements from the Indian state
have been overwhelmingly male centred and have shown little regard
for emancipatory politics for the women of the group.

Muslim women in India are particularly affected by what Ayelet
Shachar calls the paradox of multicultural vulnerability, which most
affects women's rights within the family. Where the state concedes a
certain degree of autonomy to the group in matters of the legal regulation of the family, as in the case of Muslim personal law, then it is
women within the group who are subject to systemic and sanctioned
discrimination within the group.[170] Adding women to the group-state
equation necessarily disrupts simplistic understandings of accommodation of difference and forces us to reconsider dichotomous categories. The uncritical accommodation of group difference privileges
existing hierarchical arrangements within the group and, in the arena
of family law, disproportionately disadvantages women and puts at
risk their citizenship rights.[171]

In such a reproduction of collective identity, Muslim women's rights
are deeply compromised. This tension between a policy of multiculturalism and equal citizenship is further aggravated by the fact that
this infringement of women's rights is not accidental but emphatically
inherent.[172] Muslim personal law perpetuates the subordination of

---

168   *Ibid.* at 9.
169   Lister, *Citizenship*, 66–90.
170   Shachar, *Multicultural Jurisdictions*, 45.
171   *Ibid.* at 47.
172   *Ibid.* at 49. An example of the relevance of these arguments, in the broader context
      of pluralist democracies grappling with questions of gender equality and the
      accommodation of difference, is the recent experience in Canada with the pro-
      posal to introduce Shariat law in the adjudication of family disputes in the
      province of Ontario.

women and reinforces the gender status quo. At another level, family law serves to circumscribe the application of general, secular rights to Muslim women by strictly demarcating the boundaries of the group and not permitting easy exit from the group. The effect of the state policy of uncritically retaining the personal law system as an integral part of minority rights is that Muslim women are simultaneously included and excluded and are located in marginal spaces while group boundaries are reified. Moreover, it serves to strengthen identity politics as the basis of citizenship rights, even as it excludes Muslim women from equal citizenship.

It is in this respect that Young's argument against the discourse of universal citizenship, wherein groups rather than individuals are the basis of citizenship rights, might inadvertently strengthen identity politics, construct groups as homogeneous, and reify group boundaries.[173] For Muslim women, this understanding of group rights has meant that those within the group who are more powerfully positioned have been accepted as representing the interests of the entire collectivity.[174] Will Kymlicka's understanding of the accommodation of group rights is useful for understanding the situation of Muslim women. The insights of his theoretical analysis reveal that 'laws justified in terms of external protections can open the door to internal restrictions.'[175] External protections are intended to protect the group from the impact of any decisions of the larger society that may affect the group's particular identity or culture, whereas internal restrictions are intended to protect the group from internal challenges to custom or tradition. Thus, through what Kymlicka has called external protections to the group, the group is able to impose internal restrictions on the women of the group that are explicitly harmful to women's fundamental rights.[176] In the context of Muslim women, this has meant that the Indian state has sanctioned the perpetuation of discriminatory personal law that does not conform to constitutional norms as an expression of the preservation of minority rights, notwithstanding that, as a result, Muslim women's rights are undermined.

Examining the tension between democratic commitment to religious liberty and the fact that autonomous religious communities often deny

173   Young, 'Polity and Group Difference,' 114.
174   Yuval-Davis, *supra* note 107 at 86.
175   Kymlicka, *Multicultural Citizenship*, 35–43.
176   *Ibid.* at 35.

basic liberties to classes of people on the basis of race, caste, or sex and also looking at the concurrent problem of inter-group and intra-group inequality, Martha Nussbaum considers the limitations of both secular humanist feminist and traditionalist feminist approaches and proposes an alternative way of thinking about justifiable limits.[177] Using the individual capabilities approach, she advocates a UCC, proposing that government may interfere with religion if it can show a compelling interest, and she argues that protection of the central capabilities of citizens constitutes a compelling interest. Thus, singling out women for differential treatment in a central area of human functioning or in a way that stigmatizes and humiliates them gives rise to a compelling state interest in eradicating discrimination. Nussbaum argues for a uniform civil code, for free egress from one religious tradition into another, for guarantees of sex equality within religious systems, and for parity among them. These requirements are not an assault on religious freedom, she concludes, 'but a deeper defense of its basic principle.'[178]

For Muslim women the situation is truly complex. If they forward claims for equality within the family, they are cast as betrayers of the community. Invariably, as happened to Shah Bano, they are presented with an either-or situation, where they are forced to choose between their rights or their culture. Such culture-driven arguments serve to obfuscate the manner in which 'culture' and 'religion' are deployed as political arguments to consolidate the strength of the group and demarcate its boundaries. In this complex situation, the state has disregarded the fact that Muslim women are active participants in the culture of their group and have as great a stake and interest in its continuance. It is a misconception, thus, to uncritically separate the interests of Muslim women from the interests of the group, or to present the two as mutually exclusive. Certainly, the agenda of anti-communalism and the hostility of the majority community and the threat of assimilation are as real to Muslim women as to Muslim men. It is in this climate of anti-Muslim hostility that Muslim women are invariably forced to forward the group agenda rather than pursue their gender rights.

It is therefore critical to pay attention to the difficulties women experience when confronted by a forced choice between the obligations and

---

177 Nussbaum, *supra* note 85.
178 *Ibid*. at 383.

duties that a state owes to all women as equal citizens and the conflict with the demands of faith as portrayed by religious leadership, specifically the contention that to claim legal equality within the family is a challenge to community integrity and thereby a threat to religion. We must remain committed to 'the democratic accommodation of religion, carefully attending to national differences in the role religion plays in particular democratic societies and institutions.'[179]

For Muslim women in India, who are vulnerable as a consequence of this multicultural paradox, the challenge is to re-envision current methods of accommodating difference.[180] It is critical to reformulate how the state deals with the problem of inequality within the group. It needs to rethink its policy of allowing reform only when it is initiated from within, while its definition of who represents the community is a reification of existing power inequalities. Otherwise, the policy of multicultural accommodation can become an accomplice in the erasure of women's voices.

Further, we need to challenge the group's control over defining who constitutes a good Muslim and using it as a means of blocking women's demand for change and controlling exit from the group. We must refuse to accept the binary of 'your culture or your rights' put forward by group leaders and tacitly accepted by the state. The state must encourage groups to subject discriminatory personal law to a thorough scrutiny and to measure the norms against both international and national principles of women's basic rights. As Shachar maintains, the state and groups must discard 'the legitimizing of intra-group subordination in favour of empowering once-vulnerable insiders.'[181] Shachar calls this the theory of joint governance whereby the mandate of multiculturalism is honoured, but not at the expense of vulnerable members within the group, through the notion of a differentiated citizenship.

In the context of forwarding Muslim women's rights, it is crucial to be mindful of the economic and political context of the accommodation of difference and how it affects the women of the group. We need to re-imagine the UCC as a means of forwarding Muslim women's claims to more equitable family laws while not succumbing to the

---

179 Nancy L. Rosenblum, 'Pluralism, Integralism, and Political Theories of Religious Accommodation,' in Rosenblum, *supra* note 85, 3 at 4.
180 Shachar, *supra* note 170 at 148.
181 *Ibid*. at 149–50.

temptation of identity politics. It is important to retain a meta-under-standing of the systemic nature of gender discrimination in India while paying attention to local contexts. Arguably, the lack of reform of personal law and the refusal to enact a UCC together have served to exclude women from the ideal of equal citizenship. To perpetuate the notion that a UCC must necessarily be universalizing is to underesti-mate the importance to women of all communities of just and equi-table laws, and to reject a UCC is to fall into the trap of identity politics, which serve to divide women and inhibit collective action.

Reclaiming the Nation

Andrew Parker argues that a nation uses 'some element of alterity for its definition' and is ineluctably 'shaped by what it opposes.'[182] In the immediate post-colonial years, Indian leaders were concerned equally with establishing a secular, pluralist, inclusive democracy and with establishing a modern nation that paid special attention to equality in opposition to the imperialist gaze and the colonial understanding of a hopelessly divided and hierarchical society. For nationalist leaders, it was critical to establish secular nationalism versus religious commu-nalism as a fundamental organizing principle. Yet the foundational ambivalence in the construction of secularism as the Other of commu-nalism, when, in fact, the idea of secular nationalism contained within itself the seeds of communalism and differentiation along group lines, has had serious implications for women's rights.[183]

Invariably, the state has demonstrated a reluctance to uphold the principle of gender equality when it appears to conflict with the state's perception of the preservation of minority rights. The granting of equal citizenship to women upon Independence did not translate into the prioritizing of women's issues on the national agenda. Always retaining the context in which post-colonial India came into being, we need to understand these issues to more accurately situate the struggle for women's equality. The notion of equal citizenship, where women are political subjects, stands in sharp contrast to women's identity in the family, and arguably, women's invocation of their rights as citizens is, particularly for Muslim women, in direct repudiation of their iden-

---

182 Andrew Parker, Mary Russo, Doris Sommer, and Patricia Yaeger, 'Introduction,' in Parker et al., *supra* note 152, 1 at 5.
183 Pandey, *The Construction of Communalism*, 241.

tity as family subjects.[184] The failure of the post-colonial Indian state to uphold women's rights and its complicity with ideologies and practices that privilege male patriarchy have been harshly criticized by the women's movement. As Rajeswari Sunder Rajan argues, 'The masculinity of nationalist ideology, the fiction of citizenship, and the progressiveness of law are all exposed by women's issues like the Shah Bano case ... The nation therefore is a space that, while it may be expected to offer an alternative to women's absorption into family and community structures, often simply functions in extension of them to define their "belonging" in a fashion identical to theirs.'[185] Indeed, the exclusion of women from equal citizenship results in creating a tension in women's strategies in the struggle for equality. Whereas, on the one hand, 'to call upon traditional conceptions of citizenship and equal rights to challenge the current subordination and exclusion of women is to call upon a tradition so deeply implicated in that very exclusion and subordination; but to fail to do so would be to abandon a tool – both rhetorical and institutional – that has been used throughout the world in emancipatory struggles.'[186] Arguably, the discourse of citizenship offers the possibility of freeing women from the coercive aspects of a religious identity that is ascribed by community and state and from which there is no exit. This space of citizenship offers women a location from which to articulate their rights, rather than to claim protection of either community or state. The idea of citizenship offers Muslim women a site from which to reclaim a selfhood.[187] The brief freedom Shah Bano enjoyed in appealing to the secular law at least temporarily offered her the possibility of moving beyond the constrictions of an ascribed identity and circumscribed rights based on personal law enforced by the community and sanctioned by the state.

The realm of constitutional law has a counter-hegemonic potential that points to the possibility of using concepts of equality before the law and equal protection of the law to challenge existing power structures and gender hierarchies. The law constitutes women not only as gendered subjects but also legal citizens with equal rights and entitled to the equal protection of law. It is this contradiction that can create a space from which to challenge inequalities. Indeed, the values of legal

---

184   Sunder Rajan, *supra* note 67 at 5.
185   *Ibid.*
186   Nedelsky, 'Citizenship and Relational Feminism,' 131.
187   Sunder Rajan, *Scandal, supra* note 2 at 168.

liberalism that the law be universally applicable, and that it equally protect all citizens constitute its counter-hegemonic potential that Muslim women's advocates can use to forward rights claims.[188]

According to the analytical insights of Ran Hirschl and Ayelet Shachar, a major obstacle to ensuring the complete participation of Muslim women as equal citizens of the Indian nation is the '(mis)perception that advancing gender equality necessarily compromises other important values of the state, such as the preservation of collective identity, state security, or religious diversity. As long as the promotion of women's rights and the promotion of other constitutive norms are seen as mutually exclusive, even the most eloquently worded rights legislation cannot guarantee women's equal treatment and human dignity.'[189] This understanding underscores the need to challenge misleading dichotomies between women's rights and other constitutional rights. It highlights the importance of recognizing women as equal citizens in the ethnic/religious pluralistic society of India with its 'diverse communities of identity and interest.'[190]

The notion that religiously differentiated communities necessitate the continuance of the personal law system is part of the ideological apparatus of the state, supported by those such a policy inevitably recognizes as the representatives of the community: self-appointed male conservative leaders. This religious identity is ascribed and discursively created and is hopelessly imbricated in the pattern of patronage and distribution of favours that arise from state-sponsored benefits for recognized groups to accommodate difference. By subscribing to the homogeneous concept of community put forward by conservative Muslim leaders, the state is reifying a neo-colonialist discourse in its understanding that a single tradition of religious authoritarianism speaks for the entire community.

The risk of a simplistic policy of multiculturalism is that it might reify cultural communities as homogeneous, with fixed boundaries, and deny difference within the group. As Himani Bannerjee argues, this denial of difference within the group silences women and other marginalized people as culturally inauthentic and deviant. In addi-

---

188 Kapur and Cossman, *supra* note 15 at 41.
189 Ran Hirschl and Ayelet Shachar, 'Constitutional Transformation, Gender Equality, and Religious/National Conflict in Israel' in Baines and Rubio-Marin, *Gender of Constitutional Jurisprudence*, 205 at 229.
190 *Ibid.*

tion, it serves to privilege the voice of religious leaders, *Imams* and *Ulema*, as the authentic representatives of the community, while secular and Muslim feminists and Muslim reformists challenging discrimination in family law are not so favoured.[191] This leads to the possibility, as we have seen in *Shah Bano*, that too much decision making power is transferred to unelected, traditional male leaders.[192]

In an effort to be culturally sensitive, the voices of those marginalized are silenced, while the voices of those who stand to gain from the preservation of the status quo are privileged. This is particularly relevant in the context of Muslim women's rights. Any argument that seeks to deny the basic validity of minimum standards of accountability and responsibility of national governments in disregard of both national constitutional norms and internationally acknowledged standards must pay close attention to whose interests are being harmed and whose served by a rejection of basic minimum standards, especially with reference to women's human rights. The argument that human rights cannot be universally applied does nothing to provide for an emancipatory normative vision for those who are marginalized and disenfranchised by their own state. Once again, the question of universalism versus particularism is raised, and this argument fuels the setting up of a dichotomy between tradition and modernity and shelters those representatives of a society whose voice is powerful, allowing them to claim cultural or religious particularism as a shield against women's rights. The state's ideology of the protection of minority rights, a sweeping inclusionary but not assimilationist policy of the recognition of India's diversity, can truly be progressive only when it is linked to a proactive state policy that is committed to broader universalist goals provided for by the *Constitution*, particularly gender equality. The need, therefore, is to forward the struggle for both the universal and the particular.[193]

Identity politics that reifies communal and religious divisions to prevent the construction of coalitions across difference ultimately disserves women's rights. The alliance of Muslim women's groups with the larger women's movement as well as with other progressive, reformist movements is critical to challenging those seeking to deny

---

191   Himani Bannerjee, 'Multiple Multiculturalisms and Charles Taylor's Politics of Recognition,' in Saunders and Haljan, *supra* note 121, 35 at 37.
192   Werbner, *supra* note 121 at 55.
193   *Ibid.* at 49.

women's rights.[194] The state has demonstrated its reluctance to address even the most pressing reform issues facing Muslim women, highlighting their abandonment to the control of the patriarchal community.[195] A regular response to Muslim women's efforts to organize is the pejorative assertion that they are not 'true' women, not 'true' Muslims; any demand for change is a threat to the culture of the community, a betrayal of the community. As an illustration of this refusal to acknowledge women's claims, while Shah Bano was reviled as not being a true Muslim woman, in contrast, her husband was hailed as a good Muslim by leaders of the community. Shah Bano was portrayed as betraying the community and threatening its integrity. Eventually, she was compelled to repudiate the Supreme Court decision in her favour and to recant her testimony. She was forced to assert her Muslim identity, simultaneously rejecting any gender-based rights claims. She wrote a public letter declaring that as a true believer she now understood that her actions had been wrong, and that as a good Muslim she was rejecting the Supreme Court decision. Significantly, she thanked the religious leaders for 'saving' her.[196]

There is a substantial body of work, signifying the broad spectrum of the various positions adopted by secular feminists, Islamic feminists, and Muslim reformists on the need for reform and on how best to advance Muslim women's rights, whether within a traditional Islamic framework, or within a reformed understanding of Islam or indeed in a secular context. Some Muslim feminists argue that change can occur only within the context of Islam.[197] They advocate feminist rereadings of the Koran, emphasizing those aspects which affirm

---

194 Kazi, *Muslim Women in India*, 31.

195 *Ibid*. at 20: 'Devoid of a national or visionary leadership, the voices and experiences of Muslim women came to be usurped by male Muslims claiming to represent the community. The political opportunism of the latter combined with the failure of state programmes to alleviate women's socio-economic status, left the majority of Muslim women economically and educationally impoverished. The restricted agendas of organizations like the Jamiat-e-Ulema-e-Hind, which focus on the retention of Muslim personal law; the Jamaat-e-Islami, wishing to preserve the Sharj'a; together with the revivalist and missionary activities of the Tablighi Jamaat, which propagates a particularly rigid and puritanical Islamic doctrine, do not offer any hope of initiating debate within Muslim communities or of taking up problems with the central government.'

196 Shah Bano, 'Open Letter to Muslims,' in Engineer, *supra* note 23, 211 at 211–12.

197 Maha Azzam, 'Gender and the Politics of Religion in the Middle East,' in Yamani, 217 at 227–8.

women's rights, and challenging others as incorrect and based on male, patriarchal interpretations of religion that are in fact contrary to the spirit of Islam.[198] A leading feminist theologian, Riffat Hassan, argues that there can be no change external to the traditional cultural and religious context.[199] In other words, change must be sought within the framework of Islam, but a progressive, reinterpreted Islam, by reading in women's rights guarantees. Whereas in Iran women have made remarkable gains within the Islamic framework, given the political context of the Islamic revolution and the nature of government in Iran this was arguably the best response for Iranian feminists, who indeed subverted the discourse from within to wrest greater rights for women.

As Ziba Mir-Hosseini argues, a feminist rereading of the Shariat (Muslim canonical law) and the Koran is essential when Islam is the political discourse of the state. In the context of Iran's being an Islamic Republic, for feminists seeking to widen women's rights, it is critical to claim legitimacy within this framework to challenge the state's appropriation of Islam. It is only this method, argues Mir-Hosseini that can challenge the state on its own terms.[200] Afsaneh Najmabadi's position is slightly different from that of Riffat Hassan. She suggests that we should focus on a postmodern feminism in terms of cooperation on issues without making generalized claims about women's equality or women's rights. Najmabadi challenges the dichotomy between Islamic feminists and secular feminists. She argues that the example of Iran demonstrates that the links between Islamic and secular feminists are crucial to the success of the movement to enlarge women's rights within the Islamic discourse of the Iranian state. Indeed, Najmabadi was among the first to challenge the dichotomy between religious and secular feminists. Characterizing Islamic feminism as a reformist movement, she argues that it has opened up a dialogue between religious and secular feminists.[201] Equally significant, some religious feminists have also moved away from rejecting western feminism and feminist thought. They have also declared, while challenging the clergy as the only rightful interpreters of 'true' Islam, that all those

---

198 Kandiyoti, 'Islam and Patriarchy,' 23 at 23; Mayer, *Islam and Human Rights*, 100.
199 Hassan, 'Feminist Theology,' 65.
200 Ziba Mir-Hosseini, 'Stretching the Limits: A Feminist Reading of the Shari'a in Post-Khomeini Iran,' in Yamani, *supra* note 197, 285 at 289.
201 Najmabadi, 'Feminism in an Islamic Republic,' 73, 77.

affected by the law in question, both Muslims and non-Muslims, have the right to interpret religious law.[202] Thus, religious and secular feminists have joined forces in the struggle to improve women's legal status. Similarly, Mir-Hosseini challenges the hostile binary constructed between religious and secular feminists, noting that Islamic feminists have shown 'their willingness to join forces to protest against the gender biases of a law which is derived from the Sharia.'[203]

Together with feminists, Muslim reformists constitute an important ideological current, contributing to the ongoing debate on Muslim women's rights. In contrast to Islamist fundamentalists, who deny the reinterpretation of the Shariat, reformists advocate a progressive reinterpretation of Islamic law through the Islamic principle of *ijtihad*, or doctrinal reinterpretation, compatible with human rights and women's rights.[204] Prominent among them are Ustadh Mahmoud Mohamed Taha, Abudallahi An Na'im, and Asghar Ali Engineer. Ustadh Taha, a well-known Sudanese reformist, advocated adherence to the early verses of the Koran, known as the Meccan verses, rather than the later Medinan verses acknowledged to be less favourable to women's rights. Persecuted for his progressive views, he was imprisoned and executed in 1984 at the age of seventy-six.[205] His work has been carried on by An Na'im, who, while maintaining that it is important to retain the cultural framework of Islam, advocates the evolutionary principle of Koranic reinterpretation to read in women's rights. He asserts that Islamic law is not immutable, but that, in fact, religious texts must be open to constant reinterpretation.[206] Significantly, An Na'im emphasizes that religious dogma should not be the basis of women's legal status. He highlights the importance of both religious and secular advocacy of women's rights, challenging the problematic dichotomy between eastern and western, tradition and modernity.[207]

Engineer calls for the progressive reinterpretation of the Shariat, denying the fundamentalist contention that Muslim personal law in

---

202 *Ibid.* at 72, 66.

203 Mir-Hosseini, *supra* note 200 at 318.

204 Marie-Aimée Helie-Lucas, 'The Preferential Symbol for Islamic Identity: Women and Muslim Personal Laws,' in Moghadam, *Identity Politics and Women*, 391 at 392.

205 Anonymous, 'Ustadh Mohamad Taha,' 93, 94.

206 An Na'im, 'Human Rights in the Muslim World,' 13, 17, 49.

207 An Na'im 'Dichotomy between Religious and Secular Discourse,' 54.

India is immutable and cannot be reformed.[208] In supporting the Islamic doctrinal principle of *ijtihad*, like An Na'im, Engineer moves beyond the position of some Muslim feminists, who rely on certain verses of the Koran while discounting others, to emphasize that Shariat principles must be reformulated in the spirit of evolutionary Islam rather than by seeking to elevate verses that are favourable to women over those that are not. In agreement with other reformists, Engineer advocates the reformulation of women's rights through a progressive reinterpretation within the context of normative Islam.[209] He critiques the *Ulema*, particularly members of the Personal Law Board, for their refusal to initiate much needed reform, especially in the areas of marriage, divorce, and maintenance.[210]

By resuscitating early Islamic history, Islamic feminists hope to formulate an indigenous feminist project, or at the very least to encourage a progressive reading of women's rights in Islam. However, continuing to debate the issue of women's rights within the ideological boundaries of 'true' Islam could result in encouraging ahistorical analyses of the situation of women, ignoring the complex and varied economic and social contexts of the lives of Muslim women.[211] While retaining the cultural legitimacy of the Islamic framework may indeed be desirable theoretically, the experience of women in India has shown that to root the demand for change solely within the Islamic framework is to retain religion as the sole defining authority of women's lives and status. Seeking equality on a religious terrain is to remain confined within the parameters of theological debate and the issues as defined by the fundamentalists, which do not allow for emancipatory spaces for women's liberation, at least in the case of India.

Indeed, it has been argued that, giving up feminism as a secular discourse results in accepting that there is an essential homogeneous 'Islamic' position on women in which women's difference is constructed in their primary social roles as mothers and wives. This could delegitimate much of the important work that feminists in their societies have accomplished during the last century and

---

208   Engineer, *supra* note 91.
209   Engineer, 'Islam,' 6, 9–16.
210   Engineer, *supra* note 91 at 58, 59.
211   Kandiyoti, *supra* note 198 at 23, 24.

more.[212] Moreover, the difficulty with constructing women's struggles within the boundaries of their communities' religion and culture creates racialized exclusions towards women who are not part of these collectivities but are part of their pluralist societies. It is imperative, therefore, to have 'secular spaces,' which Homi Bhabha has titled 'subaltern secularism,'[213] in which women from different communities can coexist and struggle together while having the space and autonomy to choose which elements of their traditions (and which interpretations of those traditions) to keep and which to cast aside.[214]

In the context of India democratic secularism is one of the options, rather than a sole focus on Islam, for a paradigm within which struggles can be located. In India, we must be wary of an identity politics that forecloses alliance with the struggles of other marginalized groups and inhibits coalition building across the political spectrum. Yet with regard to their rights, experience has shown that Muslim women have been excluded from decisions. However, this is a complex issue; there is no right answer to this debate and the possibility for women to enter such 'secular spaces' is highly variable. Specific historical conditions dictate the form and substance of particular feminist struggles.[215]

There is a necessary interaction of religious reinterpretation and secular thought and activism. Nonetheless, as Valentine Moghadam observes, 'It is, at any rate, very difficult to win theological arguments. There will always be competing interpretations of the religious texts, and the power of the social forces behind [them] determines the dominance of each interpretation.'[216] Moghadam goes on to acknowledge the limits of religious reinterpretation: 'Thus, although religious reform is salutary and necessary, it is important to acknowledge its limitations. Women's rights and human rights are best protected in an

---

212 Yuval-Davis, *supra* note 107 at 124. Women Living under Muslim Laws Network (WLUML) is an international solidarity network of women living in Muslim communities. It was founded in 1984 with the specific objective of challenging the denial of rights to women justified in the name of Islam. WLUML identifies commonalities between women in Muslim communities, while at the same time challenging the myth of one homogeneous Muslim world by identifying diversities across Muslim countries and communities.

213 Bhabha, 'Subaltern Secularism.'

214 Yuval-Davis, *supra* note 107 at 124.

215 *Ibid.*

216 Moghadam, 'Islamic Feminism and its Discontents,' 1160.

environment of secular thought and secular institutions, including a state that defends the rights of all its citizens irrespective of religious affiliation.'[217] Moghadam does not subscribe to the view that women's rights can be advanced only in the context of Islam. She calls for the separation of religion from secular governance, arguing that religion should not form the basis for family law.[218]

In India, the experience of the *Shah Bano* controversy highlights the ambivalent alliance between religious and political leaders, which ensures the silencing of the voices of change. Women's rights advocates' and reformists' attempts to decentre the clergy's claim to be the sole interpreters of Islam have met with little success. One of the issues on which the fundamentalists campaigned against the *Shah Bano* decision was the interpretation of Shariat law by the Supreme Court. Although the interpretations of laws on maintenance relied on by the Supreme Court in themselves were uncontroversial and, in fact, widely accepted by Muslims worldwide as authoritative, the *Ulema* contended that they were wrong and un-Islamic.[219] When Arif Mohammed Khan, a government minister who himself was a Muslim, supported the court's interpretation of Muslim women's rights, the *Ulema* dismissed him as a layperson, unauthorized to interpret the Shariat. The refusal of the *Ulema* to address women's disadvantage continues today, with the outright refusal of the religious leaders, particularly the Personal Law Board, to address the pressing issues of polygamy and triple divorce.[220] In such a context, it might be a more effective policy for women's rights advocates to pursue a strategy that separates the definition of women's legal status from hegemonic patriarchal interpretations of Muslim law.

The challenge is how best to forward Muslim women's claims to equality without drawing criticisms of westernization, imperialism, and neo-colonialism. Undoubtedly, the strategy adopted will vary from society to society, depending in great part on the choices available to women in each society as well as on the prevailing political context. In the case of India, an effective way to assert women's rights is to take advantage of the legitimacy of the *Constitution*, which mandates gender equality and equal citizenship, to choose a secular framework to establish that which women are entitled to, rather than to

217   *Ibid.*
218   *Ibid.* at 1163.
219   Engineer, *supra* note 23 at 36.
220   Engineer, *supra* note 91 at 58, 59.

present counter-arguments and reconstruct opposing foundational myths to resist fundamentalists and to displace the Islamist discourse.

Women's rights in India may be better forwarded and better protected in a secular democracy. Insisting on the primacy of religion in the definition of women's rights in the family results in privileging, however inadvertently, the essentialized religious identity of women, while disregarding the common experience across all personal law of women's disadvantage and subordination. Such an approach plays into the hands of those who seek to limit women's rights to a fundamentalist religious understanding rather than subscribing to universal minimum guarantees of rights. Moreover, this understanding continues to tie women to an essentialized notion of identity and to limit the ideological spaces within which women can search for and claim an emancipatory discourse. Further, it prevents other critical issues from being raised.[221] It fails to interrogate the conflicts around structural disadvantage within the community. We need to have a feminist legal analysis of all the factors that contribute to the complexities of women's disadvantage, not simply to focus on the preservation of religious community but also to include women's experience of class, economic situation, and ethnicity. Ultimately, rather than a concern with ideology, it is feminist praxis that must be the focus, as we need to situate women's material reality in specific historic locations.[222]

Indeed, internal reform of personal law may preclude the need to have a UCC. To this end, progressive and reformist reinterpretations of religious law are crucially important. Yet, until such progressive change occurs, 'the Uniform Civil Code must continue to function as the site of desire and the sign of the unified legal subject.'[223] At the same time, it is essential to have revisionary rereadings by feminists and reformists of religious texts and to support the reform of religion from within. In the interests of legal equality, it is critical to work towards closing the gap between religious and secular law and to move towards reform of both. As Nayereh Tohidi argues, a 'reformist or women-centred interpretation of religious laws should be considered not as an alternative to secular democratic demands, but as a component of more holistic social change.'[224] We need to foster dia-

221 Nesiah, *supra* note 150 at 19.
222 Moghadam, *supra* note 216 at 1165.
223 Pathak and Sunder Rajan, *supra* note 56, 576.
224 Tohidi, 'Issues at Hand,' 288.

logue across difference rather than to see difference between Muslim women and other Indian women as necessitating 'separate but equal' personal laws. The case for a UCC can only be made stronger by the understanding that ultimately 'women's struggles become, simultaneously, also struggles for broader, encompassing democratic civil and political rights.'[225] To advocate a UCC and to call for the separation of religion from law is not an assault on religion but rather a recognition that, in the context of India, religion as it is currently interpreted is patriarchal and discriminatory towards women.

As Edward Said argues, the ideological concern with identity, whether of minority or of majority collectivities, inevitably is bound up with the particular interests and agenda of the group. It is crucial to understand Muslim identity in India not as a unitary identity, as portrayed by conservative male leaders, but, in fact, as complex and varied. It is such an understanding of culture that can be sensitive to the reality of historical experience. Indeed, as a consequence of the colonial encounter, all cultures are influenced by each other, belying claims of singularity and purity. Cultures must be understood as 'hybrid, heterogeneous, extraordinarily differentiated, and unmonolithic.'[226] Insisting on the integration and connectedness of the colonized past with the post-colonial present, colonizers and the colonized, and between culture and imperialism, Said underscores the interdependence of ideologies of imperialism and nationalism.[227]

It is crucial to disrupt naïve belief in the unchanging purity and historicity of culture and identity, nation, and self.[228] In India, the project of nationalism was a self-conscious cultural nationalism, created in opposition to the imperial orientalist construction of civilizational backwardness.[229] The dialectical engagement between centre and margin is highlighted in the manner in which the imperialist rhetoric of western superiority and oriental inferiority was used by nationalists and anti-colonialists in the construction of a cultural nationalism. Thus, Gandhian cultural resistance appropriated to itself the essentialist understanding of the orient as spiritual and consensual in order to reconstruct an authentic, cultural identity in opposition to western

---

225 Werbner and Yuval-Davis, *supra* note 103 at 7.
226 Said, *Culture and Imperialism*, xxv.
227 *Ibid.* at 61.
228 Said, *Orientalism*, 332.
229 *Ibid.* at 331.

materialism and individualism. On the other hand, nationalist leaders
sought to rebuild the post-colonial state as secular, and they committed to equality in alterity to the imperialist understanding of Indian
society as divided by caste, religion, and gender.[230]

The insights of post-colonial theory expose the discursive constructedness of simplistic binaries of us/them, western/Indian, colo-
nizer/colonized, Muslim/Other, and they emphasize the manner in
which knowledge flows in both directions. This is what Stuart Hall
calls 'two way cultural traffic'[231] The colonial encounter and the evolution of Anglo-Muhammadan law in India have ensured 'that the
colonial past is always indelibly present in ostensibly pure Indian cultural forms ... the assumption by the tragic self of the purity of Indian
cultural and legal forms obscures the already ever present West, and
its deep influences on the very construction of tradition.'[232] Post-colonial theory's strategies of historicization and disruption of dichotomous categories reveal the extent to which 'there is no place of pure
Indianness, no place that exists in a pure form prior to the moment of
colonial intervention. This strategy of historicization begins to reveal
the extent to which Indian culture is very much a hybrid cultural form
– produced in and through the colonial encounter. It helps refute the
idea of cultural authenticity, displacing it with an insistence on cultural
hybridity.'[233] By disrupting Manichean categories of here/there and
us/them cultural binaries and revealing the hybridity of Indian
culture, these theoretical insights help in resisting challenges to the
feminist emancipatory project through accusations of cultural inau-
thenticity, and they establish the political legitimacy of women's struggle.[234] The strategies of historicization and interrogation of the tradi-
tion/modernity binary reveal the cultural hybridity of India and
undermine claims to a pure, cultural authenticity. At the same time,
these strategies locate the discursive struggles for women's rights
within the colonial encounter and within Indian history. This understanding serves to deconstruct the notion of home and the world as a
way of viewing culture and tradition. It reveals that, in fact, tradition
also emanates from outside the culture, further demonstrating the

---

230 Gandhi, *Postcolonial Theory*, 78.
231 Cossman, 'Turning the Gaze Back on Itself,' 541.
232 *Ibid.* at 534.
233 *Ibid.* On hybridity, see Bhabha, *supra* note 125.
234 Cossman, *supra* note 231 at 538.

hybridity of culture and the constructedness of tradition. In addition, this understanding shows the manner in which gender relations themselves are discursively constructed and negotiated and are not simply given.[235]

The insights of post-colonial theory reaffirm that it would be misconceived to herald the demise of meta-narratives. Whereas postmodernism emphasizes the disappearance of meta-narratives of emancipation and enlightenment, post-colonial theory highlights the reality that these grand narratives remain and provide the historical and political context for an emancipatory politics.[236] The argument is not that local and specific concerns are not relevant; on the contrary, it reiterates the interconnectedness of the universal and the particular.[237] This understanding is intended not as a rejection of difference but rather as a means of challenging the notion that difference inevitably means hostility to the Other, and a rejection of reified cultural essences. [238]

At the same time, we must heed Gayatri Spivak's warning, drawn from Foucault's argument against the valorization of marginality, against privileging the voice of the oppressed simply because it is oppressed. [239] This may well serve to perpetuate and reify, and thereby exclude certain discourses and cultures as perpetually marginal.[240] Related are the issues of positionality and the politics of location of the speaker. In the context of Spivak's and Foucault's cautioning against the dependence of the centre on the margin, Leela Gandhi questions whether, indeed, it is possible to talk about and for marginalized positions only from post-colonial locations. Further, speakers for post-colonial positions have to be wary of the dangers of co-option.[241] This danger is amplified from the perspective of Third World women. For a progressive feminist politics, it is critical to be mindful of the construction of Third World women as the ultimate victims of both

---

235 *Ibid.* at 540–1.
236 Said, *supra* note 228 at 349.
237 See, generally, the group of researchers known as the Subaltern Studies Group led by Ranajit Guha. The objective of this group is 'to promote a systematic and informed discussion of subaltern themes in the field of South Asian studies.' Guha, *Subaltern Studies*, vii.
238 Said, *supra* note 228 at 350.
239 Foucault, *History of Sexuality*, 98, cited in Spivak, *Outside in the Teaching Machine*, 59.
240 Spivak, *supra* note 239 at 55.
241 Gandhi, *supra* note 230 at 59.

nationalist and western patriarchies.[242] Spivak contests the location of such women in an identifiable margin that renders them ultimately 'Exotic Others' in the service of the centre. In being wary of reproducing a neocolonialist difference, Spivak warns of the dangers of thus reifying the gendered subaltern.[243]

The dichotomies of public and private, nation and religious minority, uniform and personal laws, and group and individual have served to exclude women from equal citizenship. The challenge before us is to reconceptualize the relationship of the state to women's equal citizenship based on the principle of democratic choice that guarantees equal rights and upholds gender justice while respecting group difference. Arguably, recasting the debate, drawing from the insights of post-colonial theory, could address issues of gender justice without undermining the claims of communities. In the final analysis, any decision must be based on the state's own ideology, and the state must make a choice that might require it to uphold principles of equality and freedom from discrimination, even if it means abandoning discriminatory personal law and state legitimization of inequality.[244]

The challenge before us is to develop a framework that can include the knowledge and experience of women in all their complexity and diversity. The challenge is to reformulate the way in which we understand the notion of a UCC and to see it as a search for hidden perspectives, for knowledge from the margins, rather than to conceive of it as another hegemonic discourse seeking to obliterate difference.[245] We must strive towards an understanding of the space of secular citizenship as empowering for women, as providing the possibility of a counter-hegemonic discourse. The idea of citizenship as a space of subaltern secularism offers Indian women of all faiths and communities the potential for creating alliances across difference while being able to choose, exercising agency, which aspects of culture and tradition to retain and which to set aside.[246]

We need to reformulate our understanding of a Uniform Civil Code of family laws as a notion that must be constantly revisioned and

---

242 *Ibid.* at 82.
243 Spivak, *supra* note 239 at 55; Spivak, 'French Feminism,' 137.
244 Hasan, *supra* note 22 at 87.
245 Sandra Harding, 'Introduction: Standpoint Theory as a Site of Political, Philosophic, and Scientific Debate,' in Harding, *supra* note 126, 1 at 4 -10.
246 Bhabha, *supra* note 213.

rethought to include the perspective of women while rejecting at the same time any essentialism. Pragmatism requires that the legal disadvantage of women be addressed, although doing so might mean that the state must take the lead despite the possibility of paternalism. For oppressed groups, the concept of a UCC can offer an emancipatory space, removed of essentialist notions of difference. Avoiding the trap of universalism versus cultural relativism should not lead to the rejection of a unified vision of the basic non-negotiable rights of women, nor should oppressive cultural practices be shielded from scrutiny on dubious grounds of cultural particularism.

The public/private split, whereby the rights of Muslim women within the family are used as a bargaining chip between state and community leaders, has left Muslim women as the terrain on which community identity is negotiated. At the same time, their voices have been silenced in the presumed interests of the group. It is critical to recognize that women are equal participants in the culture of the community and have as great an interest in its continuance. Thus, when women call for a change in their legal status, such as an end to polygamy, or call for the need to address spousal support for divorced Muslim women, then the state needs to pay close attention to these demands and to give them legitimacy as women's signal for change.

Male leaders of the community invariably seek to block Muslim women's challenges to the personal law as a dangerous and ill-conceived threat to group integrity that undermines and fractures the presentation of the Muslim (male) subject to the larger society.[247] Muslim women's rights advocates must demand 'not only simple legal reform but also actual social transformation; the prize has become social, economic, and political equity, not formal equality.'[248] Consequently, it is important to challenge the premises and practices that dispense power and patronage in society as well as those that disempower Muslim women. Such challenges, by their very nature, implicate complacent understandings of gender justice and minority rights and disrupt structurally oppressive gender-biased approaches to law reform. We need new ways of framing the complex relation-

---

247 Kimberlé Williams Crenshaw, 'The First Decade: Critical Reflections, or 'A Foot in the Closing Door,' in Valdes, Culp, and Harris, *Crossroads, Directions*, 9 at 11.

248 Francisco Valdes, Jerome McCristal Culp, and Angela P. Harris, 'Battles Waged, Won, and Lost: Critical Race Theory at the Turn of the Millennium' in Valdes et al., *ibid*. 1 at 4.

ships between law and the everyday experience of family life. Through all of this activity we need to remember the lives of women like Shah Bano, who experience discrimination within the family, emphasizing that this is not only a theoretical dialectical engagement but, in fact, a very real aspect of the lived reality of Muslim women.

At a moment when upholding women's rights in South Asia in the face of increasing religious and patriarchal controls poses what may be one of the greatest moral challenges of the twenty-first century, it is necessary to raise the question of Muslim women's rights in India, while interrogating notions of cultural diversity to challenge that particular representation of culture premised on the subordination of women.[249] To create a dialogic process that is truly inclusive, we must develop a more sensitive, nuanced understanding of challenges to the universal self-image and identity of the post-colonial Indian nation by expanding norms and claims that resonate as well with the claims of the excluded.[250] To do so, we need to understand the space of constitutional law as a site of discursive and real challenge to given notions of women's rights, identity and the accommodation of difference. Indeed, Muslim women's rights as equal citizens of the nation must move beyond formal guarantees of equality to a genuine attempt to democratize the structures of representation, to provide mechanisms for the effective representation and recognition of the distinct voices and perspectives of all its constituent groups, and to include the voices of Muslim women in the dialogue between community and state.[251]

At the same time, we must remain mindful that dialogue is not necessarily in itself empowering, and it often reinforces and mirrors existing gender and power hierarchies and supports existing privilege. The challenge, therefore, is to reconceptualize a politics based on an enhanced notion of democratic dialogue that is more generous and receptive and more sensitive to different ontological and aesthetic assumptions. Forwarding women's rights and equality within the family calls for an understanding of gender that goes beyond the simple antinomy of victim and benefactor, of personal law and a uniform civil code. Indeed, we need to reconceptualize a uniform civil code, which in the context of India's religious plurality is not merely a battleground for opposing notions of gender rights and group rights,

---

249   Kristof, 'When Rapists Walk Free.'
250   Barbara Saunders, 'Preface,' in Saunders and Haljan, *supra* note 121, 9 at 9.
251   Young, *supra* note 173 at 124.

but rather both a space for ongoing discussion and negotiation and a notion that is also a mechanism for the resolution of difference and the enforcement of gender equality.[252]

In the aftermath of colonialism, India must be wary of a complacency that reproduces a neocolonialist political amnesia, repeating – but not surpassing – the past.[253] The colonial state rejected the idea of equal citizenship for the 'natives' in a discourse that equated, ultimately, racial difference with political exclusion. Whereas the Indian nationalist movement originated in response to this exclusion of the native subject, arguably, in independent India, the combined religious and gender differences of Muslim women have served to exclude them from equal citizenship. The Indian state must move away from a simplistic discourse of post-colonialism and assertions of national progress and modernity to truly engage with the continuing struggle for subjectivity, rejecting the continuing exclusions of post-colonial society that disenfranchise not only Muslim women, but indeed all marginalized groups within Indian civil society.[254]

---

252 David Haljan, 'Introduction: Whither Multiculturalism?' in Saunders and Haljan, *supra* note 121, 11 at 13.
253 Lyotard, 'Postmodern Explained to Children,' 90.
254 Gandhi, *supra* note 230 at 170.

Bibliography

Books and Articles

Agnes, Flavia. *Law and Gender Inequality: The Politics of Women's Rights in India*. New Delhi: Oxford University Press, 1999.

Alcoff, Linda. 'Cultural Feminism versus Poststructuralism: The Identity Crisis in Feminist Theory' (1988) 13 *Signs* 404.

All India Democratic Women's Association (AIDWA), Memo, *People's Democracy*. Weekly organ of the Communist Party of India (Marxist), 29:6, February 2005.

Amnesty International Report, 'India: Justice, the Victim – Gujarat State Fails to Protect Women from Violence.' AI Index: ASA 20/001/2005, January 2005.

An Na'im, Abdullahi. 'Human Rights in the Muslim World: Socio-Political Conditions and Scriptural Imperatives: A Preliminary Inquiry' (1990) 3 *Harvard Human Rights Journal* 13.

– 'The Dichotomy between Religious and Secular Discourse in Islamic Societies.' In Mahnaz Afkhami, ed., *Faith and Freedom: Women's Human Rights in the Muslim World*. Syracuse: Syracuse University Press, 1995. 51.

Austin, Granville. *The Indian Constitution: Cornerstone of a Nation*. New Delhi: Oxford University Press, 2000.

Badran, Margot. 'Dual Liberation: Feminism and Nationalism in Egypt, 1870s-1925' (1988) *Feminist Issues* 8:1 15.

Baines, Beverley, and Ruth Rubio-Marin, eds. *The Gender of Constitutional Jurisprudence*. Cambridge: Cambridge University Press, 2005.

Baird, Robert D., ed., *Religion and Law in Independent India*. New Delhi: Manohar, 1993.

Bartlett, Katherine T. 'Feminist Legal Methods.' In Kelly D. Weisberg, ed., *Feminist Legal Theory: Foundations*. Philadelphia: Temple University Press, 1993. 551.

Basu, Aparna, and Bharati Ray. *Women's Struggle: A History of the All India Women's Conference 1927–2002*. New Delhi: Manohar, 2002.

Basu, Srimati. 'Shading the Secular: Law at Work in the Indian Higher Courts' (2003) 15(2) *Cultural Dynamics* 131.

Baxi, Upendra. 'The State's Emissary: The Place of Law in Subaltern Studies.' In Partha Chatterjee and Gyanendra Pandey, eds, *Subaltern Studies VII*. New Delhi: Oxford University Press, 1992. 230.

Bhabha, Homi. *The Location of Culture*. London: Routledge, 1994.

– *Nation and Narration*. London: Routledge, 1990.

– 'On subaltern secularism' (1995) 6 *WAF (Women Against Fundamentalism) Journal* 5–7.

Bhargava, Rajeev. ed. *Secularism and Its Critics*. New Delhi: Oxford University Press, 1999.

Bhattacharjee, A.M. *Matrimonial Laws and the Constitution*. 2nd ed. Calcutta: Eastern Law House, 1996.

– *Muslim Law and the Constitution*. 2nd ed. Calcutta: Eastern Law House, 1994.

Brunt, Rosalind. 'The Politics of Identity.' In S. Hall and M. Jacques, eds, *New Times*. London: Lawrence and Wishart, 1989. 150.

Chatterjee, Partha. *The Nation and Its Fragments: Colonial and Postcolonial Histories*. Princeton: Princeton University Press, 1993.

Chaudhuri, Maitrayee. *Indian Women's Movement: Reform and Revival*. Delhi: Radiant, 1993.

Chowdhry, Geeta. 'Communalism, Nationalism, and Gender: Bhartiya Janata Party (BJP) and the Hindu Right in India.' In Sita Ranchod-Nilsson and Mary Ann Tetrault, eds, *Women, States and Nationalism: At Home in the Nation*. London: Routledge, 2000. 98.

Cook, Rebecca J., ed., *Human Rights of Women: National and International Perspectives*. Philadelphia: University of Pennsylvania Press, 1994.

Cossman, Brenda. 'Turning the Gaze Back on Itself: Comparative Law, Feminist Legal Studies, and the Postcolonial Project' (1997) *Utah Law Review* 525.

Coulson, N.J. *A History of Islamic Law*. Edinburgh: Edinburgh University Press, 1964.

Crenshaw, Kimberlé. 'Demarginalizing the Intersection of Race and Sex: A Black Feminist Critique of Anti-Discrimination Doctrine, Feminist Theory and Anti-Racist Politics' (1989) *University of Chicago Law Forum* 139.

Daly, Mary. *Beyond God the Father: Toward a Philosophy of Women's Liberation*. Boston: Beacon Press, 1973.

– *Gyn/ecology: The Metaethics of Radical Feminism*. Boston: Beacon Press, 1978.

David, Deidre. *Rule Britannia: Women, Empire, and Victorian Writing*. Ithaca: Cornell University Press, 1995.

Derrett, J.D.M. *Religion, Law and the State in India*. New Delhi: Oxford University Press, 1999.

Dhagamwar, Vasudha. *Towards the Uniform Civil Code* (Bombay: N.M. Tripathi, 1989)

Dhavan, Rajeev. 'Religious Freedom in India' (1987) 35 *American Journal of Comparative Law* 209.

– 'Introduction.' In Rajeev Dhavan and Thomas Paul, eds, *Nehru and the Constitution*. Bombay: N.M. Tripathi, 1992. i.

Dhruvarajan, Vanaja, and Jill Vickers, eds, *Gender, Race and Nation: A Global Perspective*. Toronto: University of Toronto Press, 2002.

Diwan, Paras. *Muslim Law in Modern India*. Allahabad: Allahabad Law Agency, 1977.

Dutt, R. Palme. *India Today*. London: Victor Gollancz, 1940.

Engineer, Asghar Ali. 'Islam – The Status of Women and Social Change.' In Asghar Ali Engineer, ed., *Problems of Muslim Women in India*. Bombay: Orient Longman, 1995. 6.

– 'Maintenance for Muslim Women,' *Hindu* [India], 7 August 2000.

– 'The Need for Codification and Reform in Muslim Personal Law in India: Problems Faced by Muslim Women.' Women Living under Muslim Laws Network (1999) Dossier No. 22, 56.

– 'Triple Divorce – Need For Change,' *Journal of the Centre for the Study of Society and Secularism*, 21 June 21 2004.

– ed., *The Shah Bano Controversy*. Bombay: Orient Longman, 1987.

Everett, Jana Matson. *Women and Social Change in India*. New York: St. Martin's Press, 1979.

Forbes, Geraldine. *The New Cambridge History of India, IV.2. Women in Modern India*. Delhi: Cambridge University Press, 2000.

Foucault, M. *History of Sexuality*. Vol. 1, Trans. Robert Hurley. Harmondsworth: Penguin, 1978 [1984].

Fyzee, Asaf A.A. *Outlines of Muhammadan Law*. 4th ed. Delhi: Oxford University Press, 1999.

Galanter, Marc. *Competing Equalities: Law and Backward Classes in India*. Berkeley: University of California Press, 1984.

– *Law and Society in Modern India*. Delhi: Oxford University Press, 1994.

Gandhi, Leela. *Postcolonial Theory: A Critical Introduction*. Delhi: Oxford University Press, 1998.

Great Britain. Indian Statutory Commission (Simon Commission). *Report II*, 53 [1930].

Griffiths, Gareth. 'Representation and Production: Issues of Control in Post-Colonial Cultures.' In Harish Trivedi and Meenakshi Mukherjee, eds, *Interrogating Post-Colonialism: Theory, Text and Context*. Shimla: Indian Institute of Advanced Study, 2000. 21.

Guha, Ranajit, ed. *Subaltern Studies*. Vol. 1. Delhi: Oxford University Press, 1982.

Hall, Stuart. 'Minimal Selves.' In *Identity: The Real Me*, ICA Document 6. London: ICA, 1987. 44.

Harding, Sandra, ed. *The Feminist Standpoint Theory Reader: Intellectual and Political Controversies*. New York: Routledge, 2004.

Harris, Angela. 'Race and Essentialism in Feminist Legal Theory' (1990) 42 *Stanford Law Review* 581.

Hasan, Zoya, ed. *Forging Identities: Gender, Communities and the State*. New Delhi: Kali for Women, 1994.

Hassan, Riffat. 'Feminist Theology: The Challenges for Muslim Women' (Fall 1996) 9 *Critique: Journal for Critical Studies of the Middle East* 53.

Haynes, Douglas, and Gyan Prakash. 'Introduction: The Entanglement of Power and Resistance.' In Douglas Haynes and Gyan Prakash, eds, *Contesting Power: Resistance and Everyday Social Relations in South Asia*. Berkeley: University of California Press, 1991. 1.

hooks, bell. 'Sisterhood: Political Solidarity between Women.' In Sneja Gunew, ed., *A Reader in Feminist Knowledge*. London: Routledge, 1992. 27.

Jacobsohn, Gary J. *The Wheel of Law: India's Secularism in Comparative Constitutional Context*. Princeton, N.J.: Princeton University Press, 2003.

Jayal, Niraja Gopal. *Democracy and the State*. New Delhi: Oxford University Press, 2001.

Jayawardena, Kumari. *Feminism and Nationalism in the Third World*. London: Zed, 1986.

– *The White Woman's Other Burden: Western Women and South Asia during British Rule*. New York and London: Routledge, 1995.

Jeffery, Patricia, and Amrita Basu, eds, *Resisting the Sacred and the Secular: Women's Activism and Politicized Religion in South Asia*. New Delhi: Kali For Women, 1999.

Kandiyoti, Deniz. 'Identity and Its Discontents: Women and the Nation.' Women Living under Muslim Laws Network (2004) Dossier No. 26, 45.

– 'Islam and Patriarchy: A Comparative Perspective.' In Nikki R. Keddie, ed., *Women in Middle Eastern History: Shifting Boundaries in Sex and Gender*. New Haven: Yale University Press, 1992. 23.

– ed., *Women, Islam and the State*. Philadelphia: Temple University Press, 1991.

Kapur, Ratna. *Erotic Justice: Law and the New Politics of Postcolonialism*. London: Glasshouse Press, 2005.

– ed. *Feminist Terrains in Legal Domains: Interdisciplinary Essays on Women and Law in India*. New Delhi: Kali for Women, 1996.

– 'The Tragedy of Victimization Rhetoric: Resurrecting the "Native" Subject in International/Post-Colonial Feminist Theory' (2002) 15 *Harvard Human Rights Journal* 1.

Kapur, Ratna, and Brenda Cossman. *Subversive Sites: Feminist Engagements with Law in India*. New Delhi: Sage, 1996.

Kazi, Seema. *Muslim Women in India: Minority Rights Group International Report*. London: Minority Rights Group International, 1999.

Kirpal, B.N., Ashok H. Desai, Gopal Subramanium, Rajeev Dhavan, and Raju Ramachandran, eds. *Supreme but Not Infallible*. New Delhi: Oxford University Press, 2000.

Kristof, Nicholas D. 'When Rapists Walk Free,' *New York Times*, op-ed, 5 March 2005.

Kumar, Radha. *The History of Doing*. New Delhi: Kali for Women, 1993.

Kymlicka, Will. *Multicultural Citizenship*. Oxford: Clarendon Press, 1995.

Larson, Gerald James, ed. *Religion and Personal Law in India: A Call to Judgment*. Bloomington: Indiana University Press, 2001.

Lateef, Shahida. *Muslim Women in India: Political and Private Realities, 1890s-1980s*. New Delhi: Kali for Women, 1990.

Liddle, Joanna, and Rama Joshi. *Daughters of Independence: Gender, Caste and Class in India*. London: Zed Books, 1986.

Lister, Ruth. *Citizenship: Feminist Perspectives*. London: Macmillan, 1997.

– 'Feminist Theory & Practice of Citizenship.' Unpublished paper presented at the annual conference of the DVPW (German Political Science Association), Mainz, September 2003.

Lyotard, Jean-François. *The Postmodern Explained to Children: Correspondence 1982–1985*. Es. Julian Pefanis and Morgan Thomas. Sydney: Power Publications, 1992.

Mayer, Ann Elizabeth. *Islam and Human Rights: Tradition and Politics*. 3rd ed. Oxford: Oxford University Press, 1999.

Mayo, Katherine. *Mother India*. New York: Blue Ribbon Books, 1930.

Mazumdar, Vina. 'Political Ideology of the Women's Movement's Engagement with the Law.' Occasional Paper No. 34. New Delhi: Centre For
Women's Development Studies, 2000.

Minow, Martha. 'Feminist Reason: Getting It and Losing It.' In Katharine T.
Bartlett and Rosanne Kennedy, eds, *Feminist Legal Theory: Readings in Law
and Gender*. Boulder, CO: Westview Press, 1991. 360.

– 'Foreword: Justice Engendered' (1987) 101 *Harvard Law Review* 10.

– *Making All the Difference: Inclusion, Exclusion, and American Law*. Ithaca:
Cornell University Press, 1990.

– 'Surviving Victim Talk' (1993) 40 *UCLA Law Review* 1411.

Moghadam, Valentine M. ed., 'Against Eurocentrism and Nativism: A
Review Essay on Samir Amin's Eurocentrism and Other Texts'
(Fall/Winter 1989) 9 *Socialism and Democracy* 81.

– *Identity Politics and Women: Cultural Reassertions and Feminisms in International Perspective*. Boulder, CO: Westview Press, 1994.

– 'Islamic Feminism and Its Discontents: Towards a Resolution of the
Debate' (2002) 27 *Signs* 1135.

Mouffe, Chantal. *The Return of the Political*. London: Verso, 1993.

– 'Democratic Citizenship and the Political Community.' In Chantal Mouffe
ed., *Dimensions of Radical Democracy: Pluralism, Citizenship, Community*.
London: Verso, 1992. 225.

Mukhopadhyay, Maitrayee. *Legally Dispossessed: Gender, Identity and the
Process of Law*. Calcutta: Stree, 1998.

Mullally, Siobhan. 'Feminism and Multicultural Dilemmas in India: Revisit-
ing the Shah Bano Case' (2004) 24 *Oxford Journal of Legal Studies* 671–92.

Najmabadi, Afsaneh. 'Feminism in an Islamic Republic: "Years of Hardship,
Years of Growth."' In Yvonne Yazbeck Haddad and John L. Esposito, eds,
Islam, Gender and Social Change. New York, Routledge, 1998. 59.

Narain, Vrinda. *Gender and Community: Muslim Women's Rights in India*.
Toronto: University of Toronto Press, 2001.

Nedelsky, Jennifer. 'Citizenship and Relational Feminism.' In Ronald Beiner
and Wayne Norman, eds, *Canadian Political Philosophy*. Toronto: Oxford
University Press, 2001. 131.

Pandey, Gyanendra. *The Construction of Communalism in Colonial North India*.
New Delhi: Oxford University Press, 1990.

Parashar, Archana. *Women and Family Law Reform in India*. New Delhi: Sage,
1992.

Parker, Andrew, Mary Russo, Doris Sommer, and Patricia Yaeger, eds. *Nationalisms and Sexualities*. New York: Routledge, 1992.

Pathak, Zakia, and Rajeswari Sunder Rajan. 'Shahbano' (1989) 14 *Signs* 558.

Pearl, David. *A Textbook on Muslim Personal Law*. 2nd ed. London: Croom Helm, 1987.

Phillips, Anne. *Democracy and Difference*. Cambridge: Polity Press, 1993.

Ray, Bharati. *Early Feminists of Colonial India: Sarla Devi Chaudhurani and Rokeya Sakhawat Hossain*. New Delhi: Oxford University Press, 2002.

Razack, Sherene H. *Looking White People in the Eye: Gender, Race, and Culture in Courtrooms and Classrooms*. Toronto: University of Toronto Press, 2001.

Rivera, Jenny. 'The Violence against Women Act and the Construction of Multiple Consciousness in the Civil Rights and Feminist Movements.' In Nancy E. Dowd, and Michelle S. Jacobs, eds, *Feminist Legal Theory: An Anti-Essentialist Reader*. New York: New York University Press, 2003. 352.

Rosenblum, Nancy L. ed. *Obligations of Citizenship and Demands of Faith: Religious Accommodation in Pluralist Democracies*. Princeton: Princeton University Press, 2000.

Rudolph, Lloyd I., and Susanne Hoeber Rudolph. *The Modernity of Tradition: Political Development in India*. New Delhi: Orient Longman, 1999.

Said, Edward W. *Culture and Imperialism*. New York: Vintage, 1994.

– *Orientalism*. New York, Vintage, 1979).

Sangari, Kumkum, and Sudesh Vaid, eds. *Recasting Women: Essays in Colonial History*. New Delhi: Kali For Women, 1993.

Sarkar, Tanika. 'Semiotics of Terror: Muslim Children and Women in Hindu Rashtra,' *Economic and Political Weekly* (Mumbai) 37:28, 13–19 July 2002, 2872–76.

Saunders, Barbara, and David Haljan, eds. *Whither Multiculturalism: A Politics of Dissensus*. Leuven: Leuven University Press, 2003.

Seervai, H.M. *Constitutional Law of India*. 3rd ed. Vol. I. Bombay: N.M. Tripathi, 1983.

Shachar, Ayelet. *Multicultural Jurisdictions: Cultural Differences and Women's Rights*. Cambridge: Cambridge University Press, 2001.

– 'Religion, State, and the Problem of Multiculturalism' (2005) 50 *McGill Law Journal* 49.

Shiva Rao, B. *The Framing of India's Constitution: Select Documents*. Vol. 2. Bombay: N.M. Tripathi, 1967.

Smart, Carol. 'Feminism and Law: Some Problems of Analysis and Strategy' (1986) 14 *International Journal of the Sociology of Law* 109.

– *Law, Crime and Sexuality: Essays in Feminism*. London: Sage, 1995.

Smith, Donald Eugene. 'Emerging Patterns of Religion and Politics.' In Donald Eugene Smith, ed., *South Asian Politics and Religion*. Princeton: Princeton University Press, 1966. 21.

Spivak, Gayatri Chakravorty. 'Can the Subaltern Speak?' In Cary Nelson and Lawrence Grossberg, eds, *Marxist Interpretations of Culture*. Basingstoke, UK: Macmillan, 1985. 271.

– *A Critique of Postcolonial Reason: Towards a History of the Vanishing Present*. Cambridge: Harvard University Press, 1999.

– 'French Feminism in an International Frame.' In *In Other Worlds: Essays in Cultural Politics*. New York: Methuen, 1987. 134.

– *Outside in the Teaching Machine*. New York, Routledge, 1993.

Sunder Rajan, Rajeswari. *The Scandal of the State: Women, Law, and Citizenship in Postcolonial India*. Durham: Duke University Press, 2003.

– ed., *Signposts: Gender Issues in Post-Independence India*. New Delhi: Kali For Women, 1999.

Taylor, Charles. 'Examining the Politics of Recognition.' In Amy Gutmann, ed., *Multiculturalism*. Princeton: Princeton University Press, 1994. 25.

Tohidi, Nayereh. 'The Issues at Hand,' in Herbert Bodman and Nayereh Tohidi, eds, *Women in Muslim Societies: Diversity within Unity* (Boulder, CO: Lynne Reinner, 1998. 277.

'Ustadh Mohamad Taha: 12 Years after His Execution.' Women Living Under Muslim Laws Network (1997) Dossier No. 18, 93.

Valdes, Francisco, Jerome McCristal Culp, and Angela P. Harris, eds. *Cross-roads, Directions, and a New Critical Race Theory*. Philadelphia: Temple University Press, 2002.

Varma, S.K., and Kusum, eds. *Fifty Years of the Supreme Court of India: Its Grasp and Reach*. New Delhi: Oxford University Press, 2000.

Vickers, Jill McCalla. 'Memoirs of an Ontological Exile: The Methodological Rebellions of Feminist Research.' In Angela Miles and Geraldine Finn, eds, *Feminism – From Pressure to Politics*. 2nd ed. Montreal: Rose Books, 1989. 37.

Washbrook, D.A. 'Law, State and Agrarian Society in Colonial India' (1981–2) 15 *Modern Asian Studies* 649.

Waylen, Georgina. 'Analysing Women in the Politics of the Third World.' In Haleh Afshar, ed., *Women and Politics in the Third World*. London: Routledge, 1996. 1.

Williams, Patricia. 'Alchemical Notes: Reconstructing Ideals From Deconstructed Rights' (1987) 22 *Harvard Civil Rights, Civil Liberties Law Review* 401.

Woolf, Virginia. *Three Guineas*. London: The Hogarth Press, 1938.

Yamani, Mai, ed., *Feminism and Islam: Legal and Literary Perspectives*. Reading: Ithaca Press, 1996.

Young, Iris Marion. *Inclusion and Democracy*. New York: Oxford University Press, 1990.

– *Justice and the Politics of Difference*. Princeton: Princeton University Press, 1990.

– 'Polity and Group Difference: A Critique of the Ideal of Universal Citizenship.' In Iris Marion Young, ed., *Throwing Like a Girl and Other Essays in Feminist Philosophy and Social Theory*. Bloomington: Indiana University Press, 1990. 114.

Yuval-Davis, Nira. 'Beyond Differences: Women, Empowerment and Coalition Politics,' in Nickie Charles and Helen Hintjens, eds, *Gender, Ethnicity and Political Ideologies*. London and New York: Routledge, 1998. 168.

– *Gender and Nation*. London: Sage, 1997.

Yuval-Davis, Nira, and Pnina Werbner, eds. *Women, Citizenship and Difference* (London: Zed Books, 1999).

Newspapers

Deccan Herald [India], 3 February 2005.

Times of India, 3 February 2005.

Cases

Abdullah Khan v. *Chandni Bi*, AIR 1956 Bhopal 71.

Ahmedabad Women's Action Group (AWAG) v. *Union of India*, (1997) 3 SCC 573.

Ahmed Kasim Molla v. *Khatun Bibi*, ILR Calcutta 833.

Ammini E.J. v. *Union of India*, AIR 1995 Kerala 252.

Apparel Export Promotion Council v. *A. K. Chopra*, AIR 1999 SC 625.

Bai Tahira v. *Ali Hussain Fidalli*, AIR 1979 SC 362.

C.B. Muthamma v. *Union of India*, AIR 1979 SC 1868.

Chairman, Railway Board v. *Mrs. Chandrima Das*, AIR 2000 SC 988.

C. Masilamani Mudaliar v. *Idol of Sri S. S. Thirukoil*, (1996) 8 SCC 525.

Dagdu v. *Rahimbi Dagdu Pathan and Others*, II (2002) Divorce and Matrimonial Cases 315 (FB), Bombay High Court.

Danial Latifi v. *Union of India*, (2001) 7 SCC 740.

Fuzlunbi v. *Khader Vali*, AIR 1980 SC 1730.

Githa Hariharan v. *Reserve Bank of India*, (1999) 2 SCC 228.

Gurdial Kaur v. *Manghal Singh*, AIR 1968 Punjab 396.

Harvinder Kaur v. *Harmandar Singh Choudhary*, AIR 1984 Delhi 66.

Indra Sawhney v. *Union of India*, AIR 1993 SC 477.

In re Amina, AIR 1992 Bombay 214.

Itwari v. *Asghari*, AIR 1960 Allahabad 680.

John Vallamattom v. *Union of India*, AIR 2003 SC 384.

Jorden Diengdeh v. *S. S. Chopra*, AIR 1985 SC 935.
Krishna Singh v. *Mathura Ahir*, AIR 1980 SC 707.
Lily Thomas v. *Union of India*, AIR 2000 SC 1650.
Madhu Kishwar v. *State of Bihar*, (1996) 5 SCC 125.
Maharishi Avadesh v. *Union of India*, 1994 Supp 1 SCC 713.
Mary Roy v. *State of Kerala*, AIR 1986 SC 1011.
Mary Sonia Zachariah v. *Union of India*, (1990) (I) KLT 130.
Matthew v. *UOI*, (1999) 1 Kerala LJ 824.
Mohammed Ahmed Khan v. *Shah Bano Begum*, AIR 1985 SC 945.
Pannalal Bansilal Pitti v. *State of A.P.*, (1996) 2 SCC 498.
Reynolds Rajamani v. *Union of India*, (1982) 2 SCC 474.
Sarla Mudgal (Smt.) President, Kalyani and Others v. *Union of India and Others*,
    1995 3 SCC 635.
Shamim Ara v. *State of U.P. and Another*, 2002 SOL Case no. 514.
Srinivasa Aiyar v. *Saraswathi Ammal*, AIR 1952 Madras 193.
State of Bombay v. *Narasu Appa Mali*, AIR 1952 Bombay 84.
State of Kerala v. *N. M. Thomas*, AIR 1976 SC 490.
Swapna Ghosh v. *Sadananda Ghosh*, AIR 1989 Calcutta 1.
Usman Khan Bahamani v. *Fathimunnisa Begum*, AIR 1990 AP 225.
Vishaka v. *State of Rajasthan*, AIR 1997 SC 3011.
Zohara Khatoon v. *Mohammed Ibrahim*, AIR 1981 SC 1243.

Statutes

The Constitution of India, 1950.
The Child Marriage Restraint Act, 1929 (Act No. 19 of 1929) [1 October, 1929].
The Christian Marriage (Amendment) Act, 2001[Act No. 51 of 2001] enacted on
    20 September 2001.
The Dissolution of Muslim Marriages Act, 1939 (Act No. 8 of 1939) dated 17
    March, 1939. *Gazette of India*, Part V, 1938. *The India Code*, 1958, Vol. VI, Part
    ix, 211.
The Government of India Act, 1919, 9 and 10 Geo. 5 Ch. 101.
The Government of India Act, 1935, 25 and 26 Geo. 5 Ch. 42.
The Indian Criminal Procedure Code, 1973 (Act No. 2 of 1974) 25 January 1974
    as amended by *The Criminal Procedure Code Amendment Act*, 2002.
The Indian Divorce Act, 1869 (Act 4 of 1869) dated 26 February 1869 as
    amended by *The Indian Divorce (Amendment) Act*, 2001, [Act No. 49 of 2001]
    enacted on 20 September 2001.
The Muslim Personal Law (Shariat) Act, 1937 (Act No. 26 of 1937) dated 7
    October, 1937. *The India Code*, 1958, Vol. VI, Part ix, 205.

The Muslim Women's (Protection of Rights on Divorce) Act, 1986 (Act No. 25 of 1986), *The Gazette of India, Extraordinary*, Part II, Section 1, dated 19 May 1986. [*Muslim Women's Act*]

The Travancore Christian Succession Act, 1902 [Act 2 of 1902].

Debates and Reports

Constituent Assembly Debates: Official Report, Vol. 7 (4 November 1948 to 8 January 1949).

Towards Equality: Report of the Committee on the Status of Women in India. New Delhi: Government of India, Ministry of Education and Social Welfare, Department of Social Welfare, 1974.

Index